ROUTLEDGE LIBRARY EDITIONS:
COMEDY

Volume 2

NEW PERSPECTIVES ON WOMEN AND COMEDY

NEW PERSPECTIVES ON WOMEN AND COMEDY

Edited by
REGINA BARRECA

R Routledge
Taylor & Francis Group

LONDON AND NEW YORK

First published in 1992 by Gordon and Breach, Science Publishers, Inc.

This edition first published in 2022
by Routledge
4 Park Square, Milton Park, Abingdon, Oxon OX14 4RN

and by Routledge
605 Third Avenue, New York, NY 10158

Routledge is an imprint of the Taylor & Francis Group, an informa business

British Library Cataloguing in Publication Data
A catalogue record for this book is available from the British Library

ISBN: 978-1-032-20971-5 (Set)
ISBN: 978-1-032-22672-9 (Volume 2) (hbk)
ISBN: 978-1-032-22680-4 (Volume 2) (pbk)
ISBN: 978-1-003-27371-4 (Volume 2) (ebk)

DOI: 10.4324/9781003273714

Publisher's Note
The publisher has gone to great lengths to ensure the quality of this reprint but points out that some imperfections in the original copies may be apparent.

Disclaimer
The publisher has made every effort to trace copyright holders and would welcome correspondence from those they have been unable to trace.

NEW PERSPECTIVES
ON WOMEN AND COMEDY

Edited by

REGINA BARRECA

University of Connecticut
Storrs, USA

GORDON AND BREACH
Philadelphia Reading Paris Montreux Tokyo Melbourne

Gordon and Breach Science Publishers

5301 Tacony Street, Drawer 330
Philadelphia, Pennsylvania 19137
United States of America

Post Office Box 90
Reading, Berkshire RG1 8JL
United Kingdom

58, rue Lhomond
75005 Paris
France

Post Office Box 161
1820 Montreux 2
Switzerland

3-14-9, Okubo
Shinjuku-ku, Tokyo 169
Japan

Private Bag 8
Camberwell, Victoria 3124
Australia

Library of Congress Cataloging-in-Publication Data
New perspectives on women and comedy / edited by Regina Barreca.
     p. cm. -- (Studies in gender and culture ; v. 5)
   Includes bibliographical references and index.
   ISBN 2-88124-533-1. -- ISBN 2-88124-534-X (pbk.)
   1. American wit and humor--Women authors--History and criticism.
2. English wit and humor--Women authors--History and criticism.
3. Women and literature--United States. 4. Women and literature-
-Great Britain. 5. Women comedians--United States. 6. Comic, The.
7. Comedy. I. Barreca, Regina. II. Series.
PS430.N49 1992
817.009'9287--dc20   91-42544

CONTENTS

Acknowledgements   vii

List of Contributors   ix

1. Making Trouble: An Introduction
   Regina Barreca   1

2. What to Do with Helen Keller Jokes: A Feminist Act
   Mary Klages   13

3. Just Kidding: Gender and Conversational Humor
   Mary Crawford   23

4. Roseanne Barr: Canned Laughter—Containing the Subject
   Siân Mile   39

5. Belly Laughs and Naked Rage: Resisting Humor in Karen
   Finley's Performance Art
   Maria Pramaggiore   47

6. *Sylvia* Talks Back
   Kayann Short   57

7. Why Women Cartoonists Are Rare, And Why
   That's Important
   Betty Swords   65

8. Return the Favor
   Laura Kightlinger   85

9. The Parallel Lives of Kathy and Mo
   Brenda Gross   89

10. The Politics of Humor: An Interview with Margaret Drabble
    Ian Wojcik-Andrews   101

11. Wendy Cope's Struggle with Strugnell in
Making Cocoa for Kingsley Amis
Nicola Thompson   111

12. A Duel of Wits and the Lesbian Romance Novel *or* Verbal
Intercourse in Fictional Regency England
Catrióna Rueda Esquibel   123

13. Louise Erdrich as Nanapush
Sharon Manybeads Bowers   135

14. Confirming the Place of "The Other": Gender and Ethnic
Identity in Maxine Hong Kingston's *The Woman Warrior*
Khani Begum   143

15. Feminist Humorist of the 1920s:
The "Little Insurrections" of Florence Guy Seabury
Thomas Grant   157

16. Irony and Ambiguity in Grace King's "Monsieur Motte"
Zita Z. Dresner   169

17. Violence and Comedy in the Works of Flannery O'Connor
Mark Walters   185

18. Laughter as Feminine Power in *The Color Purple* and
A Question of Silence
Judy Elsley   193

19. The Goblin Ha-Ha: Hidden Smiles and Open Laughter
in *Jane Eyre*
Robin Jones   201

20. The Art of Courting Women's Laughter
Bette Talvacchia   213

21. The Ancestral Laughter of the Streets:
Humor in Muriel Spark's Earlier Works
Regina Barreca   223

Index   241

————ACKNOWLEDGEMENTS————

The first people who should be thanked are the brilliant contributors to this volume; I owe them gratitude for all their support and willingness to provide spectacular work. It is important, too, to acknowledge the importance of the work done by the contributors to *Last Laughs: Perspectives on Women and Comedy*.

I am delighted to recognize the assistants who worked to put *New Perspectives on Women and Comedy* together: Allison Hild—wickedly smart, stunningly efficient and remarkably patient; Laura Rossi—quick-witted, dynamic and organized; and Rose Quiello—intelligent, inspirational and irreplaceable. Wendy Martin was an early inspiration, and I am grateful to her for allowing this "daughter" of *Last Laughs* to appear as part of Studies in Gender and Culture. I also want to thank Kendra Hansis as well as everyone in the English department and the Research Foundation at the University of Connecticut for their continued and effective assistance and support.

Regina Barreca

CONTRIBUTORS

REGINA BARRECA is author of *They Used to Call Me Snow White, But I Drifted: Women's Strategic Use of Humor*, editor of *Last Laughs: Perspectives on Women and Comedy* and editor of *Sex and Death in Victorian Literature*. She is an associate professor of English at the University of Connecticut, Storrs, where she teaches feminist theory and modern British literature. She is completing a book of essays called *"Untamed and Unabashed": Women's Humor in Literature.*

KHANI BEGUM teaches modern British, continental and ethnic literatures and feminist criticism at Bowling Green State University, Ohio. She has written on Lawrence Durrell and James Joyce, and is currently engaged in a feminist study of D.H. Lawrence and James Joyce.

SHARON MANYBEADS BOWERS is an Assiniboine-Haida-Chippewa-French Canadian and Norwegian from Montana who describes herself as an international woman temporarily sequestered in Iowa for the past forty years. She does storytelling in schools and hopes to be involved with a Native American studies program. Currently she is the manager of a Cultural Center while pursuing a PhD.

MARY CRAWFORD is a professor of psychology and women's studies at West Chester University of Pennsylvania. She received her PhD in experimental psychology from the University of Delaware. Her books include *Gender and Thought: Psychological Perspectives* (1989) and *Women and Gender: A Feminist Psychology* (1992). In addition to numerous scholarly works, Professor Crawford has written on women's issues in popular periodicals such as *MS.* magazine.

ZITA Z. DRESNER, associate professor of English at the University of the District of Columbia, is coeditor of *Redressing the Balance*, an anthology of American women's humor, and has contributed articles on women's humor to a number of journals and books.

JUDY ELSLEY received her PhD in literature from the University of Arizona, Tucson, and is presently employed as an assistant professor at Weber State College, Ogden, Utah. She has published a number of articles on quilting as it intersects with feminist theory.

CATRIÓNA RUEDA ESQUIBEL is a Chicana lesbian from southern California and northern Mexico. Her master's thesis, "Loving the Other Woman: Contemporary Lesbian Romance Novels," grew out of "A Duel of Wits...." A PhD student in the history of consciousness program at the University of California, Santa Cruz, Catrióna is currently researching and compiling a bibliography of all published material by and about Latino and Chicana lesbians.

THOMAS GRANT teaches courses in American fiction, the American frontier, and the Jazz Age at the University of Hartford. He has published a book on Chapman's comedies and essays on Twain, Parker, White and other humorists, as well as on modern drama and film. He has twice been a Yale fellow and has received Fulbrights for work in Germany (1980–1981) and Portugal (1992).

BRENDA GROSS is an assistant professor of English at Barnard College, where she teaches courses in feminist comedy and drama. A former critic for *The Villager*, she reviews theatre for *Women and Performance* and *Theatre Journal*. Currently, she is writing a book about the Artists Theatre of New York.

ROBIN JONES is a doctoral candidate at the University of Colorado at Boulder. She teaches multicultural women's literature. Her dissertation involves literary depictions and practical strategies of multicultural pedagogy.

LAURA KIGHTLINGER is a stand-up comic currently living in New York City. She works in clubs and colleges throughout the country. Laura can be seen on the MTV Half-Hour Comedy Hour and HBO's "Women of the Night."

MARY KLAGES does stand-up academics for the English department at the University of Colorado at Boulder.

SIÂN MILE received her BA from the University of Birmingham in her native Britain and her MA from the University of Connecticut, Storrs. She is currently working towards her PhD in English at the University of Colorado at Boulder. When she's not scouring the pages of the *National Enquirer* for a thrill or two, she works on feminist literary theory, twentieth-century literature/popular culture, and contemporary British women writers.

MARIA PRAMAGGIORE teaches literature and film in the liberal studies department at Emory University in Atlanta, Georgia. A PhD candidate in interdisciplinary feminist studies at the Institute of the Liberal Arts at Emory, she is completing a dissertation on contemporary refigurations of the body in film, literature and performance.

KAYANN SHORT is a doctoral student in literature at the University of Colorado at Boulder. Her dissertation focuses on women's presses as multicultural locations for the production of feminist theory and practice.

BETTY SWORDS has been a cartoonist and writer of gags, humor essays, sketches and monologues. She also taught courses on humor at four colleges and presented papers at international conferences on humor. She's now writing a book on humor.

BETTE TALVACCHIA is an associate professor of art history at the University of Connecticut, Storrs. Her central area of research is the Renaissance.

NICOLA THOMPSON is a doctoral candidate in English at Emory University in Atlanta, Georgia. She is currently finishing her dissertation, "Gender and the Reception of Victorian Novels."

MARK WALTERS teaches English at the University of Kansas. He is a regular contributor of fiction to *National Lampoon* and is currently engaged in a book-length study of gender, humor and revenge in the novels of William Faulkner.

IAN WOJCIK-ANDREWS wrote a feminist/Marxist study on Margaret Drabble entitled *Margaret Drabble's Female Bildungsromane: Genre and Gender.* He currently teaches children's literature and literary theory at Eastern Michigan University. Recent publications include "Notes Toward a Marxist Critical Practice" and "The Family as an Ideological Construct in the Fiction of Arthur Ransome."

1

Making Trouble:
An Introduction

REGINA BARRECA

I laughed, as, indeed, it was impossible to do otherwise.

Charlotte Bronte, Villette

What you say is most generous and kind; I don't mean for a moment to correct your judgement. It is only that I have my girlish, mocking way of looking at things...

George Eliot, Middlemarch

We are not alone in the oddity of our beliefs. Our neighbor, whom we never thought would laugh when we laughed, actually does.

Fay Weldon, Letters to Alice

Carrying the twenty essays for this book down the green cinderblock hallway of my university, a concerned senior colleague paused briefly before asking, in sympathy and with great earnestness, what we were going to do about Swift and Pope in this collection on comedy. I clarified my position by explaining that, for the most part, this was a book about women writers of comedy, not about how women were presented in texts by male writers. "Yes, yes," he replied, "but my point is: *have* women done anything differently from Swift and Pope?"

1

This is a book about what women have done differently from Swift and Pope. Or Twain and James, for that matter. Or Amis and Heller. Our arguments will focus on literature by women writers. Male writers are invoked for purposes of comparison but appear as attendant lords only, their function to delineate even more precisely the roles of the main female players.

The goal of this volume (which, until very recently, was fondly known as "Daughter of Last Laughs"—a.k.a. DOLL), is to provide further information on women writers of comedy, women cartoonists, female comics and perfomance artists, and the ways that men's humor and women's humor differ in a number of settings. What we found working on *Last Laughs* was that, as comprehensive a volume as we believed it to be, there was an enormous amount of work to be done. In *New Perspectives,* several essays deal with work produced by women of color: articles concerning Native American, Afro-American and Asian-American writers illuminate these pages. A number of essays deal with women in performance, both from inside and outside "the business"; these essays can be twinned with those concerning women cartoonists, also written from both inside and outside the business. There are essays dealing with lesbian humor, humor and violence, humor and disability, humor and the supposition of women's shame; these essays take us from the Renaissance Italy to this year's Manhattan comedy clubs. Yet, despite the different perspectives and occasionally widely divergent conclusions, certain significant patterns of women's comedy reappear in almost every essay.

We cannot underestimate the continuing need to focus on the particulars of women's comedy, humor and, in addition, women's response to men's humor. It is of particular importance to place women at the center of a discussion of comedy because it has been done too rarely even in contemporary critical studies. Without being defined as such, the study of comedy has been the study of male comedy.

Why "male" comedy? Why make it gender-specific? Why not see comedy as the last frontier of the universal, humor as that glorious patch of hallowed ground where we all meet and laugh with equal joy? A charming thought, but dangerous in its attempt to seduce the reader into a belief that we all laugh at the same things, even when we happen to laugh at the same time, that we all see the same thing when we stand next to one another. Comedy, out of all the textual territories explored, is the least universal. It is rigidly mapped and marked by subjectivity. It is most liable to be filtered by history (we don't make Napoleon jokes), social class (do people on federal assistance find the line "poverty sucks" as funny as the yuppies do?), race and ethnicity (would you tell an Italian

joke at a Sons of Italy meeting if you weren't Italian?), and, it would seem
more than self-evident, gender.

For example, Peter Farb wrote an article called "Speaking Seriously
About Humor," which was published by *The Massachusetts Review* in
1981. Farb, in a standard scholarly explanation of the forms and effects of
various types of humor, offers without apology or embarrassment, as an
example of the "Spooneristic Conundrum" the following: "What's the
difference between a pygmy village and an all-female track team? The
pygmy village is a cunning bunch of runts" (773). If this is such a terrific
example of a certain form of word play, then (as the graduate student who
photocopied Farb's article for me wrote in its margin) "how come I'm not
laughing?" Farb's joke should perhaps be praised for its economy, since
it manages to be both sexist and racist at the same time. But Farb's
example is most useful in illustrating that a joke is not, in fact, always a
joke. A joke depends on the teller <u>and</u> the told, and if something is not
funny it does not mean the person listening has no sense of humor. It
might be that the person telling the joke is not funny. Women have been
told that they have no sense of humor based on those times when they do
not laugh at jokes or stories told by men.

Any one critic's definition of comedy simply cuts a swatch from a larger
fabric and proclaims it whole cloth. The writers of these essays cannot
claim to do otherwise; we can merely make our patterns available to the
reader. A critical overview of three hundred years of women's comedy
must necessarily encompass many and various conceptions of the general
term "comedy." When the central argument being made is that few of
these various conceptions are fruitful when applied to texts by women, the
necessity to explore a number of positions becomes further complicated by
the need for constant qualification, rebuttal and redefinition of these
positions. The texts under discussion are not meant to represent the
full-flowering of all women's writing, performance or art; rather, they
were chosen to illustrate particular forms of comedy and humor.

The following discussion of women writers does not seek to prove that
every woman who ever wrote, wrote comedy; it does not seek to prove
that everything every female character in every text every woman ever
wrote speaks satirically, sarcastically, ironically or with intent to subvert
(although the writers here tend to argue that there are more trouble-makers
than has been previously noted); no one argues that the ending of *The Mill
on The Floss*, for example, is really a slapstick take-off on traditional
couplings or that Virginia Woolf should have done stand-up routines. For
the most part, the writers included in this volume tend to use the term

"comedy" in a broad sense (so to speak), applying that term to the narrative structure of certain texts which refuse to take seriously the supposedly serious matters of the cultures in which they take place. "Humor" applies to those specific textual strategies where the refusal to take serious matters seriously is rendered explicit.

Bronte is capable of writing in *Villette*, for example, the sort of shocking metatextual statement we usually associate with such contemporary writers as Margaret Drabble when she interrupts her own text to instuct us: "Cancel the whole of that, if you please, reader—or rather let it stand, and draw thence a moral—an alternative, text-hand copy—" (118). The "text-hand" copy will draw much of our attention in all the works to be discussed. So will the idea of the "alternative" text. *Villette* is a particularly intriguing example of a genre-defying novel, in fact, because of the consideration of alternatives. If Monsieur Paul returns to marry Lucy, for example, then does the book become a comedy? If he dies in the storm, does the book become a tragedy? By traditional definitions, whether the sailor comes home from the sea will determine whether the waiting woman's life is comic or tragic. Is it any wonder, then, that Bronte refuses to supply the scene that would determine Lucy's textual fate? Lucy has had, according to her own account, the best years of her life while he's been away. What, in fact, would be her happy ending?

Women's humor has not so much been ignored as it has been unrecognized, passed over or misread as tragic. Because literary critics, analysts, novelists, and academics can all supply reasons why the creation of comedy by women is impossible, it does not follow that women have not created comedy. It is similiar to the situation in which experts in physics and aeronautics have explained to their own satisfaction that the bumble-bee can't possibly fly given its weight and wingspan, even as they dash about hoping not to be stung.

In other words, if you're not looking for it you are probably not going to find it. It doesn't mean that it's not there. "Universal negatives are seldom safe," explains Arabella from Lennox's *The Female Quixote*, "and are least to be allowed when the disputes are about the objects of sense; where one position cannot be inferred from another. That there is a castle, any man who has seen it may safely affirm. But you cannot, with equal reason, maintain that there is no castle because you have not seen it" (414).

The subjects of women's comedy are far from unimportant, however unofficial their designation within the dominant discourse. Most apparent during an investigation of available research materials on women and comedy has been the prevailing attitude that comedy written by women must be gentle and conciliatory. This may seem reductive but it is not misrepresentative. The number of histories of comedy which classify women's comedy in these terms confirms what I, for one, believe is central in the misreading of women's texts: the belief that women actually are incapable of producing the challenging, angry and subversive comedy that they do in fact write. Aside from a few articles which raise the possibility for this uncommon interpretation, such as D.W. Harding's discussion of Jane Austen in terms of "Regulated Hatred," or Wilt's "The Laughter of Maidens, the Cackle of Matriarchs: Notes on the Collision between Comedy and Feminism," there exists the mostly unassailed conviction that those few women who write comedies write them only with a desire to provide mild entertainment, a textual fliration, a batting of the rhetorical eyelashes.

Judith Wilt, however, unhesitatingly confronts the relationship between women's comedy and anger. Wilt argues that there is, for women, a: "boundary where comedy ceases to cheer and succor and becomes violent, destructive, murderous...."[1] Women's comedies have often been misread since they often do not adhere to the essentially conservative conventions of comedy. If comedy written by women is meant to include certain elements (reconciling gentility, soft admonitions for social lapses, sweet mirth) and if these elements are markedly absent, the work might be misread as non-comedic. This might occur despite the fact that the work contains aspects of fiction usually associated with "traditional" comedy: irony, hostility, aggression, the grotesque, explicit or implicit political agendas, for example. While providing at least some of the distinguishing signs of comedy—exaggerated characters, use of puns or wordplay, absurd situations—women writers still manage to undercut the conventions they employ by shifting the very framing devices used as definition. What can be regarded as a nominal happy ending might, for example, include a number of elements usually regarded as tragic. When the heroine of a Fay Weldon novel has burned down her house (asphyxiating a gerbil in the process, displaying a markedly unfeminine indifference to a housepet), abandoned her children, destroyed her husband's career and killed off her rival, we still regard the book—in this case, *The Life and Loves of a She-Devil*—as a comedy. It is women's comedy: "A comic turn, turned serious," as Weldon herself explains in the last line of her novel.

As the essays in *Last Laughs: Perspectives on Women and Comedy* illustrated, women's writing of comedy is characterized by the breaking of cultural and ideological frames. The woman writer's use of comedy is dislocating, anarchic and, paradoxically, unconventional. I say para-doxically because, of course, there is the constant problem of discussing works that must be grouped under a conventional heading such as "comedy" while simultaneously claiming that they subvert the elemental aspects associated with that convention. The woman writer of comedy will often mask her satire by appearing to describe faithfully a series of events, a method to which the heroine in Lennox's *Female Quixote* is devoted: "When actions are a censure upon themselves, the reciter will always be considered a satirist" (315).

The woman writer forges a comedy that allows for complexity and depth without the generally oppressive didacticism so often found in the social satire of writers from Swift to Amis. As I have argued elsewhere,[2] in comedies by women the very idea of the "universal" is challenged, confronted and, finally, shattered. Even the existentialist male writer will write from within the dominant discourse in terms of his gender. The most economically oppressed of male writers nevertheless writes from a position of privilege awarded to him by a culture that equates value with maleness in much the same way that an Anglo writer writes from a position of privilege in the Western world. Despite the fact that these observations may cause discomfort to the existentialist, economically depressed Anglo male writer—or critic—who regards his own oppression as unique, they remain valid. Nancy Walker, in her study of American women's humor, explains that "[e]ven when the white male humorist adopts for his own purposes the stance of the outsider...he writes with the authority of the insider, the person who is potentially in a position to change what he finds wrong, whether it is the law or the cut of a dinner jacket...."[3]

Certain forms of comedy can invert the world not only briefly but permanently; can strip away the dignity and complacency of powerful figures only to *refuse* to hand them back these attributes when the allotted time for "carnival" is finished. Comedy can effectively channel anger and rebellion by first making them appear to be acceptable and temporary phenomena, no doubt to be purged by laughter; and then by harnessing the released energies, rather than dispersing them. The world turned upside down can prove that the world has no rightful position at all, and that we have created our own systems of balance based on nothing more than the continuation of what has gone before, that reason and nature are no more reasonable and natural than they are cosmically ordained: this kind of comedy terrifies those who hold order dear.

Feminist criticism has, until recently, avoided the systematic discussion of comedy, perhaps in order to be accepted by conservative critics who found feminist theory comic in and of itself. Since the 1983 publication of Judy Little's excellent and groundbreaking book, *Comedy and the Woman Writer*, however, there has been a growing critical interest in feminist perspectives on women and humor. To the arguments made by such critics this book will refer with relief at the conviction that others have arrived at similiar questions and conclusions. The anxiety in writing about women's comedy has certainly been that of anxiety of authorship rather than the anxiety of influence.

Judy Little's work on Virginia Woolf, Muriel Spark and other contemporary English authors has cleared a path for others to follow. Nancy Walker's *A Very Serious Thing: Women's Humor and American Culture*, published in 1988, provides a thorough and provocative discussion of women's humor as it appears in both literature and popular culture, calling into question even those essentially arbitrary categories. Essays by Judith Wilt, Carol Mitchell, Emily Toth and others have opened the field for further inquiry, raising issues and suggesting questions. Writers like Joanna Russ and Mary Daly provide texts laced with delightfully venomous humor, employing the process even as they describe the method. *Last Laughs: Perspectives on Women and Comedy*, a collection of eighteen essays (and three cartoons) which I had the honor of editing, provides a wide range of responses to the question "*have* women done anything differently from Swift and Pope?" The following pages will continue the study of the ways in which women have laughed—often because it seems impossible to do otherwise.

It would be judicious, perhaps, to mention by way of preface the seventeenth-century writer Aphra Behn who was herself conspicuously concerned with the woman writer of comedy. Behn is perhaps best known now for her "historical" novel *Oroonoko*, but in her day she was applauded—and chastised—for plays such as *The Dutch Lover* and *The Forced Marriage*. Catherine Gallagher's discussion of Behn's embrace of the writer/whore mask and her creation of "overlapping discourses of commercial, sexual and linguistic exchange" in "Who was that Masked Woman? The Prostitute and the Playwright in the Comedies of Aphra Behn"[4] allows us to see Behn not as someone who made writing more difficult for women the way a wayward older sister makes life more difficult for her siblings (as Woolf seems to argue in *A Room of One's Own*), but as a woman "conscious of her historical role" and a playful challenge to "the very possibility of female self-representation" (LL 41). It is in the prologues, epilogues and prefaces to her plays, however, that Behn deals most directly with her position as a woman writer. Behn realized that the phrase "That it was Bawdy" was the "least and most excusable fault in the men writers," where, for similiar material she would be told "but from a woman it was unnatural."[5] If women are told that they cannot write, then obviously all that is written by women must, by definition, be criticized and dismissed as unnatural, monstrous, or abberant in order for the theory to keep hold. However, as Behn writes in *The Town Fop*, "But a monster is only so from its rarity...."

Behn knew that she appeared as a woman, not as a playwright, to her critics, and that often her work "had no other misfortune but that of coming out for a woman's: had it been owned by a man, though the most dull, unthinkably rascally scribbler in town, it had been a most admirable play" (Goreau 215). Even as she argues the point, she seems to retreat from it in frustration: "but a devil don't—the woman damns the poet" (219). Behn ridiculed the male playwrights who prided themselves on keeping to the three unities, who could only trace patterns rather than create their own: "Your way of writing's out of fashion grown./Method, and rule—you only understand;/Pursue that way of fooling and be damned" (216). [Nearly 300 years later, Fay Weldon would write "I do pity contemporary male writers, who have wives to bring them coffee and answer the phone to the bank manager, and no excuse not to undertake, not to complete, not to get published, and who find themselves with nothing to say."[6] Behn begins the "Epistle to the Reader" of *The Dutch Lover* by addressing her audience member as "Good, Sweet, Honey, Sugar-Candied Reader," appearing to curtsey and flutter in his presence. The next line, however, splices the alternative, "text-hand" copy onto the coy invitation: "Which I think is more than anyone has called you yet...I presume you have not much to do and therefore are obliged to me for keeping you from worse employment, and if you have a better you may get you gone about your business...." She describes a critic at one of her plays as,

> a sorry animal that has nought else to shield it from the uttermost contempt of all mankind, but that respect we afford to rats and toads, which though we do not well allow to live, yet when considered as a part of God's creation, we make honorable mention of them. A thing, reader...this thing, I tell ye, opening that which serves

it for a mouth, out issued such as noise as this to those who sat about it, that they
were to expect a woeful play, God damn him, for it was a woman's....[A]nd if
comedy should be the picture of ridiculous mankind, I wonder anyone should think
it such a sturdy task, whilst we are furnished with such precious originals as
him.... (Goreau 213)

"It was a woman's" play, novel, poem, story has always been the first
definition of a text created by a woman, whether the author cared to seek
that appellation or sought to deny it. Ntozake Shange summed it up in a
1989 interview with *The New York Times* as follows:

Because whatever we may perceive of ourselves, we writers or anything else we
want to be, when we go out of this building...any of these guys unloading trucks
don't see playwrights. They see—they might not even see—a woman. They might
see an expletive....Because when we go outside, we can't write a sign that says
'I'm an intellectual woman, therefore don't speak to me that way.' That's not
going to save you....

From Behn to Shange there exists a tradition of women's comedy informed
by and speaking to the experience of being a female in a world where that
experience is devalued. If the woman writer of comedy has been told that
she cannot possibly succeed in what she has set out to do, she has
nevertheless persevered in her endeavor by ignoring the good advice of
those who counsel her against her inevitable failure. Jane Austen, that
famous man *(sic)* of letters, was given terribly good advice at one point
when a gentleman suggested to her that she might write more profitably if
she could only chose a better subject, something like "an historical
romance, founded on the House of Saxe Cobourg." Austen replied that,
although the gentleman might indeed be correct in his assumption, she

could no more write a romance than an epic poem. I could not sit seriously down
to write a serious romance under any other motive than to save my life; and if it
were indispensable for me to keep it up and never relax into laughing at myself or
other people, I am sure I should be hung before I had finished the first chapter.[7]

She thanks him, of course, and apologizes, explaining that "I must keep
to my own style and go on in my own way" (453). Apologizing to and
thanking her critics, Austen seems to anticipate Fay Weldon's advice,
given to her fictional, novel-writing niece in *Letters to Alice,* to "agree
with your accusers, loudly and clearly. They will shut up sooner" (LTA
107). The apologies and thanks have for too long been misread as sincere

reflections of humble womanhood rather than as the social expedients they are; the sooner writers are left to write, they can get back to laughing at themselves and making jokes at the expense of others. As Elinor in *Sense and Sensibility* has learned, some comments do not bear answering: "Elinor agreed to it all, for she did not think he deserved the compliment of rational opposition" (255). Although Jane Austen did not have to risk being hanged for writing comedy, her comment indicates her awareness of the dangers particular to the woman with a sense of humor. The strategies used by women both to heighten and avoid such dangers form the basis for the essays in *New Perspectives on Women and Comedy*.

These essays move through performance and art to literature and sociology. They deal with how, traditionally, men use humor to shame women—as Talvacchia discusses—to how women are learning to refuse and refute that shame—as Crawford and Swords discuss. Klages faces Helen Keller jokes; Kightlinger faces the ritualized discrimination practiced by comedy clubs. Esquibel deals with lesbian humor; Begum deals with *The Woman Warrior* and a woman's need to learn to speak up, to make trouble. Gross gives us Cathy and Mo up close; Wojcik-Andrews gives us a closer look at Margaret Drabble. The other essays cover and uncover a variety of viewpoints, visions and visionaries. They introduce ideas and force us to examine old issues from a new perspective. Several will, no doubt, make you laugh, but their primary purpose is to raise new issues, not bring down the house. If they happen to bring down the house—or tear down some walls—well, that's a beginning.

NOTES

1. Judith Wilt. "The Laughter of the Maidens, the Cackle of the Matriarchs: Notes on the Collision." *Gender and the Literary Voice.* ed. Janet Todd. (New York: Holmes and Meier) 1980, 174.
2. See the introduction to *Last Laughs* for further discussion and references.
3. Nancy Walker. *A Very Serious Thing: Women's Humor and American Culture.* (Minneapolis: University of Minnesota Press) 1988, 11.
4. Catherine Gallagher. "Who Was That Masked Woman? The Prostitute and the Playwright in the Comedies of Aphra Behn." *Last Laughs.* ed. Regina Barreca. (New York and London: Gordon & Breach) 1988, 23-42.
5. Angeline Goreau. *Reconstructing Aphra. A Social Biography of Aphra Behn.* (Oxford: Oxford University Press) 1980, 215.
6. Fay Weldon. *Letters to Alice on First Reading Jane Austen.* (London: Coronet) 1984, 83.
7. *Jane Austen's Letters,* collected and edited R.W. Chapman. (Oxford: Oxford University Press) 1979, 458.

WORKS CITED

Austen, Jane. *Sense and Sensibility.* London: Penguin Books, 1972.

Bronte, Charlotte. *Villette.* London: Penguin Books, 1979.

Chapman, R.W. editor. *Jane Austen's Letters.* Oxford: Oxford University Press, 1979.

Eliot, George. *Middlemarch.* London: Penguin Books, 1965.

Farb, Peter. "Speaking Seriously About Humor." Massachusetts Review 22, no. 4 (Winter 1981) : 760-776.

Gallagher, Catherine. "Who Was That Masked Woman? The Prostitute and the Playwright in the Comedies of Aphra Behn ." *Last Laughs,* ed. Regina Barreca. New York and London: Gordon & Breach, 1988.

Goreau, Angeline. *Reconstructing Aphra. A Social Biography of Aphra Behn.* Oxford: Oxford University Press, 1980.

Lennox, Charlotte. *The Female Quixote, or The Adventures of Arabella.* introd. Sandra Shulman. London, Boston and Henley: Pandora, 1986.

Little, Judy. *Comedy and the Woman Writer: Woolf, Spark and Feminism.* Lincoln: University of Nebraska Press, 1983.

Walker, Nancy. *A Very Serious Thing: Women's Humor and American Culture.* Minneapolis: University of Minnesota Press, 1988.

Weldon, Fay. *Letters to Alice on First Reading Jane Austen.* London: Coronet, 1984.

Weldon, Fay. *The Life and Loves of a She-Devil.* New York: Pantheon, 1983.

Wilt, Judith. "The Laughter of the Maidens, the Cackle of the Matriarchs: Notes on the Collision." *Gender and the Literary Voice.* ed. Janet Todd. New York: Holmes and Meier, 1980.

Woolf, Virginia. *A Room of One's Own.* New York and London: Harcourt Brace and Jovanovich, 1957.

2

What To Do With Helen Keller Jokes: A Feminist Act

MARY KLAGES

What follows belongs to a genre of discourse I like to call "stand-up academics." In my youth, I wanted to be a regular stand-up comedian, but in college I developed an unfortunate tendency to footnote and cross-reference my jokes, so I became a professor instead. The following discussion was originally written as an after-dinner speech (once the gentlemen had retired to the parlor, and the ladies were left at table with the port and cigars), and is meant to be delivered orally. I therefore request that you read this aloud, preferably before an audience that has dined and drunk well; failing that, please read this aloud to yourself as you stand in front of a mirror. And remember, in comedy, as in life, *timing* is everything.

Be warned. The jokes included in this piece are cruel and politically incorrect, and are for scholarly consideration only. THESE JOKES ARE NOT FUNNY. Laugh at your own risk.

My title asks a question crucial to politically correct feminist behavior: what does the sensitive feminist do with Helen Keller jokes? The most obvious answer, perhaps, is simply to ignore them, or to take the teller of such jokes aside and explain, patiently and at great length, why making fun of the handicapped went out with men in tiger skins dragging women around by their hair. However, ignoring them or correcting them won't make them go away; they have become an intrinsic part of American popular or folk culture.

The next possible solution, following the "if you can't beat 'em, join 'em" school of thought, is to tell Helen Keller jokes. We all know some, surely...(here the audience is invited to contribute their favorite examples of Helen Keller jokes).

For the feminist academic, however, none of these solutions suffice. Being academics, what we do with Helen Keller jokes is (all together, now!)...ANALYZE THEM! And to do that, we first have to...Yes? In the front row? Correct! Put them into categories!

Of course, being post-modern academics, we can't just put them into any old categories we happen to have lying around the house. Our categorization of Helen Keller jokes must display our comprehensive knowledge of complicated structuralist and post-structuralist theoretical constructs.

For example (and feel free to call out the punchlines as they come up), in classifying the joke "How did Helen Keller go crazy? Trying to read a stucco wall," one could say some quite profound things about the desire to "read" the material surfaces of the physical world as texts, or about Keller's inability to interpret "text"-ural surfaces meaningfully as a figure for the alienated human subject moving blindly in a universe of incomplete or fragmentary signification, or about the significance of "wall" as both text and barrier, the enclosing substance which makes close(d) reading possible.

Or one could consider this joke—"What was Helen Keller's favorite color? Corduroy"—as a metonymic displacement of visual perception onto a tactile dimension. This category of humor might also include a similar joke—"What did Helen Keller say when she jumped off a cliff? (teller makes wild finger motions)"—which shows a displacement of speech, rather than vision, onto a tactile perceptual dimension. This category of metonymic displacement jokes might include "What did Helen Keller's parents do when they caught her swearing? They washed her hands with soap," as it demonstrates a displacement of speech from the locus of the mouth to the locus of the hands. However, I think this last joke is best reserved for a new category, one which emphasizes how this joke shifts a common hygienic practice into the arena of punitive familial relations which provide the basis for the modern disciplinary surveillance state described so well by Michel Foucault.

As we begin to get the hang of such categorization, we can move on to even more provocative areas, away from Foucault's discipline toward the realm of those sexy, slippery French feminists, whose theories enable us to see that "Why did Helen Keller masturbate with one hand? So she could moan (or read pornography) with the other" not only displaces speech and reading from a visual to a tactile dimension, but also that this displacement reveals that female sexuality itself contains a manual (digital) dimension *beyond* the register of the visual, in a place where sexual pleasure and language are *both* tangible and inseparable, where the Law of the Father cannot be seen nor heard. We could also note that "What did Helen Keller consider oral sex? A manicure" seems to deconstruct this privileged female space of tangible sex/text-uality by reinscribing female sexuality within the purview of the objectifying male gaze, which demands certain ritual enhancements of visual beauty that mark the female body as different from, and Other than, the unpainted, unadorned male body which cannot ever become the object of the blind woman's gaze.

Moving further into the realm of Lacanian linguistic theory, our next category of jokes might include all of those which produce a continual slippage or sliding of signifiers in an endless play of meaning, and which, by violating our horizons of expectation and familiarity, create endless existential anxiety by continually shifting the position of the (bourgeois) subject, forcing us to be always-already destabilized and decentered. Such fundamentally linguistic jokes include "Why can't Helen Keller have children? Because she's dead"; "How did Helen Keller meet her husband? On a blind date"; and "Did you see Helen Keller's new house? Neither did she." Also included in this category is the only truly narrative Helen Keller joke I've found:

> Helen Keller and Annie Sullivan go to a shopping mall, and Helen has with her a guide dog on a leash. When they go into a store, Helen heaves up the guide dog on the end of the leash and starts whirling the leash, and the dog, in circles above her head. A startled salesperson runs up to them and says to Annie, "May I help you?" "No, thank you," Annie replies, "she's just looking around."

Finally, there is one Helen Keller joke that deserves a category all its own, if only for the reason that it combines the elements of *all* the previous jokes/categories into one delightfully confusing tangle of/sexuality/textuality/tactility: "How did Helen Keller learn to masturbate? By reading lips."

However, at this point I must say that categorizing these Helen Keller jokes begins to become problematic. To utilize sophisticated literary, psychoanalytic, and linguistic theories to analyze Helen Keller jokes is to take them seriously, and to give them a status which they do not deserve; we are in grave danger of forgetting that they are vulgar and reprehensible, and not worth the attention of any self-respecting feminist academic.

Yet another category of Helen Keller jokes illustrates this fundamental offensiveness:

> How did Helen Keller burn her left ear?
> Answering the iron.
> How did Helen Keller burn her right ear?
> They called back.
> How did Helen Keller burn her face?
> Bobbing for French Fries.

While we could note that these jokes, too, employ certain metonymic displacements, and violations of expectations, the main thing they have in common is that they portray Helen Keller, not just as physically inept, but as downright *stupid*. Other jokes in this category include:

Do you know about Helen Keller's new book, *Around the Block in Eighty Days?*

Do you know about the Helen Keller doll? Wind it up and it walks into walls.

> How did Helen Keller's parents punish her?
> a) They moved the furniture around.
> b) They left the plunger in the toilet.

What, oh what, is the fastidious feminist academic to *do* with these last jokes? Dare we analyze them at all?

The answer being a resounding "YES," we can at least assuage our consciences by moving on to a different mode of analysis—one which looks, with great relief, not at the awful, unfunny jokes themselves, but at the reactions of audiences (*not* including ourselves, of course!) who actually laugh out loud at them.

The typical response to a Helen Keller joke, or other "sick" form of humor, is a laugh-wince, which represents a moment of simultaneous resistance and reification. The resistance occurs in the laughter, with which one recognizes, and happily participates in, a violation of social taboos and standards of polite behavior. The reification of these social standards occurs with the wince which immediately follows the laugh; the wince is an acknowledgement of the self-enforcement of the social taboo, when the laugher chides herself for laughing at something that, when you think about it, is really NOT FUNNY.

The resistance inherent in the laughter is a small moment in what V.N. Volosinov (who may or may not be Mikhail Bakhtin) calls "behavioral ideology," a form of individual resistance unconnected with any larger social-political critique.[1] With a Helen Keller joke, the listener's laughter momentarily knocks her Helen Keller off her pedestal as the representative of certain dominant-cultural values; the wince then re-establishes the listener's belief that we really should, and do, admire and respect Helen Keller, and the values she represents.

The listener's wince reaction is based on a sense of social maturity, and the recognition that mature, sensible, sensitive adults do not laugh at, and certainly do not tell, these jokes. This leads us to another area of analysis—who *does* tell these vulgar jokes, and why?

Folklorists and other academics who have studied Helen Keller jokes specifically, and other forms of offensive humor, see them as means of negotiating the changing cultural status of the targeted person or group. Thus Helen Keller jokes are told in reaction to the greater visibility of the handicapped or disabled population in mainstream American culture. Scholars argue that the number and frequency of Helen Keller jokes increased after the passage of a 1977 federal law which required that all public buildings be made accessible to the disabled, that disabled children be provided for in regular public school classrooms, and that employers could not discriminate against disabled workers. Helen Keller jokes were thus told as a sign of social anxiety about the integration of disabled people into the dominant, able-bodied culture; they appeared *in the absence of* any alternative dominant-cultural ideological frameworks of understanding the social position of disabled people. Without any representations of disabled people on television, and in other mainstream media, the negotiation of cultural change occurred in the realm of popular or folk culture, on a relatively unorganized, individual behavioral level.[2]

This theory, while interesting, has some flaws. I know from my own personal experience that Helen Keller jokes existed and were popular before the 1977 federal anti-discrimination law was passed; I remember distinctly telling Helen Keller jokes with my playground peers in elementary school in the 1960's. This theory also does not explain why Helen

Keller jokes would function in the *absence* of dominant-cultural representations of disability, as there are thousands of dominant-cultural representations of Helen Keller that are familiar to almost all Americans. Indeed, Helen Keller is virtually the *only* mainstream American representative of disability available to twentieth-century audiences.

Sociologists and folklorists tell us that Helen Keller jokes, like other "sick" humor, are told by adolescents, who are negotiating issues of "otherness," especially concerning bodily structure and physical appearance.[3] There is not necessarily any gender difference discernible in the telling of Helen Keller jokes, as boys are as likely as girls to tell them; there is, however, a gender distinction in cultural knowledge about Helen Keller, as girls are much more likely than boys to read about, and be fascinated by, the story of Helen Keller's life. While both boys and girls are likely to tell these jokes as an expression of adolescent anxiety about different bodies, girls are likely to be more aware of Helen Keller jokes as violations of standards of social propriety and etiquette, as etiquette still belongs primarily to the "feminine" sphere of influence. Girls are thus perhaps more likely than boys to recognize that the "polite" way to respond to a disabled person is not to stare, not to show any awareness of physical difference, and certainly not to make fun of them. This awareness could mean that girls, overall, are less likely to tell Helen Keller jokes because the jokes are rude; on the other hand, it could just as well mean that girls tell Helen Keller jokes more often than boys do because girls have a stronger reason to rebel against the "feminine" standards of etiquette that proscribe against such blatant rudeness.

Whatever gender distinctions may exist, it is fairly clear that Helen Keller jokes appeal to an adolescent sense of rebellion against established social codes and taboos regarding the able-bodied population's response to disabled people; they are told in flagrant violation of the dictum "DON'T MAKE FUN OF THE HANDICAPPED." That dictum, and the concomitant commands not to stare at, point at, or otherwise notice or acknowledge the difference of a disabled person, illustrate the dominant able-bodied culture's insistence on the *invisibility* of the disabled. Telling an adolescent (or anyone else) not to look at or notice disability is part of a cultural effort to *erase* disability.

Helen Keller jokes meet with social disapproval—the wince reaction, and the idea that "polite" adults don't tell or laugh at such things—because our dominant cultural attitude toward disability is strictly limited to feelings of pity, charity, and sympathy. If not completely invisible, disabled people are "the unfortunate," the grateful recipients of charitable benevolence.

This maternal, protective reaction to "the unfortunate" keeps disabled people in a childlike cultural position, necessarily dependent upon the generosity of the able-bodied. Whether invisible or pitiable, disabled people are still not recognized within dominant-cultural ideological frameworks as fully and equally human and adult.

One expression of this attitude can be found in a piece printed in *The National Enquirer,* one of the foremost purveyors of mainstream (conservative) American cultural perspectives. An article entitled "Killers and Thugs Tape Books for the Blind" described the efforts of a mass-murderer, serving a life sentence for "dismembering his mother and her best friend and murdering six young female hitchhikers," to provide blind college students with textbooks on tape. The convict noted that he had helped a blind man through three years of law school by taping his textbooks; his main satisfaction in so doing, the killer stated, was that he knew he was helping someone "less fortunate" than himself.[4]

Which would *you* rather be—a convicted mother-murderer or a blind lawyer?

The overwhelming cultural equation of physical disability with misery, suffering, and misfortune leads to the response of erasure or protection of the disabled. "Making fun of the handicapped," through things like telling Helen Keller jokes, is a direct violation of this attitude of sympathy, pity, and charity. From the dominant-cultural perspective, such jokes are "unladylike," because the teller (presumed to be able-bodied) is picking on someone weaker than she is. These jokes are also "unladylike" because they violate the codes of social etiquette, defined by a maternalistic attitude, which are enforced largely by "professional ladies" such as Dear Abby and Miss Manners, who function as arbiters of taste and behavior. This "feminine" code of etiquette is curiously reinforced by feminist theorists like Nancy Chodorow and Carol Gilligan, who emphasize women's greater involvement with sympathetic and harmonious interpersonal relations. From the perspective of "feminine" morality or simple politeness, Helen Keller jokes should *not* be told (or laughed at) because they might hurt the feelings of someone weaker and less fortunate than oneself.

It is this code of etiquette, which is a holdover from the Victorian ideology of True Womanhood, that makes the disabled invisible and unmentionable. Thus only "polite," socially sanctioned images of disabled people—such as mainstream representations of Helen Keller as an American saint—are supposed to be available as ideological descriptions of disability. Most able-bodied people know Helen Keller, and perhaps

F.D.R, or Stevie Wonder, as the *only* acceptable representatives of the disabled; all other disabled people, insofar as they don't measure up to Helen Keller (*et al.*), are unacceptable, impolite, and therefore invisible to the mainstream able-bodied population. This attitude will change, of course, as representations of disability become more prominent in mainstream media. Moving away from the traditionally acceptable forms of disabilities, such as blindness, or being perfectly formed but in a wheelchair, mainstream media are beginning to portray a fuller range of physical and mental differences, from cerebral palsy in *My Left Foot* to Down's Syndrome in *Life Goes On*. Perhaps when representations of all forms of difference become prevalent in mainstream media, the need for Helen Keller jokes will disappear.

Nevertheless, until that utopian moment, Helen Keller jokes continue to exist, to be told, and—yes, let's admit it—to be laughed at. The question that must be raised at this point is, *why* are Helen Keller jokes funny? (Of course, they aren't funny *really*, but if they were....)

Helen Keller jokes are only funny if you already know who Helen Keller is. Someone from Mars, who had never heard of Helen Keller, would have no idea what these jokes were referring to, much less why anyone would laugh at them. To "get" a Helen Keller joke, you have to know that she was (a) deaf and blind, and (b) a noble American heroine who transcended her physical handicaps to participate fully in normal American life and letters. The key to understanding and responding to Helen Keller jokes lies in knowing on some level what the dominant cultural representations of Keller point out as the moral lesson her life teaches—that handicaps are things to be overcome.

The dominant cultural image of Keller is that she is remarkable because she was *just like us,* despite being deaf and blind; she could and did function in a sighted and hearing world *as if* she were able-bodied. We honor and applaud her as a heroine for *erasing* her handicaps, for *not* being defined by her body, for making her own deafness and blindness so invisible that we can easily think of her as "one of us." Helen Keller has become the foremost mainstream representative of disability precisely because she conformed to an able-bodied norm, and lived within the terms of an able-bodied world, instead of challenging those norms and terms.

While world-wide publicity about Helen Keller did serve to increase public awareness, in the first half of the twentieth century, about the potential of disabled people, it also reified the dominant-cultural view that disabled people must conform to able-bodied standards. If they cannot conform, and be "just like us," they will remain Other, outside the acceptable norm. Very few disabled people, in reality, are like Helen Keller; her example, as the only widely-known disabled person, cannot help the able-bodied mainstream accept and cope with disabled people who *cannot* "transcend" their bodies—who, indeed, have every right to be in their bodies, and in public.

Telling Helen Keller jokes doesn't simply "make fun" of a respected American heroine; these jokes put Helen Keller back into her body by acknowledging her physicality, her deafness and blindness, and showing that she could not "transcend" her condition. In this sense, *The Miracle Worker* is the biggest (and longest) Helen Keller joke of all, because it insists on putting Keller's body, and its differences, on center stage.

Rather than showing Helen Keller conforming to able-bodied norms by erasing her body, Helen Keller jokes insist on integrating Helen Keller, complete with her deafness and blindness, into mainstream culture, into the events of everyday life. They continually point out her *inability* to be "just like us," her inadequacy to deal with the most mundane aspects of daily life. These jokes largely locate Keller at home, within the normally safe and protective confines of the domestic-female world; they refute the dominant-cultural image of Keller as an unconquerable spirit by showing her endlessly defeated by such dangerous objects as waffle irons, furniture, and soap.

Telling Helen Keller jokes thus is a form of resistance to the moral lesson her life is supposed to teach. Children, especially girls, are told that, if Helen Keller could overcome deafness and blindness, *you* should be able to overcome any lesser obstacles that you might face; if you don't, it's your own fault for not having Helen Keller-like willpower and determination. Telling Helen Keller jokes provides a form of resistance to this moral model, which blames the victim for not transcending her own limitations, by asserting that Keller could not overcome obstacles—that indeed, common household items and events were insurmountable obstacles for her. Telling Helen Keller jokes makes us feel safe, adequate, and competent, as we realize that we can successfully perform tasks, like shopping and answering the phone, that left this noble American heroine completely bewildered.

Not only do Helen Keller jokes make us able-bodied people feel good about our trivial domestic accomplishments, they also acknowledge that disabled people all have bodies—*different* bodies—and force us to look at those different bodies. This may be why the Helen Keller jokes which focus on sexuality produce an even greater laugh-wince reaction than other Helen Keller jokes: these jokes highlight the fact that *sexuality requires physicality.* These jokes, by presenting Keller as a physical/sexual being, provide an even greater contradiction to the dominant image of Helen Keller than the non-sexual jokes do. Keller is famous for being a disembodied woman, for fulfilling, in the twentieth century, the nineteenth century ideology of True Womanhood which insisted that women (white middle-class women, anyway) were pure, noble, and transcendent, lacking genitalia and sexual feelings or desire because they were closer to the angels than to mortal, animalistic, sexual, physical men. Jokes that insist that Keller masturbated, or had oral sex, shatter the mainstream image of Keller as a representative of True Womanhood, thus simultaneously exploding the ideas that women don't like sex, and that disabled people don't have bodies.

In short, Helen Keller jokes insist that disabled people, even disabled *women,* even world-famous deaf-blind American heroines, have bodies that need to be, and have a right to be, publicly visible, publicly represented, in their own terms, and with their own differences.

And thus I return to my title. What to do with Helen Keller jokes is— *TELL THEM!* Because *that's* a feminist act.

NOTES

1. See V.N. Volosinov, *Marxism and the Philosophy of Language,* (New York: The Seminar Press, 1973).
2. See Mac E. Barrick, "The Helen Keller Joke Cycle," *Journal of American Folklore,* 1980: 93(370), pp. 441-449.
3. See Alan Dundes, *Cracking Jokes: Studies of Sick Humor Cycles and Stereotypes,* (Berkeley: Ten Speed Press, 1987), esp. pp. 15-18.
4. Chris Fuller, "Killers and Thugs Tape Books for the Blind," *The National Enquirer,* April 14, 1987.

WORKS CITED

Barrick, Mac E. "The Helen Keller Joke Cycle," *Journal of American Folklore,* 1980: 93(370).
Dundes, Alan. *Cracking Jokes: Studies of Sick Humor Cycles and Stereotypes.* (Berkeley: Ten Speed Press, 1987).
Fuller, Chris. "Killers and Thugs Tape Books for the Blind," *The National Enquirer.* April 14, 1987.
Volosinov, V.N. *Marxism and the Philosophy of Language.* (New York: The Seminar Press, 1973).

3

Just Kidding: Gender and Conversational Humor

MARY CRAWFORD

Several years ago, I taught an undergraduate honors seminar on gender and language for the first time. In reading the social science literature, my students and I encountered claims that women's speech, in contrast to the speech of men, is lacking in humor and creativity. In studying speech and language, as in so many other areas, psychological science had used experimental methods to construct gender as difference.

I began to think about the use of humor in mundane conversation and how a feminist sensibility might be brought to bear on social science methods for studying humor. Nevertheless, I let my work on humor take a back seat to my more "serious" research for years. Actually, I felt rather apologetic about it; humor research didn't seem like real science. Now, having persisted despite my own misgivings, I believe that my attempts to reconcile social science methods and my own feminist vision of women's humor are instructive not only for what they reveal about gender and humor, but about psychological epistemologies and methods.

METHODS AND VALUES IN HUMOR RESEARCH

Most psychological research on humor stems from a positivist conception of science. It defines humor in terms of decontextualized phenomena, and conceptualizes gender as sex differences. By and large psychologists have acted as though the best way to understand humor is to bring it into the laboratory. In the prototypical psychology experiment on humor, subjects sit down alone in a room, are shown a series of written jokes or cartoons, and are asked to rate how funny they are on 7-point scales. The jokes themselves are varied on some dimension such as hostility or incongruity, and/or the subjects' scores on personality measures are correlated with their ratings. The goal of much of the research has been to use people's responses to humor as a way of getting at underlying cognitive processes or personality traits. The ability to create humor has hardly ever been studied. What people do with humor in ordinary social interaction has also been overlooked.

There are several limitations and biases in this research. The humorous stimuli are taken from public sources—jokes and comedy routines of professional comedians, published cartoons, and so forth. These public media encode masculinist and androcentric values. Earlier studies of hostile and sexual humor often failed to control for which sex was the butt of the sexual joke or the recipient of the aggression. The research focused almost entirely on appreciation rather than creating humor. Male research participants were the norm, and when both sexes were studied, there was often no clear theoretical reason to predict a particular pattern of differences. Therefore, sex differences were either dismissed or over-interpreted.

Moreover, psychology has regarded humor as though it were a property of individuals. For example, men very often rate the jokes in laboratory experiments funnier than women do, and this sex difference has sometimes been taken as evidence that women are more inhibited or conventional—lacking a well-developed sense of humor. But humor can also be thought of as an interactional event. It normally happens between people, and its emergence is collaborative.

Imagine that you and I are having a conversation. For you to be able to tell a joke, I have to give you the floor and signal in subtle (usually nonverbal) ways that I'm willing to let you be funny. Then I have to pay attention to your witticism—let you hold the floor. And then I have to let you know I "got it"—and know you meant it as a joke—by laughing, giving nonverbal responses such as rolling my eyes, or by adding a witticism of my own. This means that to study the dynamics of humor we need methods that can measure and evaluate interaction, preferably naturally occurring interaction, not just individual behavior.

All these factors—male oriented stimuli, androcentric biases in research design and sampling, decontextualized settings, and an individualistic focus—have resulted in a flawed, rather pathetic body of research on the psychology of humor. In it, psychology has participated in the social construction of women as a deviant and deficient group, with neither the wit to create humor nor the ability to appreciate it.[1]

Thus, I have turned to interpretive methods such as content analysis, participant observation, and discourse analysis. Most of the research I'll describe is based on one or another of these methods. My thinking has been influenced by Jonathan Potter and Margaret Wetherell's approach to discourse analysis, Michael Mulkay's discourse approach to humor, and my own attempts to integrate their methods with other context-sensitive methods and with a feminist approach to language and social interaction.

Discourse analysis deals with language as it is used. According to Potter and Wetherell (14), it takes speech—conversation, talk—"in all its messy and ungrammatical complexity"—as the most fundamental unit of analysis. It assumes that people use language, not just as a medium to convey ideas, but to *do* things socially. The approach assumes that humor, which is perhaps a cross-cultural universal, exists because it has important social interactional functions.

Michael Mulkay has analyzed humor as one of two basic modes of discourse. The serious mode is our "normal" one, the one in which we conduct the ordinary business of our social world. In it we make certain assumptions about reality. As serious speakers, we assume that there is one reality that every normal person can see and experience in much the same way, and that it exists independently of our descriptions of it. Ambiguity, inconsistency, contradiction and the existence of more than one interpretation are problems or mistakes that must be resolved.

The humorous mode, in contrast, depends on the active creation and display of multiple interpretations, multiple meanings. Humor is "controlled nonsense"; when people do humor they collaborate in temporarily creating a world where everything has more than one meaning. And even as they create it they deconstruct it—for example, the assumptions within a joke are undermined as the joke proceeds to its punch line.

Humor occurs when there is a sudden shift between (or unexpected juxtaposition of) two incongruous interpretive frames or schemas. Jokes first create a reality and then undermine it. The shift at the punch line of a joke is always covert and implicit—otherwise we would end up in serious mode, where people try to clarify and resolve hidden meanings. We all know what happens when someone doesn't "get" a quip or a joke, and the teller proceeds to explain it. Once explained in serious mode, the joke is too overt to be funny anymore. Humor uses incongruity but doesn't resolve it completely or literally—that's the job of the serious mode. Take for example, the following joke:

> An old man was watching the evangelist on TV. The evangelist said, "Faith can cure all ills! Yes, brother and sister, faith can heal the sick, faith can bring you the glory of health and the wonders of wealth! Faith can do anything." He went on and on like this, and the old man watched and listened. Then the evangelist said, "Yes, faith is all-powerful, and I can prove it. Just put your hand on your TV screen, and the healing rays of faith will come through from Jesus through me to you. Faith can work miracles! Yes, brother, do it, put your hand on the screen, and touch the afflicted part, and you will be healed. You will be healed!"
>
> So the old man wheeled his wheelchair over to the TV and put one hand on the screen and the other on his crotch. Just then his wife came in and said, "He said he could cure the sick, not raise the dead!"

In this joke, the phrase "raising the dead" shifts from a religious frame to a sexual one. But the shift is covert. The punch line leaves the new sexual schema implicit. A direct, literal explanation of the semantic pivot around "raising" the dead/an erection would not be funny. By the way, this joke is atypical among sexual jokes because the male, and not the female, is objectified and made the butt of the joke. Women tend to think it's funnier than men do.

The humor mode, Mulkay claims, is a subordinate mode of discourse. We're expected to (and do) operate in the serious mode most of the time, with only occasional flights into the humor mode. One piece of evidence for this claim is that we can say in conversation, "Hey, I was just kidding" but not "Hey, I was just being serious." Yet, although it's subordinate, every culture has a humor mode. And just because it's not serious doesn't mean it's trivial. On the contrary, humor can be used to accomplish very serious conversational work.

When humor is conceptualized as a form of discourse—a potent, action-oriented medium in its own right—the questions that psychologists can ask about it change dramatically. Instead of asking how we can measure humor "objectively" or what it reveals about attitudes, cognition, or personality structures, we can ask, How is the discourse of humor put together, and what do speakers gain by this construction?

A LITTLE DATA AND A LOT OF STEREOTYPES

Discourse-oriented research takes the humor mode itself as the object of study, asking questions about how people enter into this mode and what social purposes they attempt to achieve with it. This approach also invites an integration of research on conversational humor with other research on gender and conversational interaction.

Several aspects of social humor can be illustrated with the following fragment of discourse:

(1)	Steve:	So should we do that? should we start
	Deborah:	sure
	Steve:	with the white?
(2)	Peter:	Didju hear about the—lady, who was asked,
(3)	Deborah:	I'm gonna get in there, right?
(4)	Chad:	Okay.
(5)	Peter:	Didju hear?
(6)	David:	We have to sit boy girl boy.
(7)	Chad:	Boy girl boy?
(8)	Peter:	Didju hear about the lady who was asked,
(9)	Chad:	There's only two girls.
(10)	Deborah:	What?
(11)	Peter:	Did you hear about the lady who was asked...Do you
	Chad:	Boy girl boy
	Peter:	smoke after sex?
(12)	David:	I don't know I never looked. *(nasal tone)*
(13)	Deborah:	And she said? What?
(14)	Peter:	I don't *know* I never *looked*
(15)	Deborah:	Oh *(chuckles)*.

This talk, taken from a study by Deborah Tannen (1984, 88-89), was recorded as a group of friends prepared to seat themselves at a Thanksgiving dinner. The analysis is largely Michael Mulkay's (59-60).

First, I should point out that this fragment illustrates the messiness of mundane conversation. It looks very different from the dialogue in novels or films. Readers old enough to remember the Watergate tapes will recall the incoherence of published passages. If one wanted to see Nixon exposed as an idiot, it was quite gratifying. The bad news is that, transcribed, speech almost always looks somewhat incoherent. Few of us are the eloquent verbal performers we like to think we are.

In this fragment, people are gathering around the table and trying to decide where to sit. (In transcribing conversation, two people talking at the same time is indicated by having one's words underneath the other's on the same line number.) Deborah (line 3) says, "I'm gonna get in there, right?" and Chad (line 4) replies "Okay." David contributes (line 6) "We have to sit boy girl boy." This conversation continues in lines 7 and 9. Meanwhile, Peter tries to tell a joke. His first attempt is in line 2, with the formulaic "Didju hear..." but he is interrupted. Undaunted, he tries again in line 5, with the same opening. And again in line 8. Finally, on his fourth attempt, he overrides Chad's interruption and manages to get his set-up line out: "Did you hear about the lady who was asked "Do you smoke after sex?" (line 11)—only to have David (line 12) steal his punch line. Deborah, however, comes to Peter's rescue by giving him an opportunity to say his punch line after all (line 13) and to get his reward—the ritual chuckle that signifies that he has successfully told a joke (line 15).

There is a lot going on in these fifteen brief lines. Peter has to work hard to get the group's permission to tell his joke—he persists through three failed attempts and one theft of punch line. Yet, with Deborah's help, he achieves his little moment in the limelight.

Fine-grained analysis of conversation is useful, especially when assessed in relation to cultural representations of gendered speech. In the popular culture of joke books, comic strips, and comedy routines, women talk all the time, talk too much, and monopolize talk. Andy Capp moans, "Lor, will she never stop?" A wizard, consulted by a man who says his wife has been cursed by a witch and hasn't spoken in weeks, offers $500 for the exact wording of the curse. A long-suffering husband (in the driver's seat, of course) asks his chattering wife, "Want me to pull over at a rest stop and let you shut up for a while?" Women, it is clear, need to be silenced. In a comic postcard, a man is depicted driving a car while a woman sits blank-eyed beside him with a large auto muffler protruding from her mouth. The man is saying cheerfully, "New muffler really keeps the car quiet, eh honey?" (A feminist friend sent me this postcard for my collection, with the note, "How about the airbag in the driver's seat?")

Stereotypes about speech are central to gender stereotypes. Sandra Bem's Sex Role Inventory, a very widely used measure of individual gender-typing, lists several traits specifically descriptive of speech style: on the "feminine" dimension are *shy, soft-spoken, does not use harsh language;* on the "masculine" dimension are *assertive* and *defends own beliefs.* These items represent behaviors that are more valued in one sex than the other, in the eyes of college students. All are intended to be positive attributes, for women and men respectively. They represent an ideal of femininity and masculinity.

According to stereotype, males should be experts in the serious mode. What could be more serious than masculine attributes? Curiously, though, women are not thought to be the experts in the humor mode. Instead, the stereotypical representation of women's humor is one of deficiency. Women are said to be uncreative in generating humor; to be incompetent tellers of jokes and stories, forgetting the punch line or obscuring the point; in general, to lack a sense of humor. As with the representation of women's speech more generally, examples are easy to find in popular culture. In a recent *Rose is Rose* syndicated comic strip, the husband tries to share the Sunday comics with his wife, who totally fails to comprehend the humor. "I don't get it," she complains. "It doesn't make sense.... Do the panels read from left to right?" Baffled, he muses "I'm actually *married* to this entity...."

However, we know from gender-and-language research that to the extent that there are sex differences in communication style, they are contrary to the stereotype of the talkative, domineering female speaker. At least among white middle-class speakers, there are strong conversational norms that encourage men to shine and women to support. For example, research by Donald Zimmerman and Candace West showed that in mixed-sex pairs, up to 97% of the interruptions are men interrupting women. In same-sex pairs, women and men are about equally likely to interrupt their partner. Men also talk more and take more than a "fair share" of conversational time in mixed-sex groups. Men have been observed to talk more than women in informal social groups, structured discussion groups, classrooms from elementary to postgraduate levels, even when talking alone into a tape recorder in laboratory experiments—indeed, in virtually every setting and combination of people that has been studied.[2] Moreover, Pamela Fishman's research shows that they tend to control what will be talked about in conversation. Women introduce more topics, but men decide which topics will be picked up and developed. In an old *New Yorker* cartoon, a man and woman sit across a table gazing into each other's eyes. "But enough about me," he says. "What did *you* think of my last book?"

It can be funny to see these norms violated. A Sidney Harris cartoon published in the *Chronicle of Higher Education* depicts a man and a woman in conversation at a party. The man's gambit, "Wasn't it Kierkegaard who said "We perceive life through the filter of our lives, and though the world remains virtually unchanged, we see it changing continually?'" receives the deadpan reply "No, Kierkegaard never said anything like that." This humor is gendered in that it would not be as funny if the sexes of the actors were reversed. Applying the gender role reversal test shows us that the humor in this interaction indeed rests on implicit assumptions about what is conversationally appropriate for women and men. Feminist humorist Nicole Hollander often creates humor by mocking expectations of supportive stroking from women. In a panel from a *Sylvia* strip, a man strikes up a conversation in a bar with the line, "You know the kind of woman I could really go for?" Sylvia responds, "Is there anything I can say to prevent you from sharing these thoughts with me?"

Researchers need to analyze examples of women's humor in conversation, along with others' responses. We need to look at how and whether people collaborate with women when they initiate humor. As David and Deborah and their friends illustrate in the Thanksgiving dinner fragment, in order for an individual to make humor he or she must be given the floor. Others must signal that they know the speaker is in the humorous mode. Are women's signals that they are in the humorous mode ignored, just like their topic shifts? Do their potential contributions go unrecognized? How often do they get the sort of support that Deborah gave Peter so that he could have his little moment in the spotlight?

ACCOUNTS OF HUMOR PREFERENCES AND PRACTICES

It is important to test theories about conversation against people's own accounts of what they do and why they do it. I began my empirical research on humor by asking for women's and men's perceptions of their use and appreciation of humor.[3] My students and I developed a lengthy exploratory questionnaire covering many aspects of humor creation and appreciation. (Representative items include the following: "I like to watch cartoons on TV." "It doesn't bother me if a joke makes fun of a racial or ethnic group." "I like to create word plays and puns.") We asked a heterogeneous sample of over 200 people to complete it by rating how true each item was for them on a 5-point scale.

The ratings were analyzed using factor analysis, a statistical technique that shows which items cluster together to form common dimensions in individuals' responses. Ten important factors, or dimensions of humor, emerged. Women and men were more alike than different in their perceptions, responding similarly on factors that tapped creative spontaneity, ability to tolerate being the butt of humor, and enjoyment of cartoon and sexual humor. Gender-related differences emerged on four factors: Women were higher in anecdotal humor—telling stories about things that had happened to themselves and their friends. Men were higher in hostile humor, jokes, and slapstick comedy.

In another part of the study, I asked 141 people to write a narrative about someone they knew who had an outstanding sense of humor. Participants were free to write about either a male or female. Their preference was very striking. Men wrote about males by a 5:1 ratio, and women by a 2:1 ratio. A content analysis of their responses revealed agreement between women and men respondents that the most important characteristics in a good sense of humor are creativity, caring, and a basis in real-life events. Males used the creativity dimension more than females did. Both men and women were also more likely to talk about creativity when talking about men than women.

The narrative part of the study shows that when people are asked to think of someone with an outstanding sense of humor, they overwhelmingly think of a man. They consider a "good sense of humor" to be gender-linked. Men simply have more of "the right stuff," perhaps because they're believed to be more creative. Men and women apply these evaluations to themselves, too. In the questionnaire part of the study, men rated themselves as having a better sense of humor than women rated themselves.

EXPLANATIONS AND THEORIES OF GENDER AND HUMOR

There are two schools of thought about why these differences in conversation, and conversational humor, exist. Why is it that men talk more, hold the floor, tell the Polish and Jewish-American Princess and prostitute jokes, interrupt women, and ignore women's contributions to dialogue? Why is it that women tell more personal stories, support others in the conversational spotlight, and collaborate more than they compete?

One explanation, originated by Daniel Maltz and Ruth Borker and recently popularized by Deborah Tannen (1986, 142-151; 1990), is that women and men have learned differences in conversational goals. For women, the primary goal of conversation is intimacy and for men the goal is positive self-presentation. Because of these gender-linked conversational goals, the interaction climates in all-female and all-male groups are very different. As Mercilee Jenkins (10) put it, "Men in their groups seem to be saying, "I'm great. *I'm great, too.* Gee we're a great bunch of guys." In contrast, women seem to be saying, "Did this ever happen to you? *Yeah.* Oh, good, I'm not crazy."

Given the differences in women and men's goals for friendly conversation, Jenkins proposes that their humor can be expected to serve different functions. Women's humor supports a goal of greater intimacy by being supportive and healing, while men's humor reinforces "performance" goals of competition, the establishment of hierarchical relationships, and self-aggrandizement.

Mercilee Jenkins has studied gender differences in humor style through participant observation, and her results fit very well with what my respondents said about themselves. The males in my sample reported greater production and appreciation of hostile (racist, sexist, and aggressive) humor and greater enjoyment of set-piece jokes. Jenkins comments about her participants (6):

> Joking for men establishes them as credible performers and affords them an audience for whom they demonstrate their prowess. Their jokes are less personal, like their social groups, and they can be told in a variety of settings. Men can develop a repertoire of jokes which they can use to compete with other men for audience attention and honors. Their jokes are exclusive in that they more often put down others or are told at the expense of others. The teller rarely identifies with the butt of the joke....

This description recalls the Thanksgiving dinner fragment, with Peter inserting his joke into the conversation even though it had nothing to do with the setting or topic, and David stealing his punch line.

The women in my research, more than the men, said they were likely to tell funny stories about things that happened to them and their friends. Jenkins (6) characterizes women's humor as follows:

> ...much more context-bound. It is more often created out of the ongoing talk to satisfy the needs of [a] particular group of women. Since the goal of interaction is intimacy, there is not the same need to compete for performance points...[women's] humor includes and supports group members by demonstrating what they have in common.

Differences between men and women in conversational goals is a relatively uncontroversial interpretation. According to this view, men and women are just different. They speak in different voices (quite literally) because they seek to gain different things from talk. Women just want to be friends and men just want to look good in front of the other guys. A related but distinct (and less benign) explanation is in terms of conversational dominance. According to this view, gender inequality is created, re-created, and maintained not just at the macro-level (who's in the

Congress, on the Supreme Court, and doing the hiring and firing at the office) but at the micro-level, too. Men control conversation and dominate discourse in order to control and dominate the meanings that women can give voice to. Women are literally silenced by men's appropriation of conversational time and topics. The maintenance of gender hierarchy in social interaction has been called "doing gender." It remains a major force in perpetuating gender inequalities.[4]

Sex differences in interruption, topic control, and amount of talk fit the dominance framework rather nicely. However, perhaps the most compelling evidence for this framework comes from Michael Mulkay's analysis (134-151) of the content and function of men's sexual humor about women, an analysis I will describe in some detail.

First, Mulkay looks at the representation of women in men's sexual humor, using as data the collections of dirty jokes made by folklore researchers and observations of comic routines in pubs. He shows that the assumptions underlying men's sexual humor, and the way it represents male-female relationships, not only express male dominance but strengthen it.

There appear to be four basic principles in men's sexual humor:

1. The primacy of intercourse—all men want is sex.

2. The availability of women—all women are sexually available to all men even when they pretend not to be.

3. The objectification of women—women exist to meet men's needs, and are, or should be, passive.

4. The subordination of women's discourse: women must be silenced. (One formula for a dirty joke is to "floor" a woman, to render her speechless by turning an innocent statement she makes into a sexual one).

It is easy to find examples of male sexual humor based on these four principles. Readers familiar with the routines of comics such as Andrew Dice Clay will be able to think of an abundance. On a quick trip to the local shopping mall, I found a birthday card asserting that "Women are like dog shit: the older they get the easier they are to pick up." Currently, a popular format for sexual humor is "beer is better than women" one-liners. To my knowledge, they first appeared in mimeographed form on college campuses, but soon moved to T-shirts, bumper stickers, and formal publication. Examples from a recent book include "Beer is better than women because...

...beer doesn't expect an hour of foreplay before satisfying you.

...you can try dark beers and lite beers without upsetting your parents.

...a beer doesn't change its mind after you've taken off its top.

...a beer never wants to stay up afterwards talking about respect.[5]

In this humor, the male voice always triumphs over the female. Mulkay (137) says it well: "In men's dirty jokes, it is not only women's bodies and services that are at men's disposal, but also women's language." He suggests that the same principles operate in humor use as in representation. Humor in conversation can be used by men to silence women, negate their personhood, and maintain conversational control. For example, Christine Griffin (173) recorded a conversation in a train in which three women were discussing their work as reference librarians. The male companion of one interrupted with the following joke:

"What's the difference between a feminist and a bin liner? A bin liner gets taken out once a week."

The joke, which was totally unrelated to the women's topic, was greeted by silence, not laughter. Having interrupted the flow of conversation, the man then introduced a different, unrelated topic, and took an active part in the conversation.

Mulkay analyzes humor use by drawing on James Spradley and Brenda Mann's classic ethnographic study of cocktail waitresses. In the bar under study, all the cocktail servers were women and all the bartenders were men. The bartenders had legitimate authority over the waitresses, but were also dependent on them. Men initiated and benefitted from joking in this situation. They used it to reinforce their control over the women and deal with problems in maintaining their authority (for example, when they had made a mistake in an order). They made fun of the women's bodies with remarks like "It'd look better if you had some tits. Who wants to pull down a zipper just to see two fried eggs thrown against a wall?"[6]

For women, humor was a source of frustration because it was asymmetrical—women had much less latitude in what they could say, and they knew it, as illustrated by the following reconstruction of a conversation among waitresses:

> Rob made some reference about my chest.
> Same here. But I don't know what we can do to get him back.
> Maybe we could all get together and try grabbing him.
> That's silly. We aren't strong enough and they would just make a joke about it.
> We could all ignore him, but that wouldn't work because he would just pick at us until we responded. If we ignore him, we're admitting defeat.
> There's no way we can get them back. We can't get on their level. The only way to get them back is to get on their level and you can't do that. You can't counter with some remark about the size of his penis or something without making yourself look really cheap.

Mulkay (149) concludes from his analysis of "bar talk" that "men's informal humor constantly denigrates women's bodies and stresses their inferiority as social beings." Lest the reader think that only bartenders do this sort of thing, it's worth noting that in a recent sex discrimination case against the Wall Street investment firm Goldman Sachs, an employee, Kristine Utley, testified that the office humor was a source of sexual harassment. Memos introducing new female employees were illustrated with nude Playboy pinups, and other company memos contained "beer is better than women" jokes, for example "...because a beer always goes down easy."[7]

One advantage of the humor mode, at least for the dominant group, is that people can use humor to convey messages that they can then deny, or develop further, depending on how the message is received by the hearer. Because it is indirect and allusive, the humor mode protects the jokester from the consequences that his or her statement would have if conveyed directly in the serious mode. Hospital humor, for example, enables staff and patients to interact around the taboo topic of death. When old Mr. Jones says jokingly to the nurses, "I won't be wearing out those shoes," and a nurse replies, "Oh, Mr. Jones, you'll be wearing your dancing shoes by next month" everyone involved can deny that the patient's impending death was mentioned. When the taboo topic is framed as a joke it does not become part of the "real" discourse.[8]

In parallel fashion, when someone sends the message "I consider women to be less than full human beings" framed as humor, it is difficult for others to reject or even directly address the message. After all, sexist intention can easily be denied. "I was only joking." "Can't you take a joke?" "Lighten up." "Just kidding." One simple reason women may appear less humorous is that they are unwilling to participate in their own denigration. This is not the same as being prudish or lacking a sense of humor. In my own research, I framed the questions I asked so that sexist and sexual humor were distinguished from each other. The women reported that they liked sexual—but not sexist—humor.

Although women and men differ somewhat in conversational style generally and in their use of humor in conversation, I want to caution that these are not categorical differences. Often, the psychological demonstration of a gender-related difference is over-interpreted: "All women are X, all men are Y." The differences I'm talking about are average group differences. What I want to accomplish in future research on conversation is a better understanding of what social goals are met when women and men use humor in ordinary interpersonal interaction.

A PARADOX AND SOME NEW DIRECTIONS

There is an interesting paradox in the stereotype of the humorless woman. There seems to be no real reason for the culture to represent women as lacking a sense of humor. After all, humor is clearly a subordinate form of discourse. Much as we enjoy the wit or the clown, we award public power to those who can perform competently in the serious mode (with a few exceptions, of course—Dan Quayle leaps to mind). The general rule cross-culturally is that any behavior or task that is low status is assigned to women or, conversely, anything assigned to women becomes low status. Simple logic tells us that humor should be the specialty of women. Just as we have been allowed to specialize in the "subordinate" forms of visual art (quilts, ceramics, watercolors, lace making) the devalued forms of writing (diaries, romance novels, and domestic novels) and the low status, underpaid work of the society (caring for children, the ill, and the elderly; serving food and cleaning up), women should get assigned that most trivial, low-status form of creativity, spontaneous conversational humor. The prototypical class clown should be a girl, not a boy, and the prototypical raconteur a woman. Why, then, the cultural representation of women as humorless?

The answer may lie in the subversive potential of humor. Humor can be used to introduce and develop topics that would be taboo in the serious mode, while protecting the speaker from the serious consequences of having broken a taboo. What a wonderful opportunity for a subordinate group. Perhaps creating humor is culturally specified to be something that women cannot and must not do precisely because of the subversive potential of women's humor.

NOTES

1. For a fuller critique of pre-feminist experimental research on humor see Crawford, 1989.
2. Graddol and Swann review and summarize research on gender and amount of talk.
3. Crawford and Gressley, 1991.
4. West and Zimmerman originated the term. Unger and Crawford analyze the social construction and maintenance of gender inequality in interaction with reference to sex as a salient cognitive category, attributions for success and failure, tokenism, and perceived leadership in Chapters 5 and 12.
5. Brooks et al. (unpaged).
6. This and the following quotation from Spradley and Mann are taken from citations in Mulkay (148; 145).

7. Utley's testimony was reported by Kocol (33).
8. Mulkay describes research on the function of humor in the workplace, including hospital humor (73-92).

WORKS CITED

Bem, Sandra L. "The Measurement of Psychological Androgyny." *Journal of Consulting and Clinical Psychology* 42 (1974): 155-62.

Brooks, M. L., Donna E. Hanbery, Ivor Matz, Tam Westover, and Craig Westover. *Beer is Better Than Women Because....* Watertown, Mass.: Ivory Tower, 1988.

Crawford, M., and Diane Gressley. "Creativity, Caring, and Context: Women's and Men's Accounts of Humor Preferences and Practices." *Psychology of Women Quarterly* 15 (1991): 217-231.

Fishman, Pamela. "Interaction: The Work Women Do." *Social Problems* 25 (1978): 397-406.

Graddol, David, and Joan Swann. *Gender Voices.* Oxford: Basil Blackwell, 1989.

Griffin, Christine. "'I'm not a Women's Libber But...': Feminism, Consciousness, and Identity." *The Social Identity of Women.* S. Skevington & D. Baker (Eds.). London: Sage, 1989. 173-93.

Jenkins, Mercilee. "What's So Funny? Joking Among Women." *Proceedings of the First Berkeley Women and Language Conference.* N. Caskey, S. Bremner, & B. Moonwomon (Eds.). Berkeley, CA: Berkeley Women and Language Group, 1985.

Kocol, Cleo. "Taking Responsibility." *The Humanist* 49 (1988): 33-34.

Maltz, Daniel N., and Ruth A. Borker. "A Cultural Approach to Male-Female Miscommunication." *Language and Social Identity.* J. J. Gumperz (Ed.). Cambridge, England: Cambridge UP, 1982. 196-216.

Mulkay, Michael. *On Humor.* Oxford: Basil Blackwell, 1988.

Potter, Jonathan, and Margaret Wetherell. *Discourse and Social Psychology.* London: Sage, 1987.

Spradley, James P., and Brenda J. Mann. *The Cocktail Waitress.* New York: Wiley, 1975.

Tannen, Deborah. *Conversational Style: Analyzing Talk Among Friends.* Norwood, N.J.: Ablex, 1984.

___. *That's Not What I Meant.* New York: William Morrow, 1986.

___. *You Just Don't Understand.* New York: Ballantine, 1990.

Unger, Rhoda K., and Mary Crawford. *Women and Gender: A Feminist Psychology.* Philadelphia: Temple University Press, 1992.

West, Candace, and Donald H. Zimmerman. "Doing Gender." *Gender and Society.* 1 (1987): 125-51.

Zimmerman, Donald H., and Candace West. "Sex Roles, Interruptions, and Silences in Conversation." *Language and Sex: Difference and Dominance.* Ed. B. Thorne and N. Henley. Rowley, MA: Newbury House, 1975.

4

Roseanne Barr: Canned Laughter— Containing the Subject

SIÂN MILE

Roseanne Barr closes her 1987 stand-up routine with an "unbecoming" attempt to un-become her assigned gender identity. She tells her audience that "a lot of people" come up to her "all the time" and say, "God Roseanne, you're not very feminine." She then asks us, with somewhat unconvincing innocence, "Can you believe that they would say that to *me?*" "So I say to them," she concludes, "Suck My Dick!"

Barr, of course, does not have a literal "dick." To act non-"femininely," however, implies that one is acting in a "masculine" fashion—a behavior expected of a man (who presumably has a penis). If Barr is acting as a man "should," she should, it would seem, have a "dick." The visual image of Barr with a phallus, however, is clearly a ridiculous one—but one which nevertheless exposes the notions of "feminine" and "masculine" as terms and as performances which, as Butler suggests, have no basis in the physical body (336). Barr can act as though she has a "dick," and "do" the masculine gender even if she doesn't have the "correct" bodily parts; in the Halloween episode of her sitcom last year, she "did" just that—she

39

dressed up and passed as a man. Barr reconstructs her gender identity and leaves us with the possibility of a new configuration—a woman with a phallus (figurative or otherwise). In July of 1990, when Barr grabbed her crotch after singing the National Anthem, it was this configuration which offended, and which George Bush felt moved to call "disgraceful."

Despite the flak, Barr remains a comic female subject who refuses to let her subjectivity be limited by her body or by cultural constructions of "correctly" gendered behavior for that body. Hers is a process of un-becoming—unraveling the "feminine"—which is, for a woman, indecorous, unseemly and highly "unbecoming" behavior. Hers is an iconoclastic laugh which "isn't submissive" and "isn't deferential" and, therefore, "isn't ladylike" (Walker 76). Barr has no "feminine" patience for what is made (up) for her. As this clever "dick" example shows, she can clearly do her own construction work.

The job pays well. Barr has created her self in three primary ways—she has constructed three narratives/discourses over which she has creative control and with which she has, up until now, quite successfully gone to market. She presents herself as the stand-up comic of the "act," as well as the "realistic" housewife (whom *Redbook* calls "America's funniest housewife") in her #1 sitcom *Roseanne*. And most recently, Barr has produced herself as the "writer" and, more particularly, "the woman," in her autobiography, *Roseanne: My Life As A Woman*. Her subjectivity is not defined by traditional notions of Housewifery, Motherhood, and Femininity in any of these creations—rather, these institutions are critiqued, dismantled and rendered irrelevant to the definition of the female self.

It would be naive, however, to suggest that Roseanne Barr is in control of her "identity". Her self becomes further de-centered and diluted by the supermarket tabloids who, almost weekly, try to neutralize Barr's social and sexual critique by manufacturing descriptions of her as "terrible, asinine, stupid, thoughtless, lewd, sleazy, and sordid" and "a disgrace to American womanhood" (*Globe* 10-2-90). She is marketed by them in such a way as to shift the focus from Barr's radical re-constructions of "womanhood" and from the object of her comedic laugh to the highly "inadequate" bearer of it. The laugh is thus contained and a new Barr constructed to both destroy her exchange among other women (to use Irigaray's terms) and to bolster the very institutions and institutional self she tries to dismantle.

But first, the good news. Barr is a subject who has gone public—she has taken the joke out of the framework and relative safety of the domestic realm and moved into the public sphere. Barr's is a comedy looking for a mass audience, looking for validation. After spending years incarcerated inside the house, she now seeks the open space of comic discourse.

Her comic discourse, however, is of a kind not normally expected of women. There is none of what Regina Barreca ironically describes as "normal" for a woman, that is, "reconciling gentility, soft admonitions for social lapses, sweet mirth" (10). Barr's comedy is hard, vicious, and bitter—a woman's "comedy paired with anger" (Barreca 5). This humor, "coming from a man, would be considered assertive," but, "coming from a woman, [might well] be considered aggressive, even hostile" (Walker 76). "Indiscriminate niceness," Anne Beatts suggests, "is not conducive to humor" (184) and Barr's comedy is certainly not "nice," but it is not self-denigrating either; it does not attack women themselves but rather the cultural frames which surround them. It mocks traditional roles and oppressive values rather than, as Naomi Weisstein points out, the women burdened by them (88). With no holds Barr-ed, Roseanne un-houses herself.

She is no longer a housewife, but it is as a housewife that the public primarily knows her. Her success is based on a character called "Rose-anne" whom she created first for her stand-up routine and then for her sitcom. Even though Barr says this character "is me," the real location of Barr's subjectivity has changed. The "real" Roseanne is now a comic/ actress/ "celebrity"; the television other is a fictional projection. Housewif-ery is subsequently challenged as a basis for self definition on two levels. First, Barr represents a life beyond what she calls, "laying on that couch, eating those bon bons, watching them soap operas"—she has become something else. She has un-become her traditional role in what many tabloid readers clearly consider an unbecoming way.

Furthermore, in her work itself, she has marketed her housewife and managed to critique and articulate quite publicly the housewife's lot. She makes her discontent with such a lot quite explicit at the start of her stand-up act. "It's a thrill to be out of the house," she says, "I never get out of the house, I never go no place, I never have no fun ever ever ever ever 'cos I'm a housewife." The house is clearly a never-never land for Barr—or at least should be. "Nobody ever helps me," she says, "I have to do every goddamn thing by myself." Her sitcom house is not kept up and when someone remarks that she has a nice name, she replies, "Yeah, it means underpaid." She shows a distinct unwillingness to be defined by how well she cleans—"I don't even care about that cleaning stuff anyway— the day I worry about cleaning my house is the day *Sears* comes out with a riding vacuum cleaner." Roseanne is prepared to leave the housework very much to Beaver. In more ways than one, she brings down the house. She brings down the house by, in fact, bringing down the house (with laughter).

Through her comic constructions, Barr attempts to rewrite the house-wife's discourse—to redefine the "I." She recasts her as what she defines as a "Domestic Goddess"—a term which she says is more "descriptive" than housewife and which she knew would be worth "billions":

> I remember my Mom and all the neighbor ladies reading *Fascinating Womanhood* when I was young, and how there was a chapter on manipulating your old man by becoming a "Domestic Goddess"...Perfect Wife, Homemaker etc. I said [to my sister], "What if I say "Domestic Goddess" as a term of self-definition, rebellion, truth-telling?" (Barr 172)

It is as this character and out of the house that Barr can acknowledge "the truth"—"I found a stage where I began to tell the truth about my life," she says, "because I couldn't tell the truth off the stage" (Barr 202). At any rate, this particular redefinition serves, ironically enough of course, to remind us of the adulation/worship that a housewife does *not* revel in and at the same time, assigns the role more status and cosmic relevance than it normally has. Barr also uses the term to ironically accentuate the fact that this goddess resides in anything but a "heavenly home" where little, if anything, is sacred. In one episode of the *Roseanne* sitcom, when Barr's sister tells her to "go to hell," Barr replies, "This *is* hell!" This is a place beyond domestic bliss, "two days past happy," and in this hell, Barr also refuses to acknowledge the sanctity of the institutions of "Mother" or "Svelte"—she rejects them as similarly useless in defining the female subject.

On the institution of Motherhood, Barr has much to say. She does not valorize the "Mother," but describes her role quite simply. "When my husband comes home at night," she says, "if those kids are still alive, hey, I've done my job." She has no truck with the bother of nurturing or with psychologists who say, "Never hit your children in anger." Barr replies, "Like when *would* be a good time to hit them?" She is, she says, the mother her kids never had—a subject who may be more valuable absent than present.

Just as Barr neither valorizes nor sentimentalizes Motherhood (which must come as a shock to the French feminists), nor does she prostrate herself before the sacred "Svelte." She declares that "fat moms are better than skinny moms" and she angrily notes that whereas a man's overweightness is rarely noticed, a woman's is, because "everything about women is supposed to be smaller." She rejects those who might elevate themselves through being svelte—"If you're fat," she says, "just be fat and shut up. If you're thin, fuck you!" Barr affirms her female body through laughter—svelte or not, *she* is validated.

Such rejection of traditional gender defined roles and appearances constitutes the forging of a new female subjectivity—more defined here by what it is *not,* rather than what it is. It is, if nothing else, an unusual articulation. Barr's "chainsaw" style of comedy violates a "feminine" silence which has traditionally been kept. Nina Auerbach remarks that "historically men have preferred women's tears to their more threatening laughter" (Gagnier 137); McGhee, that "women are neither expected nor trained to joke in this culture" (225) and Gagnier, that "men desire to control women's humor just as they desire to control women's sexuality" (137). As Walker suggests, this urge to control, to "disallow," is rooted in the desire to maintain the status quo:

> Humor isn't submissive, it isn't deferential; it comes from the intellect rather than
> the emotions—in short, it isn't ladylike. It is perfectly fine, of course, for a woman
> to laugh at a man's jokes—*required,* in fact—but for a woman to be a satirist,
> or a comic, or even to recount the slapstick adventures of a typical day in the life
> of the homemaker ... is to step outside woman's "normal" role as passive recipient
> of cultural expectations and take on the role of truth-teller and gadfly. (76)

Barr has "stepped outside" and taken Gagnier's "imaginative disruption through humor in the relative privacy of discourse among women"(145) and made public the private joke.

If women are not expected to attempt humor, nor are they expected to succeed at it. Barr, however, succeeds in defining the female self as both public *and* as capable of creating the laugh—as capable of being the location of laughter. The credits at the start of *Roseanne* actually fade-out to the sound of her laughter. This is humor, as Weisstein calls it, "with a defiant celebration of [its] own worth"(90); a Medusa's laugh, "breaking up the truth" as Cixous would have it (245). Barr also laughs at her own jokes—laughs with us—and so makes herself funny.

As we reel from her domestic blitz, we see the split between what Barr once was—a housewife—and what Barr is now—an unhoused "I" in the affirmative. Perhaps like Cixous and Clément's hysteric, she "crosses a dangerous line" to a place where "all laughter is allied with the monstrous" and where "her laugh keeps a wide gash bleeding in the man's breast" (33)—this is a place where "masculine" constructions of "reality" and "subjectivity" are broken apart. And as she experiences "hell and pleasure at the same time" (34), her smile and her grimace become one and the same—it becomes clear that "breaking apart can be paradise, but for another, it is hell" (33). There is the pleasure that the transformed Roseanne *now* exacts from splitting the world open and then there is the suffering which is "the other's which is returned to her, by projection" (34). The "other" is the subject Barr once once—a housewife whose "hell" she tries to hysterically recreate and articulate.

When it comes to the supermarket tabloid, Barr faces a different kind of hell—one which she is now attempting to freeze over through litigation. The "rags" have, quite unashamedly, tried to head off Barr's popularity at the check-out stand. Tabloids such as the *National Enquirer,* the *Star,* and the *Globe* have made an attempt to re-validate the sacred female self Barr has invalidated. She is constructed and marketed as a toxic commodity: a material threat to the institutions of motherhood, marriage, heterosexuality, and femininity itself—time-honored badges of female subjectivity/ subjection.

The headlines suggest that she is a bad mother, an intolerable wife, a lesbian "sympathizer" and an obese monstrosity. The tabloids over the past year have suggested that Roseanne has driven her 14 year old to drink, encouraged her kids to drop out of school, and abused them—"Roseanne Investigated for Child Abuse" (*National Enquirer* 1-30-90). They have reported her divorce with glee, and suggested that she is promiscuous with headlines referring to her "three boy lovers" (*National Examiner* 11-14-89). This is clearly a woman whom only a drug-crazed lunatic could want to marry—"Druggie Lover Cuts Her With Broken Bottle" (*Star* 1-2-90). They go on to report her "delight" at her lesbian sister's wedding (*National Enquirer* 10-10-90) and, by implication, question her own sexual "standing." As if this weren't enough to fully appropriate the construction of Barr, they harp on the physical fact of Barr's weight. They call her a "blubbery comic" (*National Enquirer* 11-7-89) and imply that she is a monstrosity worthy of the title, therefore, of "the most hated woman in America" (*Globe* 1-9-90). The female laugh has been made material in Barr—a fact which, because of her size, cannot be ignored and so has to be dealt with. When the *Star* could no longer stand Barr's refusal to fashion her physical self to acceptable "feminine" standards anymore, it sliced her head onto a svelte bikini-clad body—everything a woman "should" be (12-19-89). Even such "respectable" magazines such as *Life* (March 1990) seem uncomfortable with such a large and loud female subject and insist on calling her "a tiny overstuffed sofa of a woman"

(105)—so putting her with the furniture right back into the house.

There is little doubt that Barr herself wants to re-construct "the mother," "the wife" and concepts of female sexuality and beauty—but not like this. The headlines sound like a broadcast of the Emergency Tabloid System and warn a woman that if she listens to Barr, her kids, husband, sexuality and body will be destroyed. It is, they imply, better to keep buying rather than, like Barr, to start selling. The tabloids contrive to invalidate Barr's political position by attacking her very person—this is not an attack on the framework but on the frame of the woman herself. Such subjection clearly attempts to undermine whatever comedic criticism the female comic attempts to make; the papers imply that Barr's perception of institutional inadequacies can be attributed to, and is a reflection of, her own personal inadequacies. They construct a subject whose private perceptions taint her public ones and whom, consequently, we cannot trust. The "problem," therefore, is conveniently localized and another cultural framework constructed to contain Barr's laughter and her configurations of identity. She cannot "contain" her self and so the press does it for her; her laughter is, in effect, canned. Such is the current state of this transitional female comic figure, multiple in her subjectivity, finding, for now, no safety in these numbers.

WORKS CITED

Barr, Roseanne. *Roseanne: My Life As A Woman.* New York: Harper and Row, 1989.

Barreca, Regina, ed. and "Introduction." *Last Laughs: Perspectives on Women and Comedy.* New York: Gordon and Breach, 1988.

Beatts, Anne. "Can A Woman Get a Laugh and a Man, Too?" *Mademoiselle.* Nov. 1975: 184.

Butler, Judith. "Gender Trouble, Feminist Theory, and Psychoanalytic Discourse." *Feminism/Post-Modernism.* Ed. Linda J. Nicholson. New York: Routledge, Chapman and Hall, 1990.

Cixous, Hélène. "The Laugh of the Medusa" trans. in *New French Feminisms.* Eds. Elaine Marks and Isabelle de Courtivron. Amherst, MA: University of Massachusetts Press, 1980.

Cixous, Hélène and Catherine Clément. *The Newly Born Woman.* Trans. Betsy Wing. Minneapolis: University of Minnesota Press, 1986.

Gagnier, Regenia. "Between Women: a cross-class analysis of status and anarchic humor." *Last Laughs.* Ed. Regina Barreca.

Irigaray, Luce. *This Sex Which Is Not One.* Trans. Catherine Porter. Ithaca NY: Cornell University Press, 1985: 196-197.

McGhee, Paul. "The Role of Laughter in Growing Up Female." *Becoming Female: Perspectives on Development.* Ed. Claire B. Kopp. New York: Plenum Press, 1979.

Walker, Nancy. "Women's Humor as Catharsis and Protest." *Women of Power* #17.
    Summer, 1990.
Weisstein, Naomi. "Why We Aren't Laughing Anymore." *Ms.* Nov. 1973.

5

Belly Laughs and Naked Rage: Resisting Humor in Karen Finley's Performance Art

MARIA PRAMAGGIORE

Karen Finley prefaces her performance with a performance; she comes out from backstage to talk to the audience about how nervous performing makes her. Seated in front of the audience, she smirks as she describes the nausea, the jitters. "You make me sick," she concludes. The laughter she provokes is tentative, nervous. With this gesture, Finley turns the tables, rendering the audience the nervous and jittery ones. I'm not sure whether she's serious or joking, whether we are to interpret this mini-performance as the "real" Karen Finley addressing her audience "before the show" or not. Isn't this the show, too?

Karen Finley made her name in New York's East Village clubs in the early 1980s and is notorious in avant-garde circles because of her reputation for inflicting abuse upon herself and her audiences. More recently, of course, Finley received national attention as a result of the

47

controversy surrounding NEA funding of art considered by some to be obscene. In a number of performances, she has poured dog food and cream over herself; she has reportedly shoved yams into unmentionable orifices on-stage. As a woman performing, Finley first calls attention to, and then breaks, every rule; she performs without clothes, yet she refuses to assume the traditional position of the female nude on display for the male gaze. She constantly foregrounds audience expectations relating to selfhood and sexuality under the conditions of phallocentric capitalist culture, and then reveals their disturbing nature. Her performances act out the links between capitalism, sexism and abuse; they disturb the audience because Finley forces a confrontation with cultural images of feminine subjectivity, primarily in the idiom of Freudian psychoanalysis.

The performance I will focus on, *The Constant State of Desire,* is a series of short fragmented narratives in which Finley acts out the physical and psychological violence our culture generates. Finley imbues this piece with a particularly ironic and reflexive sense of humor; the double nature of humor in Finley's work questions the limits of laughter. Because she refuses straight comedy, and always reminds us of some unpleasantness beneath laughter, Finley problematizes humor itself, particularly as it is implicated in sexism in our culture. Often this process focuses upon her body as a locus of both obscenity and humor. As the mark of femininity, the scandalous—and in some instances hilarious—Freudian lack, Finley's body represents the negative impression of psychoanalytic discourse of modern Western culture. Her disturbing vision of the experience of women in this culture is enacted through her always-problematic relationship to language and through the ironic display of her body. Finley's performance text and style are concerned with experiencing limits: the limits of notions of self, of language, and of humor.

FINLEY'S CRITIQUE OF FREUDIAN ANALYSIS

When asked by Richard Schechner why her performances provoke riots, Finley replied, "I think I stir people to be responsible to what's going on in their own personal lives, in their one-to-one relationships, interweaving this into the whole society's corruption" (153). Finley negotiates the gap between what is experienced as personal and as social—and does so by appealing to the psychoanalytic tradition. She manipulates and penetrates the politics of psychoanalysis, the discourse of the talking cure, paying particular attention to its putative ability to express and contain the body's experience in language. Psychoanalysis offers a dialect that not only serves to express our experiences of self, but also helps us form our concepts of self.

Finley begins her stories with a dream sequence; a woman tells her dreams to her analyst:

> She dreams. She dreams of being locked in a cage and singing loudly and off-key with her loved ones standing behind her whispering very loudly. "She has an ugly voice. Doesn't she? She has an ugly voice." Oh, leave it to the loved ones. To judge us like they do. It's always the loved ones who always interfere with our dreams. (2)

Finley's humor is characteristically double-edged; we may be amused as we recognize the absurd discrepancy between the "loved ones," who are loving in name only, and their behavior as the woman sings off-key. Yet we also experience the cruelty of the whispers that interfere with the woman's literal and metaphorical dreams. Throughout the performance, Finley seizes on family relationships as a cultural myth whose operation can be extremely dangerous, particularly in term of its psychoanalytic deployment.

In *TCSD*, the nightmare the woman remembers is a positive sign, according to the analyst and other doctors, because at the end of the dream she is able to scream. She emits a wail, a cry for help that cannot be heard but is, instead, carried around the world so another woman can hear her baby cry. This dream functions as a metaphor for women discovering their voices, only to sacrifice them to the maternal function, or worse still, to have them muffled in the safety of a doctor's office—a doctor who can neutralize pain.

> But she knew that these doctors were wrong. For these were the same doctors who anesthetized her during the birth of her children. (3)

Finley points to cultural attitudes that reduce women to their bodies; the doctors call her an animal when she nurses her children, they give her episiotomies during the birth of her child. Her body is denigrated, manipulated, and literally carved by her doctors. "No more sexual pleasure for her," Finley intones (139). She has fulfilled her role in the male economy of desire by bearing children; the excess baggage of female sexual pleasure has no place in such a system.

> But she knew that it really wasn't the doctors' fault. That the problem was in the way she projected her femininity. And if she wasn't passive, well she just didn't

feel desirable. And if she wasn't desirable, she didn't feel female. And if she
wasn't female, well, the whole world would cave in. (3)

The passage's irony and the woman's exaggeration may elicit a smirk but,
in fact, this vignette refers to the tragic irony of behavioral rules that
ensure that women properly perform femininity. Finley depicts the psyche
of a woman in a patriarchal economy which relies upon a particular
definition of femininity (as passivity) to ensure the circulation of goods and
services. This passage generalizes the dream of one woman to behavioral
rules and obligations that are the keystones of women's gendered
self-concepts. The passage is ironically humorous on one level—that one
woman thinks the world will fall apart if she isn't feminine—but tragically
ironic in the sense that women have internalized discipline and policed
their own performances as women.

Finley conjures up a character who explores the potential of feminism
from a position that avoids the personal changes that feminism calls for:

Q. Don't you enjoy women's studies classes?
A. I certainly do. All of the books. All of the subjects. But if it ever got in the
way of my being a proper hostess for Richard's business I'd give it up in a minute.
I'd sacrifice anything for my family. To the point of being a boring and phobic
person. (14)

The sacrificial character of the heterosexual family unit is apparent here,
as is the inevitable conflict between feminism and more traditional family
roles. Self-definitions are inextricable from our relationships to others,
including family members. Indeed, our assumptions about what the family
unit means affect our perceptions of sexual difference as well. In one
shocking story of an Oedipal monster, Finley parodies the absurd Freudian
reduction of female desire to the equation of penis with feces and child;
she reveals the humor and horror of this representation of female sexuality
by displacing it onto a man and by literalizing it:

My first sexual experience was at the time of my birth, passing through the vaginal
canal. That red pulsing tunnel, that alley of love. I'm nothing but a human penis.
(17)

This image provokes humor—we seem to be back on familiar territory.
The aggressive representation of male sexuality is a familiar butt of jokes.
In a post-feminist world, we may make fun of this behavior as "macho."

But Finley hits hard, refusing to let the audience accept this state of affairs without realizing that it is a consequence of both our belief systems and the very words that we use:

> And at the time of my birth I had an erection. I'm fucking my own mama at my birth. It's the smell, it's the sight of my mama that keeps me going. So I spend my adulthood driving around in my red car, the symbol of my masculinity, looking for hot mamas....(17)

Because of psychoanalysis, the Oedipal triangle is now firmly embedded in our cultural notion of the family. It is difficult to be confronted with the sheer brutality of the literal interpretation of this supposedly symbolic relationship between mother and son. We recognize, perhaps joke about, and tolerate "mama's boys." Mothers are, of course, responsible for everything related to child development—homosexuality, heterosexuality, our strengths and weaknesses—all of our neuroses are due to Mom, our first love object.

> And I take her baby, a bald-headed baby, and put Downy fabric softener on baby's head. Then I strap that baby around my waist till it's a baby dildo. Then I take that baby, that dildo, and fuck its own mama. Cause I'm nothing but a motherfucker. (18)

Finley makes us aware of the symbolic and literal dimensions of the word "motherfucker"—and reminds us of how easily we use such words. By pointing to the aggressive violation of the mother, Finley brings together the symbolic and the real, revealing how violence on the level of language is related to violence in our culture. Finley suggests this potential for violence is within all of us because it is embedded in linguistic and psychoanalytical representations of our selves.

In addition to exposing problems inherent in the Freudian system's representation of female sexuality, Finley's work raises an important political question: what would our fantasies be like without the language, concepts, and structure of psychoanalysis? We as a culture have learned a language and a mode of expression in therapy to express experiences of self. Can this language and method of expression itself damage certain groups, like women? The Freudian system is an integral part of modernity; Finley's performances indicate a need for a different language to speak about our experience of self.

CONSTANT DESIRE

> In *The Constant State of Desire* I wanted to show vignettes of capitalist consumer society where people go far out, stretch the boundaries—but still they never can be satisfied. So they take things into themselves, and this is what incest or abuse is about. (154)

In her interview with Richard Schechner and in her performance, Finley makes tangible the Lacanian notion of desire, its excessive and insatiable character. For Lacan, desire exists in the realm of the symbolic, in language. The subject constantly tries to fill the lack that language creates by its very operation. Finley portrays that process in terms of the body in relation to consumer objects in capitalist culture:

> So I take you Mr. Entrepreneur, Mr. Yuppie, Mr. Yesman and tie you up in all of your Adidas, your Calvin Klein, your Ralph Lauren, your Anne Klein, your Macy's, your Bloomingdale's. I tie you up in all of your fashion, your pastel cotton shirts of mint green and lilac and you know what? You like it. (8)

Why does Finley attack fashion? It is worn on the body. In a sense, our clothing is a sign of self in the same way that our anatomy marks us. During this part of the performance, the audience at the performance I attended laughed quite freely at "those yuppies." It seemed obvious to me that we as audience should feel just as ridiculous as the yuppies in consumer bondage. We enjoy Karen Finley's work, perhaps because we like being victimized by the marginal, the titilating thrill of the dangerous in the relative safety of experimental theater. Finley makes this point directly:

> So I open up those designer jeans of yours. Open up your ass and stick up there sushi, nouvelle cuisine. I stick up your ass Cuisinarts, white wine, and racquetball, your cordless phone and Walkman up your ass. And you look at me worried and ask "but where's the graffiti art" and I say "up your ass." And you smile 'cause you work all day and you want some of the artistic experience, the artistic lifestyle for yourself after work and on weekends. (8)

Finley plays with the psychoanalytic concept of introjection—the taking inside one's body of the object of desire. Performance artist Rachel Rosenthal also exploits this concept, performing a feast where she eats non-stop for hours, acting out her own eating disorder. Introjection is based on emptiness and desire; we need to incorporate something or someone in order to feel whole. For Finley, introjection is a material and bodily act, not merely a psychological metaphor.

> I drive down to Wall Street and break into the exchange. I go up to all the traders
> and cut off their balls. They don't bleed, only dollar signs come out. They don't
> miss their balls 'cause they're too busy fucking me with everything else they've
> got. (9)

Here rape, like "motherfucker," has both literal and figurative dimensions.
The trader's don't need balls—there are plenty of other objects with which
to figuratively abuse other people.

What Finley eventually does with their balls, she tells us, is to roll them
in chocolate and dung and sell them to yuppie children as expensive candy.
I read this plot of scandalous recycling as a metaphor for her own work.
Finley literally sells us back our own cultural debris and excrement—our
emotional distress, our need to feel alive, our belief in our difference from
the money-grubbing aesthetically desensitized yuppies. And this is why
Finley will never provide a narrative in which we are invited to laugh
uncritically; unless we also laugh, and often cry, at ourselves, we ignore
the fact that our own desires are also called into question, are also part of
the joke.

Finley's scatological jokes often rely on apparently adolescent body
humor, but proceed to an intense experience that associates humor,
humiliation and the experience of being a woman. She begins the story of
Joanne:

> Joanne, Joanne sleeps with a gun under her pillow. For every time she has
> intercourse with her husband he defecates uncontrollably as he has an orgasm....
> Even though she puts down Hefty trash bags over the carpeting and walls, lets the
> crap dry before pulling it off the plastic, she found the gun to do a better job. (11)

There are possibililites for detachment and laughter that Finley immediately
undermines. I would characterize this as grotesque slapstick if it weren't
for the association of guns and phalluses, phalluses and power. We are not
permitted to laugh for very long:

> The gun up his ass gives her such a sense of power. And for a few fleeting
> moments the tables are turned for her as she forgets the time when at gunpoint she
> was forced to perform fellatio in front of her children and pets in her own garage.
> (11-12)

The woman, whose body has been violated, who no longer wants to "take
shit" from men, only feels powerful when she is equipped with a gun. This
powerful point is made with a curious counterbalancing touch of dark
humor in the form of the pets who are forced to witness Joanne's
humiliation and violation.

FINLEY AND THE BODY

Finley's predilection for scatological images and actions serves an important function: it grounds her performance in a real body, in real time. When Finley acts out defecation on stage or covers herself with food, she materially enacts with her body the stories she tells in language. She plays out the emptiness of our cultural icons, the ferocity of the desire to possess and incorporate another, with/in a body that literally seems to turn itself inside out.

Language and the symbolic order are undermined by the reality of Finley's body and the fracturing of language and humor she employs. Her manner of performing is to go into a trance-like state and to chant rhythmically, building to crescendos. Richard Schechner describes her delivery as "a trance-like state, a blank look on [her] face, a sing-song delivery of lines" (154). Her performance style and language misuse evoke Julia Kristeva's disruptive "poetic language," which is characterized by rhythmic pulsions, ellipses and fragmentation. As Finley foregrounds the excesses and insufficiencies of bodies and of language, she inserts a postmodern female body into language. Finley's body marks her as female in our sexually stratified culture; it is a commodified art object but also a source of celebration and a site of pain and abuse. Finley explores all these aspects of bodily life, as well as the relationship between body and metaphor.

When Finley undresses onstage, she dares the audience to define her solely in terms of her body, to reduce her to her bodily functions as the doctors do to the dreaming woman. Schechner states, "You're a woman in control of yourself. It's not the sexual material in itself. You can go anywhere in this country and rent videos of hardcore porn" (152). Finley responds:

> If I was doing porn they'd be very happy. When they book me they think they're going to get some kinky chick from New York going out there shoving my tits in their face. (152)

Finley's work may, in fact, be described as too radical to be characterized as pornography; the bodily disgust she invokes prohibits the audience from realizing sexual desire. The response of an audience to Finley's body is more likely to take the form of rejection and nausea than masturbatory release.

Finley does not present her body to her audience for consumption. She undresses in a matter-of-fact manner, enjoying the audience's discomfort because she is not an object, a commodity, the traditional nude female body on display. She carries on a monologue that prevents the audience from viewing her body in a fetishized manner—telling us that her underwear were purchased at the performance art store and that they have a stain on them from her last period. She taunts the audience's voyeuristic desires, undressing quickly, efficiently—this is not strip tease. She discloses her body in order to produce discomfort at the level of the spectator whose prurient interest is flung back from center stage.

She mixes a curious batch of body paint: colored raw eggs and small stuffed animals smashed together in a plastic garment bag. She adorns herself with the crushed-up eggs using the stuffed animals as the applicators. Finally, she adds glitter and a feather boa. Finley claims she wanted to celebrate her body, using the idea of eggs: "That's what *The Constant State of Desire's* about, womb envy. Not penis envy, womb envy" (154). Her body in her performance is a fabric of pleasure for her as well as a site of pain; her body, like language, doubles itself. No static portrait, no frozen female nude, can adequately encompass the body that Finley evokes on stage in *TCSD*.

Finley's female subjectivity in performance is part of and yet exceeds her body; she evokes the multiplicity of experience, the psychosis of abusive relationships, and the inability of language to express experience. As Finley acts out the difference between language and experience, Lacan's discrepancy between need and desire, she scandalously exposes language's own lack in relation to the female body. Schechner remarks that:

> What you are presenting is a woman who is a subject expressing the sexual violence and humor that women are still supposed to be the objects of, or ignorant of, or excluded from. You don't just show it, you talk about it—the shock is in the words you use, more than the gesture. (153)

I would modify Schechner's statement; it is not so much the words Finley uses that shock as much as Finley's exaggeration, bodily materialization and deconstruction of those words. I think Finley's performances suggest that the power of words to affect us is crucially related to their material quality: the sounds that bodies form, the bodily pain and pleasure that produce words, the real pain underlying apparently benign words. Finley chooses the performance medium because her body must insinuate itself into the symbolic in order to expose the boundaries of language. She uses body and text, and body as text, as instruments with which to subvert

notions of the individual, of the audience vis-a-vis the performer. Finley
destabilizes audience laughter because humor in her work is produced by
the juxtaposition of the exaggerated, over-exposed (often female) body in
pain with an inadequate language; she hints that our language, as well as
our beliefs in the Freudian concept of the self, may perpetuate the abuse
inflicted upon female bodies in our society.

Finley's unique critique of phallocentric capitalist culture rests on her
ability to mine the seam between the words we use and our bodily
experiences of life, which are replete with pain and bodily waste. The
following passage from *TCSD* foregrounds her political critique of culture
and of art (for it contains a potshot at formalist critic Susan Sontag's work
on disease as metaphor); it also exemplifies Finley's relentless attack on
the seams of language using the seams of the body:

> I saw Mr. Reagan on the TV. There is a TV camera up his butthole looking up his
> asshole for polyps, for his colon cancer. He is so obsessed with what not to put
> up the butthole....Boy, I call your disease a metaphor. I call your disease your
> personal metaphor of being a fuckin' pain in the butt.

Here Finley reverses the operation of metaphor—a crucial attribute of
language. The humor she evokes is related to the fact that her linguistic
characterization of Mr. Reagan as a "pain in the butt" has mysteriously
materialized at the level of his body. The coincidence of words and body
are somehow satisfying, but this satisfaction is fleeting, for Finley is in fact
describing a body's—and, perhaps, a culture's—disease process.

Ultimately, Finley's ambivalent humor and linguistic deconstruction
expose a number of conflicts and contradictions she associates with being
a woman in contemporary culture. Finley does not, however, provide a
political "solution" to the problems she explores in her art; her bitter and
ironic humor only serves to take the edge off what she sees as the brutally
violent oppression of women and other marginal groups in American
culture.

WORKS CITED

Finley, Karen. "The Constant State of Desire," in *Shock Treatment*. San Francisco: City
    Lights, 1990: 2-26.
Schechner, Richard. "Karen Finley: A Constant State of Becoming," *TDR* 32(1), Spring
    1988: 152-158.

6

Sylvia Talks Back

KAYANN SHORT

SYLVIA   by Nicole Hollander

At one time or another, every feminist has found herself or himself in the uncomfortable position of being expected to laugh at a misogynistic joke, one which placed a woman or women as the "butt" of humor. If you _didn't_ laugh, you risked identification with the female position and thus becoming a "butt" yourself; but if you _did_ laugh, you always felt a little guilty for betraying a woman, a little uneasy about the ambiguous distinction between her and you, and more than a little angry for being put in such a position in the first place.

57

Of course, the situation I have just described can function as a paradigm for a current focus of feminist theory, which is often referred to as "Women's relation to language," or in psychoanalytical terms, "Women's relation to the Symbolic." As Julia Kristeva states in her essay "About Chinese Women," "the daughter...is rewarded by the symbolic order when she identifies with the father: only here is she recognized not as herself but in opposition to her rival, the mother with the vagina who experiences *jouissance*. Thus, at the price of censoring herself as a woman, she will be able to triumph in her henceforth sublimated sadistic attacks on the mother whom she has repressed and with whom she will always fight" (150). The feminist dilemma, then, is how to participate in the symbolic order without perpetuating our own oppression. Yet the answer does not lie in merely forsaking the symbolic, for as Kristeva warns, "A woman has nothing to laugh about when the symbolic collapses." But what then, we may ask, *does* a woman have to laugh about? Or, to frame the question in political terms, what is feminist humor?

To begin to answer these questions I would like to explore the cartoon character Sylvia from the strip of the same name by Nicole Hollander, first in terms of the Freudian tradition of joke telling alluded to above, and then in terms of gender as performance or masquerade and the role of the "female transgressor" in transforming the Symbolic.

In "The Purloined Punchline: Joke as Textual Paradigm," Jerry Aline Flieger explicates Freud's essay "Jokes and Their Relation to the Unconscious" as a story of unrequited desire in the classic love triangle: Boy/joke teller wants girl, but can "get" her only by exposing and embarrassing her in a hostile joke told to a (male) listener/voyeur. In this model, joke telling facilitates male bonding by necessarily excluding women. As Jane Gallop remarks, in joke telling "[m]en exchange women for heterosexual purposes, but the real intercourse is that exchanged between men" (53). What Gallop doesn't mention, however, is that the listener/voyeur is also unwittingly "the dupe," seduced by a promise of pleasure which can only be fulfilled by telling the joke to someone else: In Flieger's words, "One only receives the punch line...in order to give it away" (958). In fact, by Freud's definition, no one is really satisfied by the telling of a joke—even the joke teller gains only a fleeting satisfaction which cannot fully displace the lack of the original object of desire, the woman. Thus, a joke's function is to be compulsively repeated; it exists only to re-engender itself as the site of unfulfillment.

But what happens to this re-engendering if the woman tells the joke? And not just a woman, but a feminist woman, for I want to make a distinction between *Sylvia's* humor and that of a "woman's cartoon" such as *Cathy* which reinforces negative sexual stereotypes of women. That *Sylvia* expresses feminist politics was even admitted by *Vogue* magazine in a 1986 interview. Although it never mentioned the "F" word, it did state that Hollander's point in the comic strip was, ironically enough, "Women can be happy without conforming to anyone's standards but their own" (Witkowsky 222).

It is exactly against the tyranny of "standards" found in a magazine such as *Vogue* that Sylvia turns her devastating wit. For example, some of the most physically dangerous and intellectually degrading advertisements found in *Vogue*-style magazines are the campaigns for "feminine hygiene" products. A recent Sylvia postcard challenges the serious tone portrayed in such ads: to this television dialogue between mother and daughter— "Honey, you look troubled. Do you want to talk about it?/Mom, I don't always feel as fresh as I'd like to"—Sylvia responds with the practical suggestion: "Sit in the fridge."

On the first page of the 1988 issue of *Women's Studies* devoted to women and humor (later reprinted as *Last Laughs,* edited by Regina Barreca) a *Sylvia* cartoon appears which introduces the idea that humor is gendered. Sitting with her typewriter in the bathtub wearing a large hat and dark glasses, Sylvia types the following questionnaire: "Are you a man or a woman? *Check the things you find funny: □ Larry, Moe, and Curly. □ Men dressed up as women, but with their unshaven legs showing. □ The disparity between the Ideal and the Real." Presumably the last answer is the correct one for a woman, for it is exactly such a disparity that the current women's movement in this country has been trying to expose. American culture projects its ideal of what a woman is supposed to be, and feminists show how this image is not and can never be real. Alternately, feminists project their ideal of a non-sexist society and contrast it with people's actual conditions and experiences.

But, returning to the cartoon, is such a disparity between "the Ideal and the Real" funny? Yes, if the categories of real and ideal themselves are interrogated. As Regina Barreca explains, in feminist humor "[t]he presentation of 'realism' is less meaningful if the concept of the real is open to question" (18). Sylvia does not just attempt to explore the gap between the ideal and the real, but exposes the slippage in the categories themselves by parodying cultural inscriptions of gender roles. In *Sylvia,* gender is a masquerade, a silly act, or a peculiar habit one gets hooked on. For example, in a narrative created by Sylvia as writer, a female "supercop" confronts a man at the breakfast table about his wife's lip gloss addiction, asking him "How many times a day does she put it on? How often does she lick her lips? Is there money missing from your wallet?" (February 6, 1990). Thus, in Sylvia's world, it is not men who are the butt of her jokes, but a system which enforces gender role stereotypes, a system in which everyone—even women—is to some extent complicit.

Feminists have recently begun to articulate a theory of femininity and masculinity as performance, based not on some original or true form, but instead on a complex cultural construction which can never be attained, but can only be displaced, and therefore must always be repeated. Gender "is a repetition and imitative structure that marks from the start *a failure of adequation....*The site in which the 'ideal' or the 'original' might be located is in the performed *effects* which try—and fail—to approximate it; in other words, the 'original' is to be found in the effect of an impossible ideal produced by any given gender performance" (Butler 1-2). Rather than propose some essentialist theory about the nature of "women" or "Woman," the challenge before feminists today is to expose how such categories of identity are created, regulated, and circulated within cultures.

In *Sylvia*, gender role as performance is foregrounded by the structure of the cartoon itself, which features Sylvia as a commentator on the absurdities propagated by mass media. Most often she is talking back to a television set that proclaims some cliché view of gender, such as the frame where the TV voice declares "Someday he'll come along, the man I love..." and Sylvia finishes the sentiment with "And I'll probably be out shopping" (Hollander, *Training*).

Television functions as a metaphor in *Sylvia* for all the lies women and men are told about, in Hollander's words, "Sex, Marriage, and Other Irreconcilable Differences." *Sylvia* strips have expanded this metaphor to include other forms of mass communication, such as answering machines and videotapes, by parodying the exploitation of gender role anxiety within consumer culture. For example, women's compulsion to shop is satirized in a cartoon featuring a ringing telephone amidst tabletop clutter voicing the taped message: "Hi, this is Sylvia's materialistic desires behavior-modification hotline. Today's mantra is 'If I buy this, may my hand drop off my body.' Repeat mantra loudly until the desire for the purchase subsides or you are ejected from the store" (November 10, 1989). In another strip, titled "Sylvia's Video Date," a woman testifies, "The Sylvia dates have allowed me to lead an exciting life without leaving the friendly confines of my apartment," while the text for the product reads, "Just slip 'Video Date' into your VCR and sit back, because from the moment your date walks in the door carrying gardenias and dinner, he will be totally focused on you—45 minutes of mind-blowing attention! Comes in Blonde and Foreign" (January 30, 1990). Besides what this particular cartoon says about women's sexual fantasies and neuroses, including agoraphobia, it also comments on women's anxieties about their bodies, for at the bottom of the strip, the voice from the video asks, "Can I get you on a diet cola, my sweet?" Here Hollander exposes how, even in their fantasies, women must control their appetites.

Even before the advent of advertising, the body has been the primary site of gender role anxiety. As Lacan has shown with his picture of two doors, one marked Ladies, the other Gentlemen, anatomical difference figures gender difference, and everyone must choose one door or the other. It should be no surprise that bathroom etiquette, in particular, has been a source of humor and Sylvia, too, exposes the masquerade of gender difference as biological function by trivializing it. In a strip titled "Gender-Based Difference: How to Tell If You're a Guy or a Gal," Sylvia's questionnaire asks "□ 1. You think that an alarm which attaches to the inside of a toilet seat and is activated when the seat is left up for more than 30 seconds should be a big seller. □ 2. You think it's stupid" (March 1, 1990). In an earlier strip, the debate about E.R.A. comes down to the following question, "How's a decent woman going to relieve herself on the battlefield?," Sylvia's retort, "why don't you try holding it until peace-time?," shows how equality not only threatens the ideologies surrounding our most private biological acts, but is tied to national policies of war and peace (Hollander, *Ma*). This strip is reminiscent of another early Hollander cartoon which also satirizes the location of gender roles in the body: "If ERA passes, men will be forced to *shave* their legs and women will be compelled to wear tiny spit curls on their chests!" (Hollander, *Training*).

Besides locating the site of gender role inadequation in the media's policing of gendered bodies, the characterization of Sylvia herself exposes these myths. Sylvia challenges the stereotyped image of female commentators in the mass media today from Hollywood movie stars to TV anchorpersons. Sylvia is not young, svelte, or blonde, nor does she wear tailored business suits. Instead, she follows her own sense of fashion, be it polka-dotted party hats or furry high-heeled slippers. Neither is she obsessed with fitness. To "Wondering in Wichita," she answers with tongue-in-cheek, "I don't know of any foundation grants that enable you to take a year off to work on your body, *but* if you hear of one let me know" (October 30, 1989). Sylvia also realizes that, despite advertising's emphasis on eternal youth, age is in the eye of the beholder, as seen in her quiz, "How to Guess your own Age": "You see a frail old person crossing the street. You think: 1. 'I will not be living in this climate when I'm old...not me, oh Lord.' 2. 'I will be rich when I'm old.' 3. 'I'll probably be dead at 40.' 4. 'What old person?' (February 6, 1990).

Through characterization as a writer, Sylvia belongs to that long tradition of women who live by their wits, but her occupation also places her as a liminal figure between the private domestic world of women and the public political world of men. In fact, Sylvia is almost always home. She is, to borrow Mary Russo's term, a "female transgressor" whose unrestrained, aging female body refuses to be finally and wholly marginalized. Instead, it occupies a carnivalesque space which is often hyperbolized in the strip by the appearance of space aliens, gypsy fortune-tellers, and the devil himself. As feminists have pointed out, this space can be one of power, serving to "resist, exaggerate, and destabilize the distinctions and boundaries that mark and maintain high culture and organized society" (Russo 218). Irreverent and irrepressible, Sylvia talks back and always gets in the last word. In fact, Sylvia often supplies the punchline to what is not even supposed to be a joke in the first place, as in the frame where the TV proclaims, "Women hold up half the sky." Sounds egalitarian, doesn't it? But once again Sylvia reminds us of the disparity between the ideal and the real when she replies, "Uh huh, but in a poor neighborhood" (Hollander, *Training*).

I would like to suggest some areas for feminist investigations of humor as found in a strip like *Sylvia*. First, going back to Freud's paradigm, we may begin to look for links between the compulsive repetition of a joke based on unfulfilled desire and the compulsive repetition of gender performance created by a lack which can only act out its own failure. It is no coincidence, I think, that jokes which depend on gendered positions can only be "gotten" at the price of being "had."

Next, feminists can look at the locations of desire within feminism itself. Are we merely exchanging gendered positions and values, replacing boy for girl and girl for boy, or can we change the locus of desire around which jokes are circulated? Can we expose and transform a system of oppression without identifying something or someone as the "butt" of our humor?

Finally, is all humor funny? In the case of *Sylvia*, I think the answer may be ironically "No." For example, in the last cartoon to appear in the *Women's Studies* issue devoted to humor, Sylvia asks, "Do you have a good sense of humor? Check the situation below that tickles your funny bone: □ A Man wearing a toupee and a fat woman trying to get through a revolving door at the same time. □ People hitting each other with chickens. □ Anything with chickens." The first answer reflects traditional humor where, interestingly, both actors are identified by bodily characteristics. The second answer presents slapstick humor, more off-the-wall perhaps, but still a recognizable genre. The third answer, however, is a kind of nonsense—why chickens? What is "anything"? If I find neither of the first two answers funny, must I necessarily check the third box?

Since I've started working on this paper, many people have told me that they don't understand *Sylvia,* they just don't "get it." I have to admit, I don't always "get it" either, but maybe that's the point, for besides destabilizing the borders between public and private, real and ideal, and masculine and feminine, *Sylvia* also disrupts the dichotomy between humor and non-humor, not only in content (*what* is funny), but in form (*how* it's funny). Humor is a human construction and our reactions to it are in some way determined by cultural conditions. If our expectations are not fulfilled, we become confused. *Sylvia* provokes us to interrogate our expectations and our desires as they are circulated through the discourses of humor, of gender, and of whatever feminisms are currently "in *Vogue.*" When Sylvia's daughter Rita asks, "Ma can I be a feminist and still like men?," Sylvia answers, "Sure.... Just like you can be a vegetarian, and like fried chicken," a reply which at *second* glance disrupts our initial laughter: what *does* it mean for a vegetarian to like fried chicken? Can we not only *like* fried chicken, but eat it too? Confronted with an analogy that, in Sylvia-esque fashion, doesn't quite match up, we can only agree with Rita: "Ma, sometimes when you tell me something I get *more* confused."

WORKS CITED

Barreca, Regina. "Introduction." *Women's Studies* 15 (1988): 3-22.

Butler, Judith. "Lana's 'Imitation': Melodramatic Repetition and Gender Performative." *Genders* 9 (1990): 1-17.

Flieger, Jerry Aline. "The Purloined Punchline: Joke as Textual Paradigm." *Modern Language Notes* 98 (1983): 941-67.

Gallop, Jane. "Why is Freud Giggling?" *Hecate* 10 (1984): 49-53.

Hollander, Nicole. *I'm in Training to be Tall and Blonde.* New York: St. Martin's Press, 1979.

___. *Ma, Can I be a Feminist and Still Like Men?* New York: St. Martin's Press, 1980.

Kristeva, Julia. "About Chinese Women." In *The Kristeva Reader.* Ed. Toril Moi. New York: Columbia University Press, 1986. 138-59.

Russo, Mary. "Female Grotesques: Carnival and Theory." In *Feminist Studies/Critical Studies.* Ed. Teresa de Lauretis. Bloomington: Indiana University Press, 1986. 213-29.

Witkowsky, Kathy. "Cartoon Verite." *Vogue* (February 1986): 222, 229.

7

Why Women Cartoonists Are Rare, and Why That's Important

BETTY SWORDS

My humor research has had a personal motive: I was looking for the answer to that perennial Question: Why so few women cartoonists? For I was that rarity, a cartoonist of the female persuasion; I started selling to the *Saturday Evening Post* and other top magazines in 1955.

My studies changed forever my rather Pollyanna view of humor as a kindly contemplation of life's incongruities, to paraphrase the Canadian humorist Stephen Leacock. Instead, I discovered humor's tremendous powers: to kill as well as cure. I saw that too often men used humor as a weapon against the Others of society, and it was women who marched at the head of this Hit Parade.

Still, I realized that humor was a great natural resource, like nuclear energy, that could be used to benefit or to destroy.

"WHERE ARE ALL THE GALS?"

Actually, The Question wasn't really "perennial." It was more like every few years that a cartoonist would look around and ask, "Where are all the gals?" Someone else might answer that women were too subjective, "take everything personally, you know." Certainly they were all agreed that it wasn't discrimination. An editor would have to be crazy to reject a funny cartoon just because it was drawn by a woman! And it was back to (male) cartoon business as usual. But I was still puzzled.

Sometimes mentioned was the fact that there were some funny women writers, like Jean Kerr, and a few comedians, too. Why were women rarer in the cartoon field of humor?

If anyone knew the answer, it should be Gurney Williams, the dean of humor editors, first for *Colliers,* and then *Look,* as well as a humor writer himself. So I was delighted when he brought up The Question in a 1960 *Memos,* an occasional newsletter sent to his humor contributors. His answer?

"I don't know why there aren't more gals like Martha Blanchard, Barbara Shermund, Betty Swords, and, of course, Janice Berenstain...." Big help.

Small as the number of women cartoonists was, it was shrinking more. Cartoonist Jack Markow wrote in his Cartoonist Cues column for *Writer's Digest* in 1969: "In this space a few years ago, I mentioned these female practitioners of magazine and newspaper comic art—then a mere dozen— now more decimated by drop-outs due to retirement and marriage." I was one of Markow's "mere dozen."

But in 1974, Markow wrote that "Betty Swords is one of the very few cartoonists on the distaff side still active." *Why?*

The women's movement was close to ten years old and the numbers of women were increasing in all the other once-male-only professions: doubling in medicine, almost tripling in law. Why not in cartooning?

It was Mort Walker, creator of the *Beetle Bailey* and *Hi and Lois* comic strips, who came up with an obvious assumption: Women lack a sense of humor. "The rib that God took from Adam and donated to Eve must not have been a funny bone," said Walker, in an Associated Press story that got wide media coverage in 1976.

As proof, he pointed out that the Museum of Cartoon Art, of which he was president, had fewer than twenty women represented among thousands of male cartoonists. And most of these weren't all that funny, he said. "They range mostly from cute to soap."

"It has been proved that a sense of humor requires intelligence," continued Walker, "you must first understand a situation before you can see the humor in it." He does admit there are a few funny women: writers and comedians like Jean Kerr, Erma Bombeck, Carol Burnett, and Joan Rivers. "*But they are still exceptions to the rule (I* added the emphasis)."

Perhaps Walker was just being more honest than the other cartoonists in saying what he thought; certainly he knew the seriousness of his charges. "It's like being un-American," he admitted, in the A.P. release, to say that someone doesn't have a sense of humor. "People don't like to be told that anymore than they like to be told they have no sex appeal or they're out of toilet paper."

I don't know who was angrier about Walker's accusations: I, or the class I was teaching in humor power at the University of Denver—the women members, anyhow. Some of the men were already convinced that women had no place in humor—those who, upon seeing that the instructor was a woman, went out to check the room number to see if they were in the right place. Upon returning, they made a point of sitting in the back row, putting the maximum distance between themselves and me.

Of course women do have a sense of humor. (Who was it who said they needed one in order to put up with men?) And certainly discrimination is largely responsible for the scarcity of women in all areas of humor, but the discrimination against women cartoonists is not the usual garden variety (or not entirely).

Here's what I discovered:

THE ANSWER TO THE QUESTION

I was reading a book of comic's one-liners, *The Encyclopedia of Humor* by Joey Adams, when I became aware of a growing discomfort. People usually skim these books, but I had to read them thoroughly because I reviewed them for *The Denver Post*.

I was growing punchy from the aptly-named punch lines, when I noticed something odd about the section I was reading on Marriage:

Married life is great—it's my wife I can't stand!

She married him until debt do us part.

He was unlucky in both his marriages—his first wife left him—and this one won't!

All the jokes were not only against marriage, they were against women as well: *The fall guy was a gal.* Click.

I looked at the section on Women:

A woman's brain is divided into two parts—dollars and cents.

Women have a tough life. They have to cook and clean and scrub. That's hard to do without getting out of bed!

Under "Girls" were these gems: *She's a nice girl: won't take gifts from men—insists on cash.* And *The modern girl has what it takes to take what you've got.*

According to Adams, women (and "girls") come off as bad trouble: both vicious and avaricious.

Well, fun's fun. I checked to see what it was like when men were being zapped. The first joke under "Men" was: *A man is incomplete until he's married—and then he's really finished.*

Under "Husbands": *His wife has changed a lot since they were married—his habits, his friends—his love.* And *He'd never be where he is today without her—busted.*

What we learned about men/husbands was—*women are vicious and avaricious.* An ugly image of women was emerging.

The gags were similar to those I'd read in other joke books, and heard on TV, I realized. I needed to check further. Adams had written over a dozen joke books; Bob Orben over forty, aside from being a speechwriter for President Ford. He would be a good choice to study, too.

The jokes were much the same, except that Orben is a breast man:

Did you hear about the fellow who married the flat-chested girl for her brains? It was awful! Every morning he'd wake up and take one look at her and yell, "Quick, honey, say something smart!"

I love that phrase "pockets of poverty"—sounds like my wife's bra.

I'll bet he came up with some beauts about Betty Ford's mastectomy. Bad taste? Of course, but it hardly seems to be *good* taste to make jokes like that about his wife. (Comedian Allen King, when asked on the *Tonight Show* whether his wife objected to his jokes about her, answered "No, not as long as she gets that check every week.")

The other joke books I checked showed the same result: humor was hostile to women. But I realized that the stand-up comic, on the night club circuit, has a very different life style from the more domesticated cartoonist, whose studio is usually at home. So I checked the cartoon collections.

In a way, they were worse.

It's like the difference between radio and television: radio allows us to use our imagination in picturing people; but cartoons were the TV of humor, showing how the male humorists, themselves, regarded women. And it was awful. Parasite wives became cretinous matrons, while the battle-axe wives became ugly monsters. As for the sexy playgirls, wow! Their pneumatic breasts were raised to silicone heights of glory which defied the law of gravity, except that their behinds were equally inflated.

First, I recognized that our humor is incredibly hostile to women, who were stereotyped as tricky, lazy, greedy, and *dumb.*

Other ideas began to click into place: *Women would have to have a very low self-esteem to come up with cartoon drawings and gags that are so hateful and hostile to women.*

But what happens if they *don't* follow this ugly stereotype of women? I realized that the biggest discrimination women cartoonists face is against their ideas. In other words:

Women don't make the jokes because they are the joke.

Cartoonist Dorothy Bond got her feature on babies syndicated, but she didn't have much luck with one on secretaries. "That isn't funny!" was the common cry of the syndicate male editors. And it wasn't, by their lights. For Dotti had violated the stereotype of secretaries as dumb, bosomy babes, whose filing abilities ran the gamut from A to B. Instead, *her* bright secretaries dared to make fun of their bosses. Secretaries enjoyed not being the butt of jokes for once, and bought the book she published, when she couldn't get her cartoons syndicated.

CLICK!—THE MOMENT OF TRUTH

A "click" is a moment of truth, a recognition that women are discriminated against because they are women, and powerless in a society formed and controlled by men. It's the start of questioning all of society's basic assumptions, which are formed by men, and passed on through the media they control.

Men had usurped for themselves the right to name, as theologian Mary Daly put it. The male images of women created by cartoonists were accepted as the *truth* about women. For example: The woman driver is the safest driver, according to the National Safety Council—but not to the National Cartoonists Society. To them she's the quintessential "dumb driver," an idea so set in the concrete of comic tradition that it's become a humor shorthand: when we see a cartoon of a woman driver, we know automatically that she's a dumb driver. Just ask a man which he believes— the Cartoonist Society or the Safety Council?

At this point I can hear some male voices complaining that I'm doing just what male cartoonists complained of: taking a joke personally, for God's sake! Being too subjective. Didn't I know it was just a joke?

As if a joke weren't serious business. "Comics reflect our culture," said Berger (1). Humor is one of the best indications (or indictments?) of the culture of a country. What we laugh at is a key to our nature; and what America finds funniest is women.

It seems I wasn't the first person to discover that women were U.S. humor's chief target. Professor Jesse Bier wrote in *The Rise and Fall of American Humor* that women were always "the supreme target" of American humor, which he called the most misogynic in the world; in the classic *Enjoyment of Laughter,* Max Eastman says that in two top gagwriters' collections of over a million gags, "there are more jokes filed under 'Dumb Dames' than any other topic." And Gershon Legman notes in *Rationale of the Dirty Joke* that "this material (dirty jokes) has all been created by men, and that there is no place in it for women except as the butt."

Why America's humor is so much more misogynic than that of other countries is a good question: Bier explains it as being "true for any culture that allows women to threaten men's position—from on high, as it were."

Could it be that Bier, himself, is affected by all the male cartoons and other humor which show married women as ruling the domestic roost? Arthur Asa Berger, in *The Comic-Stripped American,* writes of "the notion that marriage is debilitating and destructive of virility and masculinity...a veritable cliche in the comics and in popular culture."

Francis E. Barcus, in his analysis of the Sunday comics, notes the husband's wimpishness and the married woman's "thirst for power." But he goes on to comment that this is just the marriage model chosen by the comics, *any relationship to the truth about marriage relationships being coincidental.* (Perhaps the cartoonists thought it funnier than the reality of domestic violence.)

UPPITY WOMEN UNITE!

It's not surprising that my Click! became an open sesame into feminism and the women's movement. But other women came through a similar door: like the infuriated one who called the NOW line early one Monday to complain, "I'm sick of the way TV ridicules women, and I want to do something about it!"

"RIDICULE implies a deliberate often malicious belittling," according to *Webster's Ninth New Collegiate Dictionary,* and is one of the most potent humor weapons—especially useful against the women's movement.

How could anyone take the ridiculous—or their complaints, no matter how justified—seriously? The uppity woman, who preferred equal rights to pedestal heights, was doubly damned. And "bra-burner" was the perfect belittling title to attach to her like "bloomer girl" for the suffragist of the nineteenth century (the change shows men's anatomical fixations of the two periods). It was immaterial that the practical bloomer costume was worn by very few women, for only the briefest period in the early 1850s, due to such vicious ridicule. And that no twentieth-century woman burned a bra. Men were the ones to name the feminist, and they named her mud.

It's fascinating—and a little frightening—to see how little has changed in the media's treatment of feminists in the two centuries. In both periods editorial cartoonists showed them as ugly misfits, bitter old maids who wouldn't care about getting equal rights if they could get a man.

Or the feminist was shown as a battle-axe wife, a monster who heaped the greatest degradation on her pipsqueak husband by making him wash the dishes *and mind the baby.*

But there is one notable change in the two centuries: in the nineteenth century the young women feminists were often shown as beautiful. Not so in the twentieth. *Definitely* not. This time around there seems to have been more hate.

But sometimes the media image worked to our advantage: in 1970, Denver's mayor appeared so grateful that a small NOW contingent didn't dance on his desk, shedding our bras and inhibitions, that he agreed to sponsor a three-day conference on women.

There I gave a workshop on humor, which was vastly different from any time I'd spoken on humor before. Partly because I was different, but so were the women.

They, as well as many of the women students I had in my later classes on humor power, were suffering from what I called *humor anxiety.* They were expected to be good sports and laugh at jokes about themselves—jokes showing them to be vicious, avaricious dummies—even when the jokes drew blood, or *they were accused of lacking a sense of humor.* "How do you handle the jokes?" was a constant question.

And there was still another question I had to answer: if ugly sexist stereotypes made it so difficult for women to become a cartoonists, *how come I was one?*

I DID IT MY WAY

Being a cartoonist was not my childhood dream: that was to draw the prettiest paper dolls in the world. Girls draw pretty; it's the boys who draw ugly and funny (I remember punch-drunk boxers as being a juvenile male specialty).

But after getting a Bachelor's in Fine Arts at the University of California at Berkeley, I went to The Academy of Advertising Art in San Francisco to study fashion illustration (*drawing* paper doll dresses?). I had planned to design dresses, but that meant years of study in New York, in a field (strangely!) dominated by men. It was difficult in 1938 to take seriously the career aspirations of young women, who'd just be getting married.

Eric Erikson claimed that women get their *identity* from the men they marry; I don't believe that's true now, if it ever was. But choosing a man meant choosing a way of life—and I chose a beaut!

I married a doodlebug. Leonard was party chief of a seismograph crew that hopscotched throughout Texas, Louisiana and Mississippi, exploring for oil. I was frustrated that I couldn't do any fashion illustration: we moved too often, usually to towns too small for original commercial art work.

EUREKA!

It was in the lobby of an ancient hotel in the Heidleberg oil fields in the wilds of Mississippi, in 1944, that I came across a *Writer's Yearbook*. It said that although most cartoonists lived near the New York publishing center, *cartooning was the only form of commercial art that could be done by mail from anywhere.* That was for me! I was certainly anywhere and everywhere and I'd always loved humor, making scrapbooks of my favorite cartoons.

The clincher was that so many men were in the armed service that *women were now welcome.*

The gags came easy. I could view the world from just off-center (which is, actually, where most women are placed) and see the humor in it. But I was operating in a vacuum, away from the advice of both cartoonists and editors. I didn't know what I was doing wrong—or even right.

I quit after about six erratic months of trying to cartoon, mail, and move, hoping the drawings would catch up with me. After we finally settled in Midland, in West Texas, and had two sons, cartoon ideas still haunted me. So I did gag-writing for features like *Dennis the Menace.*

Eventually I tried cartooning again, with the urging of the editor of a cartoon/gag-writing newsletter and the aid of a cartoon agent. Alice could report on the market news and reactions to my work, as well as save me all the time spent mailing to the different markets.

But Alice's *biggest* help to me was in knowing someone was waiting for my cartoons every week. Three was the most I could manage, even with a weekly cleaning woman. But without an agent, busy weeks could go by of caring for my four and six year old boys, a husband and house, without my drawing any new cartoons, remailing the older ones to new markets being the best I could do.

Marty Links, who drew the syndicated teenage *Emmy Lou* for so many years, wrote wistfully of the young people now who "share work domestic and economic.... Pretending I didn't work I wouldn't wish on anyone," she said. She did rent studio space with commercial artists, one of whom came to do her backgrounds and lettering, a time-saving practice I didn't learn about until much later (but it also required enough sales to warrant the expense).

Careers for married women weren't common, nor were such women catered to. Many of the rare women cartoonists quit cartooning upon marriage: Mary Gibson, Marjorie Henderson, who drew the wildly successful last-page-of-the-*Saturday Evening Post's Little Lulu.*

"Her wealthy husband didn't want her to work. Besides, she'd probably said everything she wanted to say," commented a former *Post* cartoon editor, who also spoke of another well-known woman cartoonist who quit because she married a "jealous" (and less well-known) cartoonist. Mary Petty made extremely rare appearances in *The New Yorker* after she married Whitney Darrow, Jr., another *New Yorker* cartoonist. But she did "appear" on the cover when she painted the cartoons of her color-blind husband.

My rare trips to New York brought me offers from two syndicate editors, who liked my work, to do a feature for them. But doing seven cartoons a week, *without fail,* seemed an impossibility then, along with my *real* job of wife/mother/housekeeper.

THE NEW YORK SCENE

Cartoonists living in the New York area, where they presented their work to the editors in person—and met with other cartoonists—had a big advantage. And yet, if I'd lived there I might never have become a cartoonist.

I'd been selling cartoons to some top markets for two years before I got to New York for a Look Day. Every Wednesday the cartoonists descended on the magazine offices *en masse,* and all male. I saw only one other woman cartoonist among about seventy men: I was faced with the *reality* that this was a male profession. (Those last-name-only signatures were not—usually—hiding a woman.)

All beginners take a while to learn cartooning technique, so they must face a lot of rejection. Wouldn't a woman, wouldn't *I*, have become discouraged because I felt those rejections were due to my sex rather than my ability?

Some of the cartoon editors would confirm those suspicions.

I'd been a professional cartoonist for five years when an editor told me, "You gal cartoonists are all alike. You're too kind; none of your cartoons have the slash and attack of the men's work!" Another editor looked at my work and asked me, "Isn't there anything you *hate?*" And another blurted out, *before he even looked at my work,* "Why would *you* want to be a cartoonist?" (After examining my cartoons he conceded that I *could* draw and would be welcome in his magazine.)

A woman cartoonist-by-mail would also be spared comments like the one I got from a "friendly" cartoonist: "Frankly, I feel you're stealing food from the mouths of my wife and children."

I was stunned. "Why?" I asked.

"Because you don't *have* to be a cartoonist," he said. "You're married and your husband can support you."

THE BREAKTHROUGH WOMEN

Obviously, there are many obstacles to a woman becoming a cartoonist, but if the chief discrimination is against a woman's *ideas,* what about those breakthrough women?

Well, Barbara Shermund, whom Gurney Williams mentioned, was unique for a woman cartoonist because her work appeared regularly in *Esquire,* the first of the slick men's magazines. Her women were gold diggers, amateur prostitutes who fulfilled the male stereotype of "girls" as seductive man-traps.

Martha Blanchard was often called a top "woman cartoonist," but was a top *cartoonist* by any criteria. Her work was less objectionable, but it still followed the sexist stereotypes of the cute-dumb dames who try to trap a man into marriage (as did most of the women cartoonists) and the parasite wife (though also cute-dumb): a woman modelling a sumptuous fur coat, says to her surprised husband: *It's from you!*

One of the best-known cartoonists was Helen Hokinson whose "girls" graced the pages of *The New Yorker.* These were plump matrons "of a certain age" whose minds remained childlike as they were "protected" from participation in the real world. Hokinson truly loved her "girls," for whom Richard McAllister did the gaglines, which projected the image of women-as-dummies. When Hokinson discovered that the public was laughing *at,* instead of *with,* her "girls," this shy woman took to the speaker's lectern to defend them. On her way to make another speech, she was killed in a plane crash.

But what about my cartoons?

For one thing, I avoided the stereotype problem because my cartoons were usually about kids. My first sale to *Post* has a tough little boy saying to a friend, "It wasn't so bad being sick, I made a lot of money taking medicine." I sold a lot of Dennis rejects.

But they weren't all about kids. I hated to admit it—even to myself—but I followed some of the same sexist stereotypes: The dumb bride who burbles to her husband, "Do you like the steak? I boiled it myself," and the parasite wife who surprises her husband, "I got you something for your birthday that I've been wanting for a long time."

And it's no excuse to say they were usually (male) gag-writers' ideas (even though I was a gag-writer myself, with hundreds of ideas still not drawn). I chose them because they looked like the kind of cartoon gag I often saw printed.

Gag-writers are another element that a cartoonist deals with; most cartoonists use them for one-quarter to one-half of their cartoons. Gags are submitted in batches of eight to fifteen three by five slips, and the cartoonist "holds" those she likes. When and if the cartoon sells, the gag-writer gets a percentage, usually twenty-five percent.

As soon as I appeared in *Saturday Evening Post* regularly I was inundated by a flood of gags. Most of the writers recognized I was a woman by including women in the cartoon idea (I was surprised to discover women were actually in less than half the printed cartoons) but they were *the most incredible, hostile, hateful Maggie and Jiggs, hit-him-over-the-head-with-a-rolling-pin type of gags.* Only two, out of nearly fifty gag-writers, sent anything I could stand. I used a few of the "cute-dumb dame" who's trying to trap a man into marriage, like this: "I want to get married and settle down, and he wants to stay single and live it up!" It sold to the Cartoon-of-the-Month syndicate I did some work for.

The supremacy of the battle-axe wife gags should have told me something. Then I just assumed it was only a bunch of crazies who sent me gags, not realizing these were the professional gag-writers; this was how they worked. And this was the lasting power of the stereotype.

So pervasive are cartoon—humor—stereotypes, so much a part of comic tradition, that cartoonists follow them, sometimes unconsciously. Any token woman allowed into the game must play by the rules of the game. Male-set rules.

THE SYNDICATES

Unless we subscribe to *The New Yorker,* most of us see cartoons almost entirely in the funny pages today. As advertising switched to TV, magazine markets for cartoons shrank so drastically as to disappear from many former markets. That left the syndicates to monopolize the cartoon scene.

The cartoon panels or strips in the funnies are all supplied by large syndicates, whose features are seen by hundreds of millions of viewers around the world *daily,* second only to TV in the size of their market. The larger the audience, the more conservative the humor, and the syndicates generally have conserved a lot of the bad old female stereotypes, many of which they were responsible for establishing—certainly of perpetuating.

Marty Links drew the quintessential teenage strip, *Emmy Lou* (also known as *Bobby-Sox*) for thirty-four years until 1979. It covered *Emmy Lou's* addictions to boys and clothes.

"Mostly what I knew or know about teen-agers was not printed" (1977), she wrote me. Her own three teenagers discussed Vietnam hotly; *Emmy Lou* was not allowed to. And when Links wanted to update the series in 1970 by bringing in a black person, the syndicate vetoed the idea and sent her a wire saying if she did she "would lose all her papers in the South" (*San Francisco Chronicle,* December 24, 1979).

"There's no place for (*Emmy Lou*) in today's cartoon world," said Links when she ended the strip (1979)—but oddly enough there is: *Cathy* serves as a grown-up version of *Emmy Lou.* Her interests are still clothes and guys, plus an addiction to dieting.

When the *Cathy* comic strip started in 1976 it concerned "a sweet young thing...torn between her family's traditional values and her friends' leanings toward womens' lib" (Detroit Free Press, 1976). Any reference to feminism, pro or con, has disappeared from the strip along with its rarely seen exemplar, Andrea, who is now fanatical about motherhood, instead of sisterhood.

The syndicate also "bounces" any strip where they feel *Cathy* acts out of character, saying something "blunt or cutting or sarcastic," said Guisewite in 1976. "I have to remember not to let her lash out at goofy guys."

Feminist cartoonist Genny Pilgrim Guracar adopted the pen name Bulbul to protect her family from any connection with her irreverent pen. (They were then living in a "company town.") Later, a syndicate editor saw an article in a San Francisco paper about Bulbul and her work, and asked her to do a feature for his syndicate. But it never worked out: Bulbul said they couldn't accept her feminist ideas (private correspondence, 1978). She self-syndicates her work to feminist, aging and environmental publications, and has published three books.

Nicole Hollander is another feminist cartoonist whose work originally appeared in a feminist newsletter, *The Spokeswoman,* and later in many books of her work. After she became syndicated, the number of papers dropped so low that she quit the syndicate. Currently she is more successful at self-syndication of *Sylvia.*

THE FUNNY PAGES TODAY

Even with the awareness that the woman's movement has brought, with its exposure of sexist humor, the change in humor hasn't been that great, especially in cartoons. We may have *Sylvia,* by Hollander, but we still have sexist strips like the *Lockhorns* and *Andy Capp;* and that feminist breakthrough, the house-husband, *Adam,* is more sexist than feminist. *Adam* is the personification of the lazy, lousy housekeeper image that women have been tagged with.

Most comics are still drawn by men, though there are a few more strips by women now: *Little Women* by Kathryn LeMieux, for example, deals mainly with children. Perhaps the most feminist in its ideas of the search for equality, especially in that battleground, the home front, is *Sally Forth,* drawn by Greg Howard. That it's drawn by a man may be pertinent, since a woman might have trouble expressing such revolutionary ideas without being called an aggressive bitch.

Actually, it's probably easier for a woman to become a doctor or lawyer than a syndicated cartoonist. It's men who dominate the humor field, especially the cartoons. But, aside from the disadvantage for women cartoonists, what does that mean to us?

WOMEN'S HUMOR/MEN'S HUMOR:
WHAT'S THE DIFFERENCE?

Mindess says that the results of his test on humor enjoyment show "No significant differences between the sexes on any of the categories (of jokes)." He thinks these results suggest "there is less sex-bound difference in humorous taste than is popularly supposed" (1971). As for sexual humor, both sexes rate as funniest jokes "which put down the other sex" (1971).

At least Mindess included in his test a non-sexist sex joke. Other humor tests, such as *Psychology Today's* much earlier one, did not, and found women humorless for not laughing at them. But Gershon Legman, in his monumental, two-volume study of the sex, or "dirty," joke found them universally sexist "with no place for women in these jokes except as the butt" (1975).

I find myself in strong disagreement with Mindess, though, on the reaction to degrading humor. He feels people should be able to accept them as fairy tales or other far-out fiction, and "allow ourselves to laugh even though we might feel indignant if we took them literally" (1985: 84).

If Mindess found himself as relentlessly attacked by degrading humor as women are, I doubt if he'd find much to laugh at.

If there's so little difference between what men and women find funny, as Mindess believes, why should it matter that men are the vast majority of the humorists—especially of the cartoonists? In fact, *does* it matter?

It's true that feminists have gone to great lengths to prove that most of the supposedly male and female traits are the result of *nurture* rather than nature. Yet they haven't denied that there are great differences, whatever the cause. Men, for example, are more aggressive, and competitive; women more empathetic and cooperative. How does that translate into humor?

"First, humor is play" (1963), says psychiatrist William F. Fry, Jr.; Mindess also considers playfulness one of the "more important characteristic(s) of humor." But how does that fit with men's often aggressive and cruel humor?

Eastman addresses that point by stating that it is not due to the nature of play "but to the nature of the playing beast: man."

Does that mean "man," including woman, as in mankind? Or man as in macho man—or even that now out-of-date term: Male Chauvinist Pig?

Let's see how women's humor differs.

WOMEN'S HUMOR: BOTH FEMALE AND FEMINIST

Women have always made men nervous, claims Mindess; their humor more so—especially if it's labelled "feminist."

"They (men) have assimilated the misogyny of male humor, and with some guilt they expect that feminist humor will return the treatment in kind," writes Gloria Kaufman in the Introduction to *Pulling Our Own Strings* (1980: p.14).

This excellent collection of feminist humor and satire includes female, as well as feminist, humor and draws a distinction between them.

Female humor could be called "Ain't it the truth," looking at life from the women's point of view and showing an awareness of the oppression they suffer. It's resigned. Most of my cartoons in the *Male Chauvinist Pig Calendar, 1974* are examples of this female humor.

The idea for an MCP calendar first occurred to history professor Bob Hurley in 1972. His students understood discrimination against Blacks; I worked with him and his professor wife Peggy on a humorous calendar to help the students also recognize sexist discrimination.

I'm glad that my calendar cartoon that has been the most reproduced, in exhibits and collections, and also in sociology textbooks around the world, is a counterfoil to the stereotype of the parasitic wife, so popular in male humor. A clever pantomime spread by Cobean in *The New Yorker* showed a typical parasite wife, stretched out on a chaise lounge, reading a novel and eating "bonbons." Alerted by her little boy, watching at the window, she quickly puts on an apron and musses up her hair. When her husband enters he is greeted by an exhausted-looking wife leaning on a mop. Not only a lazy parasite, but sneaky to boot.

Mine is different. At the breakfast table a woman is struggling with fighting children and a squalling baby as her husband says, "Well, I've got to go to work, even if you don't."

But feminist humor is one of hope and *change,* which is why I thought of *Changing Times* as a market for a spread of cartoons on the new look in politics in 1972: the woman candidate. Cartoon editor Robert Marshall had faith in me when the editorial board didn't. But eventually they all approved a two-page spread of cartoons which reversed every old stereotype about women and politics. (Reversal was an early and easy form of feminist humor.) I was at a party for Pat Schroeder (running for the first time for the House of Representatives) the day *CT* came out.

"I addressed the Rotary Club today," she told me, where one of the Rotarians said, "You'll never believe what was in *Changing Times* today!"

Men thought—and feared—that when women got positions of power they would act like men do, that their humor would create an opposing stereotype "a nasty and oppressive male as repulsive and disgusting as their stereotypic female," wrote Kaufman.

But instead of being the obverse of male mainstream humor, with its put-downs, feminist humor is noted for its *pick-ups*. Kaufman says that "we do not laugh at people, we bond *with* them." It's a humor of hope.

So, when we deny females and feminists the freedom of the funny pages—making it both difficult to appear there, as well as to express their own ideas—we are negating the female experience. But, more important, we are missing out on a bring-us-together kind of humor.

We also continue to perpetuate ugly, negative stereotypes of women that work to erode our self-esteem and degrade us in the eyes of the world.

WORKS CITED

Adams, Joey. *The Encyclopedia of Humor* (Indianapolis: Bobbs-Merrill, 1968).

Barcus, Francis E. "The World of Sunday Comics," in D.M. White and R.H. Abel, *The Funnies: An American Idiom* (Free Press: 1963).

Berger, Arthur Asa. *The Comic-Stripped American* (United States: Walker Publishing Co., 1973).

Bier, Jesse. *The Rise and Fall of American Humor* (New York: Holt, Rinehart and Winston, 1968).

Eastman, Max. *Enjoyment of Laughter* (New York: Simon and Schuster, 1936).

Fry, Jr., William F. *Sweet Madness: A Study of Humor* (Palo Alto: Pacific Books, 1963).

Horn, Maurice. *Women in the Comics* (New York: Chelsea House, 1977).

Kaufman, Gloria and Mary Kay Blakely, eds. *Pulling Our Own Strings* (Bloomington: Indiana University Press, 1980).

Legman, G. *No Laughing Matter: Rationale of the Dirty Joke,* Second Series (New York: Breaking Point, 1975).

Mindess, Harvey and Carolyn Miller, Joy Turek, Amanda Bender, and Suzanne Corbin. *The Antioch Humor Test: Making Sense of Humor* (New York: Avon, 1985).

Orben, Robert. *The Ad-Libber's Handbook: 2000 New Laughs for Speakers* (Garden City, N.Y.: Doubleday).

Walker, Mort. "Do Women Have a Sense of Humor?" in *Guida alla Mostra Inter nazionale dei Cartoonists* (Rapallo, Italy: 1976).

OTHER MEDIA

Holmes, Jennifer. "She Draws Comics, Paychecks—But Romance is the Bottom Line." *Detroit Free Press* (November 28, 1976).

Correspondence from Guisewite to Swords, August 10, 1977.

Concerning Marty Links: Correspondence from Links to Swords, May, 1977.

Rubin, Sylvia. "The Bobby-Sox Generation Bids Farewell." *San Francisco Chronicle* (December 24, 1979).

"Well, I've got to go to work, even if you don't."

From Male Chauvinist Pig Calendar, 1974, copyright R/M Hurley

"Congratulations! Some day you'll make a great Medical Secretary."

From Male Chauvinist Pig Calendar, 1974, copyright R/M Hurley

"A woman who..."

A woman who got her liberation together
and leaped from hearth to hustings, that's who.
Cartoonist Betty Swords, a Ms. herself,
explores the repercussions.

"But gee, hon, you're my wife. Why would you
want to be a county commissioner?"

"When she says she'll make policy and somebody else
can make coffee, she means it!"

"At least you won't have to cook for Rick while
I'm at the convention. He's a delegate, too."

"The woman's touch
was Elizabeth's idea!"

"A Women Who..." is reprinted from Changing Times The Kiplinger Magazine,
October 1972

"Why do they always go off in a corner and talk politics?"

"Confound it, man, women don't belong in public office! They're too emotional!"

MEET YOUR CANDIDATES

"I always said, give 'em the vote and they'll try to take over the country!"

"Sure, you'll vote for her just because she's a woman— and you know she's running against a brother Elk!"

"...so I said, 'Look, you've got the qualifications, right? So get in there and win!'"

"A Woman Who..." is reprinted from Changing Times The Kiplinger Magazine, October 1972

8

Return the Favor

LAURA KIGHTLINGER

I would never encourage or discourage anyone from telling jokes or committing suicide.

I'm a stand-up comic and during performances I've heard men say: "sit on my face," "dance," and "show us your tits;" in other words, I'm no different than any woman walking down the street.

I don't know why I'm a stand-up comic. I don't have any relatives in the "business." I didn't grow up with outrageously funny friends—I just liked playing with knives. In college I wrote comedy sketches for my roommate and soon after joined a comedy troupe on campus and that's where I started. My mother's single most encouraging comment after seeing my first MTV 'spot' some two years ago was, "well, you're a lot funnier than the guy who wears the glove on his head." She was, of course, referring to Howie Mandell; she was of course, dead-on in her assessment but I could feel the undercurrent of her disbelief in my talent...she really said more than she knew as far as quality vs. quantity and what sells, etc.

There's a general misconception about what the comedy "business" is like and how you "break in." I've been happy living under that misconception for a turn. My favorite example of "How It Isn't" is the time when my grandma had it all figured out for me, and she said, "Wouldn't more people know about you if you were on the Johnny Carson show?", to which I replied, "yes." And then she said, "you should just ask him (Johnny) if you could do your routine some night on his show." I said, "you know, you're right!" TV shows like "David Letterman" or "The Tonight Show" are usually a three or four (sometimes eight or nine) audition-process. A comic must be highly recommended before a talent coordinator or show producer will come out to see the comic perform in a club. The average overnight success takes six to ten years.

No one gets rich as a comic performing on a nightly basis in New York City. All city clubs pay the comics between $10 and $20 a set during the week; most comics can do between three to five sets nightly, sometimes more on weekends. The clubs pay between $40 and $70 a set on the weekends in Manhattan. A set consists of fifteen to thirty minutes of "jokes." In a comedy glut like ours, quality material is not a booking agent's/club owner's top priority. On the weekends, some club owners will shamelessly dole out a myriad of hackneyed acts for public consumption to keep the cheap laughs and drinks at their optimum.

So, how does this affect you and me? If you're an audience member, you are not going to hear a lot of thought-provoking intelligent material on a weekend night in the clubs in New York City. Interestingly enough, you will not see a lot of female comics on the bill either. Not to imply that all female comics are interesting and provocative and therefore are banished from weekend spots, but instead to say a man taking cheap shots at women, sex, etc. is more widely accepted, appealing, appreciated than a woman spouting the same.

So, what's the bright side to being a woman in a low or no brow, male dominated, monkey spankin' field like this one? THE TEN BUCKS. I hope I'm not sounding bitter; wait, here's the bright side...in case you're not a man with your blazer rolled up to your elbows you can still be a comic who cares about substance, you can tell yourself it's an art form, you can be true to your shoes and hope that your gender isn't a strike against you. (Here's where I lay down my shovel and let you look into the hole).

A female comic is still a rarity. I'd like to relate a specific but very common story about the comedy business, about wearing your sweaters outside of your pants and returning the favor. I worked in a comedy club for two years. I had the last spot or the "check spot," or as I like to call it the "what's-the-point" spot just about every night and the nights when I wasn't last, my friend Nancy was. We were, incidentally, the only female comics on the show. We never complained about sitting on the back of the bus; in fact, we kind of laughed about it and assumed it would change. Well, it did change; the last two spots were removed from the show—along with me and Nancy. We were told that the shows were going too long and they wanted them to end at midnight. So, when we gave our availability for shows for the following week we were told that we would have to re-audition. The person who gave us the news didn't necessarily take part in the decision to keep the women off the show; he was merely the mouthpiece for the sexism which, to me, is even more heinous. Let's call him B.G. B.G. was the faithful servant of the proprietor who made the initial decision to keep the club all-male; let's call him the Dwarf Man since that's his name. Days pass. B.G. leaves his position as booking agent and/or unequal opportunities lender and a woman takes his position, let's call her Katie. Katie has been in and around the comedy "scene" for a number of years and Nancy and I heaved a sigh of relief thinking we could sit with the men on the bus.

We were wrong. Even Katie told us we would have to re-audition. So, just as the women comics who acted like men in style and "substance" lost their identity, so did Katie. She took over B.G.'s position right down to the last misogynistic belief of his.

And there's another basic ugly level to this: Katie didn't want women on the show because it would draw the attention away from her. She wanted to run the show and be the shapeliest among men—literally—she tucks her sweaters inside her pants; wants to be the object of desire; and, at the same time earn the respect of any man in her position. No way. The women who tuck their sweaters into their pants are the enemy as much as the mouthpieces who carry out orders of sexism without question. It's the women who tuck in their sweaters, the ones who must be the shapeliest because of some beauty contest insecurities that will keep a man's world exactly that. When a woman has the opportunity to give an opportunity to another woman and doesn't because she may lose her own "uniqueness" in the process—this is the real disgrace; it is because there aren't enough women in demanding positions that make the situation unique to begin with. If more women could help each other become employed in certain fields, the ridiculous pressure of being "one-of-the-first-women-to" do this or that job would not exist...it would be commonplace for women to have any position that a man had and it would not be such a rare occurrence.

When I think of the entertainment industry, I imagine a black and white snapshot from the 1940's of men sitting around a table smoking cigars and playing poker at the edge of the table. Completely by accident a woman's arms and torso are in the frame placing pretzels down on the card table. The woman isn't playing the game, even though she might think she's snuck herself in; her head isn't even in the picture—she has a job like Katie. I don't think Katie understands that it will be harmful to her career to hold onto the novelty aspect of being the only woman on the job. At present, Katie may enjoy the faux respect that the male comics are giving her, but they won't remember her, they won't think anything of what she does for them because they are accustomed to that kind of treatment. A woman would appreciate it more if Katie had hired her and just may return the favor because another woman knows what it's like to be passed over. Not much has changed since the 1940's snapshot of poker players. If Katie were to hire other women she wouldn't be bringing pretzels to men playing poker, she would be playing the game with other women.

The point here is to return the favor. When you hire other women or help other women then your head is in the picture and you are participating in a game with your peers and/or contemporaries and they will return the favor just by re-establishing your good judgement.

I think that when you help other women, then it only reinforces the importance and necessity for more competent women in any and every field. What is the challenge in being a novelty—the challenge should be in becoming less novel, in bringing your gender into the fold. Return the favor—and be glad that you did.

9

The Parallel Lives of Kathy and Mo

BRENDA GROSS

Confession, cremation, Catholicism, vegetarianism, virginity, bulimia and bikini waxing are just a few of the topics touched upon in "The Kathy and Mo Show: Parallel Lives." Creators Kathy Najimy and Maureen Gaffney satirize all things female, male, feminist and sexist. They spoof dating rituals, family rituals, female rituals and religious rituals ("two Our Fathers and two Hail Mary's for eighteen years of sin?"). "The Kathy and Mo Show" highlights the complexities of contemporary life (where the ultimate female sin is not sex with a married man but with a married woman) and good-humoredly attacks the status quo with intelligence and sophistication.

Structured as a series of skits and monologues, the show opens in heaven with a dialogue between two debating angels. God has made the world but left the "minor details" to his subordinates. Having invented procreation, the angels cannot decide which sex should give birth. After arbitrarily selecting women for the honor, they worry that men will feel left out. To balance the wealth, they make childbirth *very* painful (a brainstorm: let the baby grow big inside the mother, then come out a tiny portal) and give men lots of ego. Reappearing to introduce Act II, the angels remark, "Boy, that ego thing really took off."

Gaffney and Najimy play not only angels but also Jewish senior citizens, Italian teenagers, alcoholic single mothers, hookers, celebrity wives, bulimic thirtysomething sisters and Catholic children "who are afraid of God." Like Lily Tomlin and Whoopi Goldberg, the two create characters who are laughable but not unlikable, funny but not unsympathetic.

We see the world from the eyes of a teenage girl from Brooklyn who defines love in the romantic all-or-nothing terms of her favorite movie (West Side Story). To Annette and her best friend Gina, the clichés of music and cinema hold worlds of meaning and bear repeating. "Love is a many splendored thing," says Annette. "And love is a rose but you better not pick it," Gina responds. When the two girls compare notes and discover that the "first time" was painful for them both, Annette has a revelation: "Love hurts, on all levels—I can't believe I thought of that!"

Much of the show's humor comes from characters like Annette and Gina whose self-image and dreams have been shaped almost completely by movies, advertising and other "higher authorities." These vulnerable, often literal-minded characters are especially prevalent in the skits where Catholicism comes under fire. Kathy and Mo play little girls, debating just what is and isn't in the Bible (does it really say that nuns have eyes in the back of their heads?). They scare each other silly with fantastic stories about "Pregnatory" but get bogged down in confusing Biblical details, like the logistics of God marrying all those nuns.

The sharpest skits are often those that spoof women's studies, women's theatre and other feminist subjects rarely satirized (let alone visible) on the Off-Broadway stage. We meet Syvie and Madeleine, two widowed Jewish senior citizens who get closed out of a community college Real Estate course (what else?) and take Women's Studies instead, figuring they have the "prerequisite." Enlightened by the course, Syvie and Maddie coach each other on being politically correct but also have that intimacy, dependence and rapport that only two single, senior women can have—constantly correcting and fussing over each other. The characters are funny but also authentic.

Now enrolled in Women's Performance Art, they come to a feminist vegetarian restaurant to see "Sister, Womyn, Sister." The lights go down and Kathy and Mo (both of whom are veterans of California feminist theatres) transform themselves into "Holly and Molly." After welcoming everyone to the restaurant, a "drug-free, meat-free, male-free, smoke-free environment," they perform a classic composite of bad women's theatre. Sporting white T-shirts with black female symbols, they sing an opening "tribute" to Holly Near and other feminist folksingers, then begin chanting the evening's title piece: "Sister, Womyn, Sister . . . Womyn: W—O—M—Y—N, womyn, woomyn, wooomyn, woooomyn. . . WOMB!! We are Birth! We are Afterbirth! Cut the Cord. Cut the Cord! No—DON'T!!"

"The Kathy and Mo Show" may be funny but its humor can often be pointed and political. Maureen Gaffney's pantomime of the feminine rituals of plucking, shaving, waxing and painting is both humorous and sad. The time and effort women waste in trying to live up to media hype is further developed in a monologue by Kathy Najimy about the unreachable bliss of being "Mrs. Kenny Rogers."

The show makes a limited but effective attempt to challenge the status quo on issues such as sexual preference, abortion and society's preoccupation with weight. "I find life less painful when I'm thin," a bulimic woman tells her sister, after fielding the "Put on a little weight, dear?" question from every relative at her grandmother's funeral. In another (completely serious) scene, Kathy Najimy plays a woman struggling with the complex emotional/political aftermath of abortion. She feels badly about feeling badly: acknowledging her loss seems like a nod to the anti-abortion forces.

Cremation, abortion, bulimia, homosexuality. Gaffney and Najimy wring the comedy from serious subjects without diminishing their weight. They get their political points across but with humor. Laughter lightens their agenda without lessening its significance.

"Talking with Kathy and Mo"
The Westside Arts Theatre, New York, New York, August 1989

BG: How did you get into performing?

MO: I never wanted to be a nurse or a doctor or anything else. I just wanted to be an actor. As far as comedy goes, I was always kind of funny. In high school, kids would say, "Oh, you're just like Carol Burnett." But there weren't a lot of Carol Burnett's around, so it didn't really seem like an option.

BG: Did your family encourage you?

KATHY: I can remember being in jr. high and sitting with my cousins and my aunt, talking about "what do you want to be?" So, one cousin says: "A stewardess." Another: "A cheerleader for a major football team." Another: "a registered nurse." And then they all turned to me and asked, "Well, what do YOU want to do, Kathleen?" And, with all the confidence in the world, I said, "I'm going to be an actress." And I could see them all sort of choke on their German chocolate pie and look at each other funny, like "Oh . . . RIGHT." And that little thing, boy, that gave me whatever family impetus I needed . . . .

BG: Before "Kathy and Mo," Maureen performed with "Hot Flashes," a feminist improvisation troupe and Kathy directed a women's cabaret. Now, you've moved toward a more main-stream audience. Has the change in audience affected what you do or say onstage?

MO: In "Hot Flashes," which played a lot of women's music festivals, we didn't have to worry about being loving, about being loving women together. Of course, in that group, it was always assumed that we were gay, just as in traditional society, it's assumed that everybody is straight.

KATHY: Although people still speculate about us—which probably sells tickets.

BG: Any other differences between then and now?

MO: Back then, we were also a little bit more sappy about the women's movement because we knew we'd be accepted from the minute we walked in the door. Plus, the overall feeling was more casual than now. In "Kathy and Mo," we still say what we need to say but it's "business." Even though it's comedy, it seems more serious.

BG: Why?

MO: Because we're women. We're two women who have our own Off-Broadway show that we wrote and I don't know how often that happens. Lily Tomlin and Whoopi Goldberg had their own Broadway shows but it's not the norm. Plus, we just came here. No Mike Nichols, no big producers. So it seems more serious because we feel like somewhat of an example to other women who want to do this or to people who think that women aren't smart enough to do it.

BG: How does your New York experience differ from the West Coast?

MO: There seemed to be a stronger women's community in San Diego. In New York, people do comedy shows and you know they're feminist but it's a different feeling than in California, where it's more of a family.

BG: You're both funny. Does that ever provoke a negative reaction from men or other women?

KATHY: It's nothing anyone ever said. Although some guy did tell us that when a funny woman walks in the room, men cross their legs, because it's sort of a very castrating experience for them. (Since then, of course, I usually enter the room with, "SO, DID YOU HEAR THE ONE ABOUT ...?") In fact, though, we get so many men who really embrace us in the show.

BG: So, for you, being funny is not a problem.

KATHY: No. It's actually the opposite. People expect us to be funny. It's when we're serious that people get put off because that breaks down the stereotype. It's easier for them to buy into a really narrow view of what funny women are like. They expect us all to be self-denigrating, self-hating "funny people" who have no sexuality, no personal life. Look at Joan Rivers, Phyllis Diller and Todie Fields. It wasn't that they didn't like themselves or thought they were ugly but they wanted to succeed as comedians.

MO: And all that had been in stand-up comedy was men's humor ... the assumed listeners were men and also women who had been satisfied with men's humor.

KATHY: So the only way that people would let them succeed was if they made fun of themselves. Making fun of themselves dehumanized them, made them into something acceptable. This plays into the old idea that women can't be onstage unless they're Lola Falana or dancing naked or, better yet, someone motherly, acceptable and soprano-ish. So, if you're going to be funny then you'd better "de-female" yourself and dehumanize yourself by letting us know that you can't be serious, you can't be real, you aren't feminist, you aren't sexual . . . .

BG: How much do you think that audience expectations have changed?

KATHY: They're still setting boundaries for Mo and me. Right now, there are things that I think are funny but I know that the audience will not accept.

BG: Such as?

KATHY: Sex in the nineties: relationships between men and women, women and women, men and men. I would love to deal with really sexual issues, sexual games people play at night and in the day. Also there are some really radical issues that I can't deal with here on 43rd Street and Ninth Avenue that I could, perhaps, if I were downtown. Gynecologist things, serious things, "rage" kind of things. Although, you've got to be careful of rage.

BG: Because it makes people hesitate to see or accept women's comedy?

KATHY: Yes. Reno does more in anger and that's one of the things that I really respect about her. Sandra Bernhard has thousands of people who love her and thousands of people who hate her and that's just the chance that you take.

BG: Rage doesn't sell tickets to women's comedy but you do have one skit in the show that is completely serious: the monologue about abortion. How did you decide to include it?

KATHY: That is the only forty second segment in the show that has no humor and our director Paul Benedict's initial reaction was that it should be cut. He was afraid, as anyone would be, that it was right on the line of being too "you know." He also wondered why we chose to be serious since we usually deal humorously with touchy things.

But the way that I look at it, I've been doing this show or a version of this show for a long time. Off-Broadway, I do it eight times a week. So I have to find certain things to propel me along and most of them are political, really political. And, if I start getting rid of them just because somebody might be offended or think it's too "on the line," then I'm not doing what I set out to do. And what I set out to do is what I'm passionate about. Not things that other people accept.

BG: You also frequently mention weight in the show.

KATHY: Actually, I'd like to do more. In fact, we once had a producer who asked us to cut the show's second reference to bulimia. We protested because bulimia is a big issue, it's a reality. I told him, six out of ten teenagers throw up. Putting it in again is like using "the" twice in a sentence.

BG: And you deal with women's endless attempts to impress men.

KATHY: The opinion of men is so filled with impact for women of all ages. It means so much. Even if the ugliest guy on the street says something about the way you look, you carry it with you. A person you wouldn't spit on, you wouldn't even talk to—if he doesn't like your hair, it affects you.

BG: The show focuses on women's self-images and our attempts to be what others want us to be. You capture it in "Mrs. Kenny Rogers."

KATHY: Women have such tremendous insecurity about who they are and who they are "supposed to be." It's something that men don't have to deal with, at least not in the same way. Men are supposed to be things but they are generally wonderful things. For example, they're supposed to be rich, powerful, successful. But all the things women are supposed to be take so much time and energy NOT to do. We're always thinking about, worrying about, questioning our being all the time. Restraining our natural impulses, watching people watch us. "I know I'm being strong now but I know these people think I shouldn't be strong so I know they're not liking me so I'm going to soften it up a little bit so they'll do what I say." Do you see how much energy that takes rather than to just say "I need you to do this." And all that goes on, even for the most centered, strong, well-balanced women.

BG: Even you?

KATHY: Even me. I take care of most of the business for the show and every time I go into a new city, inevitably there's a handful of people who don't like me. And no matter how much I think "okay, Kathy, this is their problem," just thinking about that, just going through that process takes up energy. I don't want any women to have to do that any more. To constantly question how they look, to constantly think about plastic surgery or ways they might fix their hair so that more men will be attracted to them. To think maybe they should talk softer or be more natural or wear more makeup. . . . I mean, when are we going to find our beings? I would like to be the real, insecure person that I am instead of always questioning who I'm supposed to be. You can get exhausted from trying to be liked, from trying to make people understand, from trying to fit yourself into a world where there's no space for you.

BG: Few men do comedy about any of these issues. Why?

KATHY: I think it's easier for women, particularly now, to deal with truths. And the truths for women are the obvious truths. Lily Tomlin does them, Whoopi Goldberg does them, Sandra Bernhard does them. There's a plethora of women doing them and I think it's because men aren't that interested in doing truths. They're interested in doing jokes which make people laugh and there's nothing wrong with that. Or, if men do truth, they just slide it around the edge of the jokes, but it never gets that personal.

        But women are getting to the point where we have all this rage, and it is personal, so we turn the rage into comedy. Whereas men, I hate to generalize but from what I've seen, concentrate more on what's going to make you laugh versus what they feel inside. They don't take it past step one to make it more personal.

BG: Would you say that men's comedy is autobiographical but in a different way than women's?

KATHY: It is and it's also very safe. Jay Leno is feminist and does some feminist stuff but it's very removed from him like, "aren't those guys in the Senate stupid?" Maybe it's men's conditioning. It's hard for them to get personal, to show that they care about things that they're talking about.

BG: So, men's humor is more audience-oriented?

KATHY: Much more audience-oriented, and less rage oriented. I guess "rage" is a 1979 word but . . .

BG: How about those men who scream? It's supposed to be rage.

KATHY: There's one man who screams who's very political: Bobcat Goldwaithe—really smart, feminist—and I think his screams come from rage. Sam Kinison, Andrew Dice Clay . . . they're screaming from their dicks. It's very misogynist, it's racist and it's homophobic.

BG: Have men and women's comedy changed?

KATHY: Women's comedy has changed but men's really hasn't had to. Women have had to say "Okay, I'm tired of talking about how ugly I am. Now I'm going to talk about something else."

BG: But we still talk a lot about men. For a funny woman, is that a hard subject to escape?

MO: It is. But, it's okay to talk about men because they're an issue. If you're a heterosexual woman, men are a big part of your life. And lesbians talk about their girlfriends. We all talk about "the other." So, talking about your boyfriend is not so bad but if that's all you talk about (or if you can only joke about how you look, how fat you are, etc.) then I can't particularly get into it. For example, I've seen Elayne Boosler before, doing boyfriend jokes. But last night I saw her and she was different. She put forth her ideas on abortion and George Bush. I found that exciting.

BG: Do you think that audiences are more accepting of feminist humor from a male comedian? Can he say things that you can't and make them palatable?

KATHY: To a point. But I also think that the way he says it and the way I say it are very different.

BG: What do you see as your next step?

KATHY: One of the reasons that I did "The Kathy and Mo Show" was so that I could have control over it. I knew what I would be saying, doing, what the material would be like, what the posters would look like, what the press release would say, what photographs would be used, all that. That's why I built this little castle. Now we're expanding—which I want to do and will do—but it's frightening because there are people with lots of money who expect you to give up control. And I'm going to have to get back into that "fighting world" again, the real world of having to explain why I don't want to portray a character like that, or why this one word or one sentence is offensive to me.

BG: Can you see doing other people's material?

MO: I'd love to—although I'm not going to do "Bimbos on Parade" or anything incredibly offensive to me. For example, the first movie that I auditioned for, they wanted me to be a slutty bar girl. I thought I could put on a tight dress but that's just not me. So I read the script again and found a smaller part with less lines but I felt better doing it. So I called and said, I cannot read for the slutty girl but I can read for the mother of two. And, I got the role. So, now, my first movie will not be of me in a tight dress, drinking, being slutty. Instead, I'll be a wife of a mobster who goes around killing people.

BG: You'll be a real role model. Are you getting called for mainly funny roles?

MO: They haven't been funny yet, which I don't mind at all. Because "funny" is the hardest thing to do. You instantly know if you're funny or not, because people laugh. You don't know if you're "dramatically correct" or not because people don't go "ah!" or anything. So, I don't mind doing dramatic stuff.

ME: What do you think is funny?

MO: Kathy Najimy—very funny. I don't know, a lot of things are funny. It's hard to say. I think truth is funny—the funny stuff comes from what really happens.

10

The Politics of Humor: An Interview with Margaret Drabble

IAN WOJCIK-ANDREWS

*This convention [MLA] seems to me to be an excellent metaphor for our social life.
I mean the first person I saw here was someone [I knew] from Cork, Dublin. It's
extraordinary.*

(Drabble, 1990)

Ironically, I hadn't intended to talk about women and comedy when I went
to New Orleans MLA. I did hope that I would see and talk with Margaret
Drabble, whose work I've read and admired since 1978 when, as an Essex
University undergraduate, I took "Anglo-American Fiction Since 1945"
with Geoffrey Thurley who had attended Cambridge with Drabble in the
late 1950s and early 1960s. During Thurley's seminar, Drabble's post-
modernist narrative techniques in *The Waterfall* (1969) seemed quite at
home alongside the works of Burroughs, Pynchon, Mailer, Murdoch,
Lessing, and others. Reading Drabble then, I would have acquainted
myself further with *The Waterfall's* subtle humor, as well as its elements
of narrative technique, outlined in Vol. 1. of *Last Laughs* by Nancy Wal-

ker in a thoughtful essay entitled "Ironic Autobiography: from *The Waterfall* to *The Handmaid's Tale*," had I known that in 1990 I would be talking about the politics of women's humor to Drabble herself.

I began by asking Drabble about her recent though continuing involvement in British left-wing politics ("A Case for Equality," the text of a speech given to the Progressive League of Fabians on 22 April 1988). But, given the laughter Drabble evoked from her audience at the panels she attended during MLA, it seemed appropriate to talk about comedy. Thus, we soon were discussing Drabble's *The Ice Age* as comedy, the writers of comedy she admires (Austen, Weldon, Waugh), and her own social experiences of humor-liminal moments when unlikely people and unlikely subjects unexpectedly come together.

W/A: Everybody was greatly amused yesterday at your reading of *The Radiant Way*.

D: I think it's because when you are reading you can point out comedy as something that is funnier than when it is being read. Also, my interpretation of that is that here everybody is at the MLA, and everybody has been working very hard and hustling around, and here is somebody smiling and reading her own work and she doesn't mind if you laugh; it's a sort of permit to laugh. I like to give readings of my work. I know what bits work and what bits don't work and that's fine. Unfortunately, I hadn't read the papers on my work that were presented during my panel. I had no idea what was coming so I couldn't really produce anything terribly coherent as a response. Ultimately, I thought this is a bit foolhardy and, as I probably said to you already, I find it difficult to read about my own work. I find it worrying. In the end I thought the papers were very interesting. It's a funny experience coming to one's work like that, having it analyzed whilst one sits there.

W/A: All of the papers were somehow related to humor. One speaker was very much concerned with word play in your fiction.

D: Well, in fact, that paper was rather difficult to take in at first, I thought, because it was very dense and if you hadn't read the books, which a lot of people probably hadn't, it wouldn't have made much sense. But there were some interesting verbal points. There is a lot of that play on words. Some of them weren't serious.

I think that some of them were very good points. It was a strange mixture. There were things I absolutely recognized and there were things that I thought were absolutely far-fetched. It would be very difficult to say so in the context but I think also it would have been difficult for them in that context to produce a violent attack on my work. They would have been more aggressive than they were but, in fact, none of them were very aggressive so it was quite acceptable to me.

W/A: An undergraduate in my class described *The Ice Age* as a "complete comedy," a "humorous representation of overwhelming despair." Most critics would consider *The Ice Age* your least humorous, most conventionally political novel.

D: Yes. I think quite a lot of it is funny. It's a very heavily ironic novel, I think. For instance, let us take the question of the dead dogs in the novel. Dogs keep dying. Now one dead dog is quite sad. Two dead dogs could be even sadder. But three dead dogs is funny and four dead dogs is ridiculous and so when you start piling disaster upon disaster there is an element of ironic comedy in the structuring of the book itself: a black comedy in the ironic mode. "Overwhelming despair" is slightly overstating it. At least, Anthony at the end, he's all right. He survives.

W/A: Yes, but he survives alone.

D: Yes, but he'll get over it. And it's probably quite good for him because he's in such a muddle to begin. It could be a criticism of the novel that I wasn't able to give it a more tragic completion, like killing off my characters. I don't like that. I like to let them live another day.

W/A: The humor is in the continuity, the interconnectedness.

D: Yes, I think so. It's to do with survival really, I suppose. Well, things can go on being quite funny while you are still alive, but cease to be funny when you die. So I guess the whole idea of survival is ironic, making the best of things, looking on the bright side of things. There is something very comic about Anthony looking on the bright side of things. I think he makes some comment about how a prison diet is good for him. That's very British humor. That is actually also true in that I know I have a friend who survived the concentration camps whose health is excellent, for as she said you have these spartan diets as a young girl. She certainly didn't indulge in anything: a very heavily regulated diet. In fact in Britain, it is said that the war generation, because we had regulation, ration books and so on, had better health than the affluent generation, such as right now. There is an ironic slant on almost everything except death.

W/A: Humor is another way of dealing with tragedy, such as the Lockerbie disaster and the King's Cross Underground fire.

D: That's right. That's right. One of the things I wanted to point out in *The Radiant Way* was that all the three women come not from exactly middle class backgrounds, peculiar backgrounds, and yet they have ended up in middle class positions. And I think that there are people who are much less regular than they look in Britain. If you look behind them, the facade, everybody is pretending to be normal.

W/A: Behind the facade of normality is the chaos, the problems of living.

D: Chaos, problems, peculiarities, eccentricities. Chaos, problems, peculiarities, eccentricities. I was talking to the editor of the local paper about the King's Cross Fire disaster. He said it is unbelievable the stories of those people who got killed. You begin to think that there are no normal ordinary people, ordinary human beings left in the world. They are so peculiar, their stories, and I suppose I find that fascinating that people are more peculiar than they seem.

W/A: Is that Fay Weldon's point: humor is a way of confronting tragedy?

D: Absolutely. Absolutely. That's exactly what she does. She exaggerates things to such a degree that it becomes ridiculous. It is a way of coping. One cannot go on feeling deeply grieved about everything in the world. Comedy is one response. Sentimentality is another, the response of the press. The day after the [Ferry] disaster we all feel sentimental but the day after you have to bounce back.

W/A: In an essay in Vol. 1 of *Last Laughs* (Ed. R. Barreca), Fay raises the point whether it is right to laugh at tragedy but, ultimately, comes to the conclusion that, as you have just said, what else are you going to do.

D: Oddly enough, I've used that in my next novel, that Ferry disaster. Well, all I've done is get a couple who meet on a Ferry four days after the disaster and there are jokes about this an unfortunate place to meet and is absolutely anti-romantic; ferry crossings used to be romantic—

W/A: —"Ferry across the Mersey"—

D: "that's right. But, I'm thinking now about women's humor. I addressed last year a Cosmopolitan dinner. It was a dinner with three women writers. It's not my kind of thing but they are rather sparkling. Anyway there were three of us all speaking. And I said to the audience something—my husband was there—and I said something about how I was dressing for this event. I didn't know what to dress for but I look around and I see that you are a mixed bunch, some dressed in up to the minute things, some of you dressed in any and everything. Well, what I did on the way over was to tear out my shoulder pads and throw them away. And everybody laughed. I *knew* they would laugh. I don't know why, though. But Michael said to me afterward, why did they laugh about that thing with your shoulder pads? I said to him that I don't know but I just knew they would. And I suppose it's because shoulder pads are a symbol of formal dressing or power dressing or whatever it is called. I thought that it was ridiculous. They were sliding all over the place and I decided that I would rather be comfortable. But I suppose that is a sort of symbolic sending up of symbols of power which is a very British thing. I mean look at the Royal Family. I mean they are grotesque, really. Well, it is a sort of soap opera, the Royal family, the greatest soap opera in the world. But I think it's arguable that it's a very dangerous one; the whole idea of hierarchy is a very bad one. Which is that Theodore Dreiser novel in which the hero—it ends badly I know as they all do—in which the hero starts off in a hotel as an errand boy and the whole world is open to him, and there is nothing wrong with him being this errand boy because he knows he is going to make good.

In England, people are born into a bracket. They accept it. They know that there is no way out. I find that very depressing. And from what I can see, it hasn't changed. There is still that defeatism at the bottom of society that there was twenty or thirty years ago.

W/A: The political nature of women's humor is its sending up of the shoulder pads as—

D: —symbols of power. Since then I realize that it is called "power dressing" and that women with shoulder pads are meant to be macho. I hadn't realized that at the time, but just felt instinctively that these shoulder pads weren't me, even though you could hardly buy anything without them in. Women's humor subverts social norms, power structures, could be, could be. But it just arrived to me as I stood there and looked at this funnily dressed audience. There were some wonderfully smart women with bubble skirts and sequins and some who had just come out in any old thing, you know.

W/A: Women writers of comedy you admire?

D: Jane Austen, of course. George Eliot is less funny.

W/A: Contemporary writers?

D: Fay Weldon is extremely funny. Mary McCarthy is terribly funny. Alison Lurie is very funny. Yes, I remember a male friend of ours saying that women had no sense of humor and Alison Lurie saying rather indignantly that her books were quite entertaining and I thoroughly endorse that.

W/A: Humor is gender specific? There's a difference in the way male writers use humor?

D: I'm sure there is. I would have to think much more seriously and at length to give you a reason why. I think that some of my use of humor has been influenced by some writers such as Evelyn Waugh, who has influenced me, and Fay Weldon.

W/A: Which Waugh novels are you thinking of? *Vile Bodies?*

D: Yes. And *A Handful of Dust*. In fact, *A Handful of Dust* is a wonderfully funny book which ends very very grimly. That particular combination of tragedy and comedy I find very appealing.

W/A: *The Ice Age* is both amusing and tragic.

D: Yes. I think that is absolutely right. I think that the tone is quite difficult to catch for young people not brought up on it. It requires a certain familiarity, a tradition of irony. I sometimes think that it is a weakness in my work and indeed in the work of British novelists generally that they can't write the Blockbuster, that great big stick-your-neck-out thing, and it's probably something to do with British education, our position in the world, the self denigratory which in fact is self-laudatory. Superiority concealed as politeness.

W/A: Is intertexuality gender-specific and do women writers use intertextual references subversively through humor? How do you use intertextual references?

D: I use them a great deal. My head is full of quotations which is inevitable if you study literature, as most of us do. And I use them mostly expecting them to be recognized but occasionally not minding if they are or not. Sometimes they are very obscure which I expect only a handful of people will spot. Only very occasionally are they in the nature of a private game. Usually, I expect people to pick them up. They are just a form of shorthand really. I don't think they are gender specific at all. Men and women use a fairly large frame of reference.

W/A: My students felt that the intertextual framework of say "The Waste Land" was used inhibitingly unlike the references used by such writers as Bronte, Woolf, Weldon, and yourself, particularly *The Ice Age*. Women writers tried to include rather than exclude the reader.

D: Yes. "The Waste Land." Eliot, and Pound, are very interesting examples of people using quotation, I think, in order to put up barriers occasionally and part of the fun of decoding "The Waste

Land" is going through the references. That's why you have all those footnotes. I suppose I would like to have my books able to read on two levels. Obviously it's more interesting if you know the references. But one doesn't want to prohibit people from reading who don't know the references. The references need to be self-explanatory or dispensable with. I would prefer people to feel included but at the same time one lays oneself open then to the charge of flattering the reader which is to allow the reader to guess along with you whereas in fact you really know a lot more than they do. I remember hearing the charge that Henry James flatters the reader because the reader is always a step ahead of the author who intends you to be a step ahead. I think that's a very interesting charge. I'm just reading Austen's *Emma* at the moment, and here, of course, the question arises how much are you meant to know of what the narrator knows. I personally would like to include the reader in most of the narrator's knowledge.

W/A: A community of knowledge and a community of place. The humor is the sense of interconnectedness. Your whole corpus is community orientated.

D: Yes, that's true and it is something I've got more and more interested in as I've gone on. Other writers have done this and I now see the attraction in the works of Trollope or Anthony Pole of writing not exactly sequels as such but of an interlinked social world where you naturally expect people to come in from other novels, which is not so much a question of writing a structured sequence but of just acknowledging that they have a common ground. We inherit the Romantic tradition of individualism and it's a dangerous one because it can isolate. A lot of the social rituals we go through now seem to be empty and meaningless. Nevertheless, we go through them. And I suppose that I am interested in the life left in the old rituals and the new rituals like a party that we forge for ourselves. And I find, I do think that we should value our communal life and enjoy it, and that we should enjoy our common humanity. But by that I don't mean that we ought to live in communes, or spend all our time in large groups. I mean the false barriers we have. Particularly in Britain, I don't think it is the same in the States, this false segmentation of the people you do speak to and the people you do not speak to, this segmentation of society in Britain. I mean I know I never notice this because I'm a woman but I never notice whether people are wearing the old school tie or the old club tie. There are a lot of influences. It's totally wasted on me because I don't know what any of those messages mean. There's a lot of that going on and I suppose that's people trying to belong to a lot of little communities. But it is also excluding other people so we come back to inclusion and exclusion. What I really enjoy in life are the unexpected moments when you make contact with someone from another social world and you realize that you do have some universal common language created through humor.

—11—

Wendy Cope's Struggle with Strugnell in *Making Cocoa for Kingsley Amis*

NICOLA THOMPSON

Making Cocoa For Kingsley Amis by English poet Wendy Cope made the bestseller list in England in 1986. Although it is perhaps a slight exaggeration to claim, as did one reviewer, that "no one in the civilized world could not have heard her name by the time the book was published" (Toomey 31), the commercial success of Cope's book suggests that its readers include a wide spectrum of the general public. In America Cope is less well known, but her parody of T. S. Eliot's *The Waste Land*—"Wasteland Limericks"—has by now become secondary reading in many modern poetry courses.

Making Cocoa is Cope's first book. Many of the poems appeared previously in publications ranging from *The Observer* to *Vogue,* and part of the book's charm lies in its stubborn refusal to play for a single audience or to conform to tidy generic categories. Cope's collection consists of personal love poems and poetic parodies of the works of male predecessors such as T.S Eliot, Ted Hughes, Seamus Heaney, Philip Lar-

111

kin, and, by implication, Kingsley Amis. In her love lyrics Cope celebrates men; in her parodies she mocks them. Between these two poetic modes and conflicting visions lies an ambivalence about stereotypical conceptions of femininity, particularly in relation to artistic creation. An exploration of these tensions seems to me crucial to reading *Making Cocoa,* and I find it surprising that her reviewers ignore this dynamic, although David Sexton in his *Sunday Times* review does grant Cope's feminism a perfunctory nod by noting that "her mockery is edged by sexual difference. Only men get the treatment" (43).

Cope's title has been seriously misconstrued by one of the book's reviewers, Bernard O'Donoghue from *The Times Literary Supplement,* who, reading the book as generally anti-modernist, interprets the title as a placating gesture, "offering something soothing to the conservative formalist" (616b). It seems to me, however, that Cope is doing something fundamentally unsoothing in debunking Amis and Larkin and the "masculine" poetics of the Movement. Cope's cocoa is laced. *Making Cocoa For Kingsley Amis* enacts a parodic deconstruction of essentialist stereotypes of masculinity and femininity as they surface in the poetics and poetry of the Movement.

The title of Cope's collection of poems along with the parodies, particularly of Larkin, highlight the *parodic* connection between Cope and the Movement—the group of poets whose anti-modernist, anti-romantic agenda dominated mid-century English poetry. The obvious similarity is that Cope, like the Movement poets, writes poetry accessible to the general reader. Part of the Movement's unofficial manifesto declaimed against the erudite references and classical allusions of the High Modernists. Larkin and Company wanted to jettison Yeats's esoteric symbolism—his "myth kitty." They wanted to deflate the cosmic agonies of Eliot (as Cope puts it in "Waste Land Limericks": "Wei la la. After this it gets deep"). And the Movement sought to avoid the rhetorical and emotional extremes of Dylan Thomas and the neo-romantics.

Despite this apparent aesthetic and ideological congruence between Cope and the Movement, there is an even more telling difference: Amis and Larkin, along with other "members," sometimes write from an exaggerated and overtly "masculine" perspective, while Wendy Cope, through her parodies of male poets and in the love poems written in her own voice, humorously mocks and directly challenges their sexist ideology.

The Movement's membership was of course exclusively made up of men, with the single exception of Elizabeth Jennings, and the degree to which she "belonged" is disputed. Robert Conquest characterizes it thus:

"'somebody once described her association with us as comparable to that of a schoolmistress in a non-corridor train, with a bunch of drunk marines—a slight slander to both sides'" (Morrison 22). This "bunch of drunk marines" often wrote "macho" literature. In their poems emotion is usually kept at arm's length; the "formal distancing of emotion" in Larkin's poetry is explicitly referred to in *Required Writing* (67), and John Press describes the Movement's anti-romanticism as a "fear of unregulated, unscrutinized emotion" (253). The absence of personal love poems from Larkin's work is also noteworthy. Amis writes disparagingly in a poem called "Bookshop Idyll" of women poets' compulsion to write always and only of love. And when they deal with sex, "Movement texts often see things from the point of view of a male seducer," according to Morrison, who cites several examples from Amis, Davie, Gunn and Larkin of what he sees as a "sexist and even misogynistic...exploitative attitude" to women (182).

In "A Bookshop Idyll" Kingsley Amis equates women's poetry with emotional self-disclosure:

> Man's love is of man's life a thing apart;
> Girls aren't like that.
>
> We men have got love well weighted up; our stuff
> Can get by without it.
> Women don't seem to think that's good enough—
> They write about it.
>
> And the awful way their poems lay them open
> Just doesn't strike them....(56-57)

For Cope, however, art, life and love are inextricable, and this is, to repeat, perhaps the most substantial difference—a difference both ideological and aesthetic—between her and the Movement poets. "I'll work," Cope explains in her "Manifesto,"

> . . . for there's new purpose in my art
> I'll muster all my talent, all my wit
> And write the poems that will win your heart. (42)

Art is prosodically linked to "heart," and the formal object is intentionally "contaminated" with the author's desire. As for the "awful way their poems lay them open," Cope responds that openness is necessary for a heart-driven poetics.

And if some bloodless literary fart
Says that it's all too personal, I'll spit
And write the poems that will win your heart. (42)

But while Cope rebels against a cultural and literary patriarchy that
sunders love, life and language, she is inescapably a product of that which
she is protesting against. Her lyrics and love poems are dominated by the
presence of men: some are addressed to a lover ("I thought you'd be a
pushover / I hoped I wouldn't hurt you / I warned you this was just a fling
/ And one day I'd desert you"). Others muse about men in general ("There
are so many kinds of awful men"), about her relationship with her father,
about the relation between love and poetry ("My love is true, but all my
verse is rotten"), or about her aesthetic debts to male writers. "Strugnell
In Liverpool" (ironically written through a male persona who is identified
with Philip Larkin, as will be demonstrated below) is prefaced by an
acknowledgement to "Allen Ginsberg, Charlie Parker, T.S Eliot, Paul
McCartney, Marcel Proust...and all the other great men who have
influenced my writing" (52). This last example demonstrates that her satire
can be subtle. Superficially this appears to be an expression of suitably
deferential gratitude. However, when we consider that the persona of this
poem is modelled on Philip Larkin, who is thoroughly if playfully deflated
in other poems, and when we recall that Larkin's regard for the "great"
writers listed is highly questionable (he would have loathed Ginsberg's
neo-romantic emotional, confessional, and rhetorical excesses), it becomes
clear that Cope is laughing as she bows before Larkin and the "great men"
listed, all members of the patriarchal artistic establishment.

As the personal, non-parodic lyrics cited above indicate, the purpose of
Making Cocoa is not just to mock male writers. In "My Lover" (36-38)
Wendy Cope uses Christopher Smart's "To My Cat Geoffrey" as a basis
from which to "consider" her lover: "For at the age of 49 he can make the
noise of five / different kinds of lorry changing gear on a hill. / For he
sometimes does this on the stairs at his place of work." The speaker
contemplates her lover's "old-fashioned masculinity," his love of football,
his elusiveness, his refusal to "miss his evening class or his choir /
practice for a woman." Essentially "he is the kind of man who has been driving
women / around the bend for generations," the kind of man who "grew up
before the permissive society" and who, therefore, will not ask his lover
what she would "like him to do." This type of man is "not too concerned
with his appearance," "lets the barber cut his hair too short," and is reluctant to involve himself with the details of a woman's appearance: "For
when I ask if this necklace is all right he replies / 'Yes, if no means

looking at three others.'" Cope's poem is an affectionate affirmation of her conventional lover, who, despite his conventionality, is willing to sit "through many lunches, discussing life and love, and never mentioning football," and who is not only happy to accept her inability to cook, but who is prepared to cook himself, and even to indulge her supremely silly craving for "smooth cocoa with bubbles on the top."

In some ways the speaker obviously associates herself with stereotypical femininity. Before she met this lover she knew nothing about football and wanted to know less; she identifies with those women who have been driven "round the bend" by men like him; she dislikes his tendency to drive fast on the motorway; she asks his opinion about her jewelry. And yet she also drinks and smokes as much as he does, she avoids cooking, and most importantly, she is detached enough to find his traditional masculinity amusing. It is her amusement as much as her affection that inspires her poetry. This love poetry is not primarily infused with sentimental ("feminine" according to "A Bookshop Idyll") ardor, but with quiet laughter.

On first reading, Cope's poem "Message" seems to reflect an acceptance of conventional sexual codes. The female speaker waits for a lover to phone her, enacting the passive feminine role, apparently finding it unthinkable that she should be audacious enough to call him again. "Message" also falls within the *carpe diem* poetic convention:

> Well, wouldn't it be nice to consummate
> Our friendship while we've still got teeth and hair?
> Just bear in mind that you are forty-eight
> And dial my number. There's no time to spare. (40)

A closer reading reveals that Cope turns sexual and poetic convention upside down in this poem. While the female speaker is publicly passive and demure, she is revealed as privately aggressive. Furthermore, Cope's conversational idiom renders the high diction classically deployed by male poet-seducers "nice," "effeminate," and hopelessly archaic.

And, to reverse the hierarchy completely, Cope confesses that if her cold lover doesn't speed things up, she will make a typically "masculine" move:

> Another kamikaze love affair?
> No chance. This time I'll have to learn to wait
> But one more day is more than I can bear—
> Love is already turning into hate.

Of course, my friends say I exaggerate
And dramatize a lot. That may be fair
But it is no fun being in this state
And very soon I'll start to look elsewhere. (40)

The genius of these simple lyrics lies in the fact that Cope uses
Movement methodology to subvert Movement ideology. The harsh honesty
of "Love is already turning into hate," and "soon I'll start to look
elsewhere," the poet's acceptance of the unromantic facts of the situation,
her refusal to indulge in disappointment, the slightly self-mocking but
even-tempered tone, her colloquial diction—all these stances and devices
come right off the top of Larkin's prescription pad. But this is a woman
speaking. The traditional object of the *carpe diem* "conversation" talks
back—or talks first—and she speaks in the blunt, matter-of-fact, unemo-
tional idiom of Movement poets. Cope's unrequited love is *less* melodramatic than Amis's "weighted up" love, and she manages to embrace the
reality without pitying the losses or lapsing into passivity. And yet Cope
also remains much more open to the experience, remains emotionally
accessible—if not vulnerable ("one more day is more than I can bear"),
remains true to a poetics designed to include the personal and emotional.

Such "emotional accessibility" may seem like thick character armor to
readers of the "confessional" poets of the United States. Cope is of course
writing from within (and from without) an entirely different tradition that
is indirectly opposed to the aesthetics of post-war U. S. poetry. To be able
to adopt a feminist stance, to maintain a poetic voice that is clearly that of
a woman, to write about intimate emotional issues from her own life, and
to do so using a "masculine" poetics, the "hard, dry verse" of T. E.
Hulme which the Movement retains, a poetics inimical to such "feminist"
strategies and themes, is no small literary or ideological feat. But as
Harold Bloom's work on poetic influence argues, one does not escape
unscathed from battles with literary predecessors. Cope's own explanation
of how she came to write parody suggests that the impulse originally
stemmed from infuriated resentment at the literary establishment's refusal
to publish her serious personal poems. In essence, poetry written in her
own voice was not considered artistically or commercially viable, and so
in order to get published Cope felt she had to construct an "exoskeleton":

When I began writing, my poems were very serious and intense....Some of them
were about love. No one wanted to publish them....So I thought....sod it, if that's
what we're supposed to do, I'll do it. I started writing parodies out of a sort of
bloody mindedness. (Spankie 36)

Alicia Ostriker in *Stealing The Language—The Emergence of Women's Poetry In America* has an interesting theory about women poets' use of parody. Ostriker states first that a division of self is part of being "a creative woman in a gender-polarized society" (60). She suggests that since the 1960's, women's poetry has often been characterized by a cold, hard tone, an "exoskeleton" which serves as a barrier between poet and reader, and which protects the woman poet from charges of sentimentality or excessive emotion (88). These remarks, as well as Ostriker's subsequent comments on parody, apply clearly to the love lyrics and the parodies in *Making Cocoa For Kingsley Amis*:

> Parody and mockery seem the flesh and blood of the exoskeletal style....The artist's stance in many of these poems seems to identify aggressive-defensiveness with the art of writing.... To approach the strategy of this style from another angle, we need look no further than Laing's observation that an ontologically uneasy person may adopt to the point of caricature, the personality of his oppressor.... An intelligent woman poet may have every reason in the world to construct, as her fortress, a perversely exaggerated version of an acceptable style. (88)

Thus the occasionally overt hostility in some of the love lyrics to the patriarchal literary establishment or to men in general ("Rondeau Redoublé" 39) is echoed in a more covert way, disguised through humor, in the parodies. By adopting a Movement "voice" Cope adopts an alien style, "the personality of her oppressor."

So Cope's "very serious," "intense" poems, some of which "were about love" were, if not given up entirely, mixed aggressively with the sort of poems "we're supposed to do." Cope turned to Ostriker's "fortress, a perversely exaggerated version of an acceptable style," parodying male poets in whose works women were at best marginalized, where such "feminine" experiences like emotion and love were relegated to a firmly peripheral status. Cope's feminism is apparent both in the deflation of acceptable male poetic styles and voices and in her own stubborn self-exposure in the personal and love poems—which she obviously refused to abandon entirely, even if she did mix love with humor as a defensive-aggressive act. Perhaps the humor in the personal poems also reveals what Ostriker would call her "ontological unease," her fear that such poems would be rejected by her readers and by the establishment as inappropriate, overly sentimental or emotional.

Naturally, the parodies in *Making Cocoa* rather than the "straight" poems have received the most critical attention and applause, apparently because even the male literary establishment enjoys hearing Eliot's imperiously prophetic voice mocked ("A Nursery Rhyme" 19), or Hughes's bloody universe ridiculed ("God and the Jolly Bored Bog-Mouse" 55). (Though the irritation of one particular reviewer at Cope's "hubris" in joking about Larkin is perhaps in reaction to the barbed nature of Cope's humor: "In 'Mr Strugnell,' he [the persona] is identified as the next occupant of Larkin's Mr Bleaney's room: that is, Larkin. It seems to me that a heavy price is paid for the hubris, risked for a small joke...the summoning of Larkin's ghost at all is dangerous here" [O'Donoghue 616b].) I have chosen two parodies to look at in greater depth: "Mr. Strugnell" and "Strugnell in Liverpool." The "Strugnell" poems are explicitly feminist, and one of them, "Strugnell in Liverpool," attacks one of Larkin's most misogynistic poems, "The Large Cool Store."

"Mr. Strugnell" is a parody of Larkin's "Mr. Bleaney," and its "aggressive-defensiveness" is evident in Cope's treatment. Cope's poem, like Larkin's, is written in four line stanzas with every other line rhyming. Note the similarities in the first stanzas:

> 'This was Mr. Bleaney's room. He stayed
> The whole time he was at the Bodies, till
> They moved him.' Flowered curtains, thin and frayed
> Fall to within five inches of the sill.
> (*The Whitsun Weddings* 10)

> 'This was Mr. Strugnell's room,' she'll say
> And look down at the lumpy, single bed.
> 'He stayed here up until he went away,
> And kept his bicycle out in that shed.' (45)

The changes are ironic: while the speaker in Larkin's poem finds the landlady noisy, ("Stuffing my ears with cotton-wool to drown / the jabbering set he egged her on to buy"), Mrs. M. in Cope's revision finds Strugnell's jazz music equally annoying:

> 'And up he'd go and listen to that jazz.
> I don't mind telling you it was a bore.
> Few things in this house have been tiresome as
> The sound of his foot tapping on the floor.'

Later in the same poem Cope refers mockingly to Larkin's poem "Annus Mirabilis." This is from the original poem:

> Sexual intercourse began
> In nineteen sixty-three
> (Which was rather late for me)—
> Between the end of the Chatterley ban
> And the Beatles' first LP. (*High Windows* 34)

And this is Cope's (or Mrs. M's) version:

> "He didn't seem the sort for being free
> With girls or going out and having fun.
> He had a funny turn in sixty-three
> And ran round shouting 'Yippee! It's begun!'"

> 'I don't know what he meant but after that
> He had a different look, much more relaxed.
> Some nights he'd come in late, too tired to chat,
> As if he had been somewhat overtaxed. (Cope 45)

Cope describes Strugnell as solitary, explaining that he liked to read popular male writers like Dick Francis or John Betjeman, but not Mrs. M's favourite popular female writers, Pam Ayres or Patience Strong. Larkin's well known fondness for jazz, Dick Francis and John Betjeman makes it clear that Cope is poking fun at Larkin through the persona of Strugnell.

> But not Pam Ayres or even Patience Strong
> He'd change the subject if I mentioned them
> Or say 'It's time for me to run along
> Your taste's too highbrow for me, Mrs. M.' (45)

Just in case we were not already sure about Strugnell's identity, Cope spells it out in the final stanza, reminding us that Philip Larkin spent his last years working as a librarian in the English town of Hull:

> And now he's gone. He said he found Tulse Hill
> Too stimulating—wanted somewhere dull
> At last he's found a place that fits the bill,
> Enjoying perfect boredom up in Hull. (46)

In Cope's revision, the focus moves away from Mr. Bleaney or Strugnell to the landlady Mrs. M, and instead of seeing Mrs. M through the derogatory lense of the speaker of Larkin's poem, where she is just referred to as "her," the perspective changes so that Bleaney's or

Strugnell's intellectual airs, elitist, and sexist attitudes are mocked from the landlady's perspective.

"Strugnell In Liverpool" is a parody of Larkin's "The Large Cool Store" in which Larkin characterizes men and women through the clothes displayed in a department store. The shirts and trousers conjure up the male weekday world of those who leave in the morning for "factory, yard and site," while the artificial fabrics and colors of the women's "Modes For Night" leads Larkin to theorize about the relations between men and women:

> sapphire, moss-green, rose
> Bri-Nylon Baby-Dolls and Shorties
> Flounce in clusters. To suppose
> They share that world, to think their sort is
> Matched by something in it, shows
>
> How separate and unearthly love is,
> Or women are, or what they do,
> Or in our young unreal wishes
> Seem to be: synthetic, new,
> And natureless in ecstasies.
>   (*The Whitsun Weddings* 21)

The perspective of this poem is obviously masculine—the women are "they" as opposed to "us," and the gap between men and women is portrayed as unbridgeable. Cope's singularly unappealing "love" poem is likewise written from a male perspective and deals with a man thinking of a woman in terms of her nylon clothes and her shampoo:

> eating my cornflakes
> plastic flowers on
> the windowsill green
> formica table lovesong
> on the radio bacteria
> in the drainpipe
> thinking of you
>
> ...thinking
> of you
> your pink
> nylon panties
> and your blue
> nylon bra
> Body Mist
> hairsmell of Silvikrin. (53)

Here Cope is clearly adopting the "personality of her oppressor" through the persona of Strugnell. Both poems have a male speaker who thinks about women in terms of synthetics, but behind the male persona of "Strugnell In Liverpool" Cope problematizes Larkin's stereotypical vision that connects women "naturally" to artifice. Her style might indeed be characterized as "perversely exaggerated." As Ostriker puts it in *Stealing The Language,* "the exaggerated style invites us to understand that it means both what it seems and the opposite" (89). Yes, Cope seems to be admitting, the world *is* denaturalized. We are surrounded—men no less than women—by the ugliness of our techno-chemical products, by our "Harpic," our "Andrex," our "green / formica." The only other life in Strugnell's apartment is perhaps pathogenic ("bacteria / in the drainpipe"). However, this artificiality is not an essentially "feminine" quality. There is no ground for the assertion that women are somehow *producers* of a nylon world through the "laws" of supply and demand, whereas men are estranged from it. Indeed, "Strugnell in Liverpool" reveals Strugnell "at home" with such a world, and even implies that his synthetic lover is a fantastic extension of his industrialized homescape. His technologized gaze produces an artificial lover, reduces her "naturalness," her body, to nylon underwear which he recalls with a truly "unearthly" pleasure.

Cope's reviewers focus on her parodies; one reviewer, Robert Nye from *The Times* in an article entitled "Max the parodist in skirts," describes Cope as the "most accomplished parodist since Beerbohm" (Nye 15). Sexton, in *The Sunday Times* says that "[O]nly the few poems which attempt pathos in her own voice fail to come off. This is an altogether welcome debut in what has previously been pretty much a male preserve" (43). (I assume he's unaware of the irony in the juxtaposition of these two thoughts.) Robert Nye, however, believes that Cope's potential is not accurately reflected in the book:

> Something in her is very much a poet, I think; but it has been depressed or deterred into parody and literary jokes by the rather dreadful specimens of the condition of poetry publicly available for inspection over the last decade or so. That would explain the sometimes virulent brilliance of the work attributed to her hold-all versifier, Jason Strugnell. (15)

Sexton, then, finds Cope's poems in her own voice unpersuasive, while Nye seems to imply that Cope's inner poetic voice gets disguised or lost through the parody. Larkin once described an *Observer* poetry contest which automatically discarded all the love poems; the urge to write parody can be attributed to a poetic establishment that views personal expression or self-disclosure in poetry as absence of high poetic seriousness. Ostriker believes that "the central project of the women's poetry movement is a quest for autonomous self-definition" (10). Cope's concession in writing parody rather than love poetry to get published is therefore a function of the criteria of acceptable poetry in England today. In an interview with Sarah Spankie, Cope speaks plaintively and self-disparagingly of her desire to write more poems in her own voice: "I'm sure I will go on writing parodies, but I hope to expose more of my own stuff too" (36). Cope's choice of words is telling: she refers to "exposing" poetry in her own voice, implicitly juxtaposing and contrasting the protective exoskeletal shell of parody with the vulnerability and risk of female self-expression and self-assertion, perhaps unmixed with the aggressive-defensiveness of her humor, delightful as that is. Although the male literary establishment needs a parodist to foreground its ideological content, we look forward to a Cope collection made up of the "very serious" and "intense" love poems the establishment wouldn't publish—perhaps entitled, *Making Cocoa for Wendy Cope.*

WORKS CITED

Amis, Kingsley. *Collected Poems 1944-1979.* New York: The Viking Press, 1980.

Cope, Wendy. *Making Cocoa For Kingsley Amis.* London: Faber and Faber, 1986.

Larkin, Philip. *Required Writing.* New York: Farrar, Strauss, Giroux, 1982.

___. *The Whitsun Weddings.* London: Faber and Faber, 1964.

Morrison, Blake. *The Movement.* Oxford: Oxford University Press, 1980.

Nye, Robert. "Max the parodist in skirts." *The Times* 13 March 1986: 13.

O' Donoghue, Bernard. "Light cakes, thin ale." *The Times Literary Supplement.* 6 June 1986: 616b.

Ostriker, Alicia Suskin. *Stealing The Language—The Emergence of Women's Poetry in America.* Boston: Beacon Press, 1986.

"Poetry Today: A Special Report." *The Times.* 6 May 1986: 30-31.

Press, John. *A Map of Modern English Verse.* London, Oxford: Oxford University Press, 1969.

Sexton, David. "Making Cocoa For Kingsley Amis." *The Sunday Times.* 16 March 1986: 43.

Spankie, Sarah. "The Poet and the Parody." *The Sunday Times.* 2 March 1986: 36.

—12—

A Duel of Wits and the Lesbian Romance Novel or *Verbal Intercourse in Fictional Regency England*

CATRIÓNA RUEDA ESQUIBEL

(Being a necessarily brief discourse on the history of criticism of lesbian romance novels, an introduction to the regency romance, and a study of the verbal dynamics and romantic conventions in Pembroke Park, "the First Lesbian Regency Novel.")

Such provocative titles as *The Romance Revolution, Goodbye Heathcliff, Loving With a Vengeance, Fantasy and Reconciliation*, and *Insatiable Appetites* are indicative of the veritable boom in academic study of the paperback romance as popular culture, patriarchal propaganda, and feminine discourse. The titles themselves seem to indicate a desire to identify with the passionate world of romantic fiction. Like that world, these works are exclusively heterosexual in content, taking little or no notice of non-heterosexuals.

In her study of fifty-two romance novels, Thurston points out that "Homosexual males appear in 24 percent of the stories, and in more than

123

two-thirds of these they are portrayed as immoral or undesirable"[1] and that "there was no mention of homosexual women in any of the stories" (75). Thurston does mention the genre of lesbian romance, but in doing so, promptly dismisses it from her study on the basis of numerical inferiority, comparing seven titles by author Sarah Aldrich to the 150 titles per month issued by the major romance publishing lines (12).

There are, of course, considerably more than seven lesbian romance novels currently available. The Naiad Press alone has seventy-seven romances in print, and when combined with the holdings of Firebrand Books, New Victoria Publishers, and The Seal Press, romances account for a large percentage of lesbian literature.

Lesbian romantic fiction has not fared any better at the hands of lesbian critics, however. In her massive and ambitious study *The Safe Sea of Women: Lesbian Fiction 1969-1989,* Bonnie Zimmerman, while acknowledging that the romance is one of the major forms of lesbian fiction, reveals a distaste for the genre.

> Romantic love stories, differing only slightly from the pulp fiction of the 1950's and 60's, are the staple offerings of certain lesbian publishers, in particular The Naiad Press. (77)

Zimmerman looks at lesbian romance only in terms of its "formation and definition of the lesbian couple"(77), and like many of the early feminist readings of heteromance, takes a combative (good feminist critic vs. evil romance) stance toward the material. She cites Russ' description of lesbian novels as "clumsy, stupid, anti-sexual, romantic in the bad sense, simple-minded"[2] and then herself adds "If we refer only to those popular romances published by a handful of overtly lesbian presses, we may well characterize the genre as 'unbearable'" (17). Academic lesbian-feminist contempt towards the genre of lesbian romance is not surprising, considering that heteromance has only recently been given quasi-legitimate status both in academic and in feminist circles.

Clearly this field deserves more attention than it has yet received. My study is on the carry-over of genre from heterosexual romance fiction to lesbian novels: focusing on the regency romance, although other genres have similarly made the transition to lesbian fiction including gothics, contemporary mystery romances, historicals, contemporary romances, and family sagas.

The genre of regency romance is traditionally credited to English novelist Georgette Heyer (1902-1974) who wrote some twenty-nine historical romances and comedies of manners, set roughly between 1775 and 1825.

> Regency romances transport readers to England, often London, to a society in which women contract suitable marriages through participation in a structured social ritual—the marriage market represented by the London season. A courtship ritual dominates the action of each book and provides a value system against which characters behavior can be measured. Some heroines flout convention more than others, but all are in danger of ostracism for inappropriate behavior.
>
> (Mussell, 56)

Popular romance author Joan Aiken adds:

> Explicit sex does not flutter the pages of a Regency novel. It is understood that off-stage the gentlemen have their doxies, light-skirts, charmers, and the like. But the wise heroine, though aware of such peccadilloes in her suitor, turns a blind eye, and is, of course, herself chaste though spirited. Heroines occasionally elope, but seldom get very far. (78)

In the Foreword to *Pembroke Park* which is styled "A Bit of a Departure: The First Lesbian Regency Novel," Michelle Martin expands on this historical description, including women's position in Regency society:

> England in 1817 is enjoying a flowering of all the arts. William and Dorothy Wordsworth, Byron, Keats, Percy and Mary Shelley, Scott, Austen—All are writing. Men are adorning themselves with as many "fripperies" as their female counterparts, showing off their legs in skintight breeches, padding their elegant coats to broaden their shoulders and chests, styling their hair as carefully as their neckcloths. Women of the ton (the nobility) uncover a good deal of their bodies, even dampening their gowns to have them cling more revealingly to their curves. Women have already become social and financial accessories, a condition which will not be effectively challenged until our own century—except by certain women....

The predictability of the regency romance, especially when penned by such of Heyer's imitators as the "prolific and long-lived Barbara Cartland, who has honed the 'poor little Cinderella' plot line to a dull edge" (Thurston, 37) is illustrated in Margaret Atwood's *Lady Oracle* in which author Joan Foster embarks on the writing of her first romance for a large publishing house:

> I made lists of words like "fichu" and "paletot" and "pelisse"; I spent whole afternoons in the costume room of the Victoria and Albert Museum.... I thought if I could only get the clothes right, everything else would fall into line. And it

did: the hero, a handsome, well-bred, slightly balding man, dressed in an immaculately tailored tweed cloak, like Sherlock Holmes's, pursued the heroine, crushing her lips to hers in a hansom cab and rumpling her pelisse. The villain, equally well-bred and similarly clad, did just about the same thing, except that in addition, he thrust his hand inside her fichu. The rival female had a lithe body like that of a jungle animal beneath her exquisitely stitched corset, and like all such women, she came to a bad end. I think she merely tripped on her paletot, going downstairs. But she deserved this, as she'd attempted to reduce the heroine to a life of shame by tying her up and leaving her in a brothel....

But I had aimed too high. My first effort came back with instructions to the effect that I could not use words like "fichu" and "paletot" and "pelisse" without explaining what they meant. I made the necessary revisions and received my first hundred pounds, with a request for more material. Material, they called it, as if it came by the yard (175).

How does this formula of hero-heroine-villain-villainess change when the regency novel is the setting for a lesbian romance? When the romance is not boy-meets-girl, or rather lord-meets-lady, it becomes a case of loving the other woman, which in Regency England is a somewhat dangerous endeavor. *Pembroke Park* is both a regency romance and a coming-out novel, for it follows the sensual awakening of Lady Joanna Sinclair, a widow and mother, and thoroughly proper lady of the ton who is confronted with the eccentric, scandalous and incredibly wealthy Lady Diana March. I would call *Pembroke Park* a romance first and a coming-out novel second, because the focus of the novel is the developing relationship between the two women, with Joanna's recognition of herself as lesbian, though of obvious importance, receiving somewhat less attention. Joanna realizes her love for Diana well before the latter recognizes that her own love is reciprocated.

The novel begins conventionally enough, with Lady Sinclair strolling along a country lane, musing upon literature, and being confronted by a stranger on horseback.

The dull rhythmic thud of hoofbeats brought Joanna's head up from her contemplation of her dusty shoes. Quickly she shaded her eyes, half expecting to find Ivanhoe galloping towards her.

There was no white stallion, however; only a large, powerfully built bay mare. And instead of a knight in shining armor, there was a fair damsel, though hardly in distress; she seemed a superb horsewoman. She was young, perhaps of medium height, dressed in brown turkish trousers tucked into riding boots, and a dark blue long-sleeved shirt and brown vest only slightly darker than the tan of her face and throat. The rider's honey-blonde hair was caught in to a thick braid that swung across her back while stray wisps floated about her face. Stunned by this apparition, Joanna stopped in her tracks and seriously wondered in Mrs. Stempel's scones had so unsettled her stomach that she was now suffering from hallucinations. (2)

The two ladies promptly fall into the conventional duel of wits:one of the most common elements of regency romance and an important part of the courtship ritual It is a means of discovering the intellectual capacities of the prospective mate, as well as a form of intimate intercourse between the protagonists. This convention originates in the novels of Jane Austen, and as developed by Georgette Heyer, frequently results in one protagonist being bereft of words by the honesty of the other.

"We haven't been formally introduced yet. I'm Diana. Diana March. I've just purchased Waverly Manor."
"You? " Joanna gasped, staring up at the woman with unconcealed shock. "Waverly Manor?"
"You're not going to be needing smelling salts, are you?" Diana March asked anxiously. "I never carry them, you know."
"No, no I...I beg your pardon, Lady March. I was...daydreaming and you caught me unawares. Welcome to Heddington."
"Thank you." Diana's grin was decidedly mischievous. "You knew I had purchased Waverly Manor?"
"Oh yes. Mr. Acton, my...my brother's solicitor, mentioned you only the other day."
"Whatever he said could not have been good." Diana chuckled. "Solicitors take an instant dislike to me. They do not approve of females giving them orders, I think. I doubt if they approve of our sex at all—we're always having to be provided for in wills that would be quite straightforward without us."
"On the contrary, Mr. Acton spoke very highly of you," Joanna said a trifle stiffly. She had regained her equilibrium.
"Did he? How odd. I should regard any future advice he may give you with the greatest suspicion, Lady Sinclair. His judgment seems to be faltering. There are no upcoming court battles I trust?"
"No, none," Joanna said faintly.
"Then my mind is at ease. Well," Diana said decisively as she gathered her reins, "it has been a great pleasure meeting you, Lady Sinclair. You've the honor to be the first neighbor whose acquaintance I've made after being in residence only two days. I daresay the calling cards will be streaming in now. It is a great trial being new in the district, you know. I always dread conversations about the weather. I can't tell you how grateful I am that you didn't mention today's absence of rain. Ciao!"
"Good...day," Joanna faltered as the bay broke into a canter and carried its unique mistress away leaving Joanna to stare after them, her body numb, her mind feverish. "Good God," she breathed. (3-4)

This dynamic to their verbal relationship continues in their next meeting, when it becomes apparent that Joanna is not so much shocked by her companion but by her own behavior when she is with Diana. Recounting neighborhood history about a hot dispute between two leading families over the unscrupulous hiring away of a prized chef which feud died only with the poor fellow in question, Joanna concludes:

> Now both families enjoy mediocre chefs and once again are on the best of terms."
> "Ah England, England," Lady March sighed rapturously, "how I have missed thee!"
> Joanna forgot herself enough to chuckle.
> "Would you like more tea?" Lady March inquired.
> "No, thank you," Joanna replied, embarrassed by her unseemly levity.
> "Well then," Lady March said, "my renovations are a fait accompli. Would you like a tour to see what my whims have wrought at Waverly?"
> "Tour?" Joanna said faintly. She had expected perhaps a discussion of gelding methods, but certainly not this.
> "Yes," Lady March said brightly. "You'd be the first. Aren't you just the slightest bit curious about the wondrous transformation a bold and daring mind can create?"
> Joanna stared at her hostess. "You are quite mad," she thought.
> "Don't be alarmed Lady Sinclair. Everyone thinks so, but it's only partially true."
> Joanna jumped and then blushed furiously as she realized she had spoken aloud.
> "I...beg your pardon, Lady March! I didn't mean..." she stammered. (28-29)

At the end of a longer interchange at Lady Sinclair's dinner party, Lady March once again disarms her new companion and leaves her speechless.

> Diana regarded her hostess with frank pleasure. "You are far more formidable than first appearances would allow," she said with quiet decisiveness.
> Joanna, who had never in her life been called formidable, could only stare.
> "Come," Diana said, taking Joanna's arm, "let us return to the Drawing Room. I am anxious to discover which of the rest of your guests will try to make love to my fortune. (52)

Lady March invites Joanna and her daughter Molly to tea, promising the latter that she will wear her most outrageous costume, which in this case is a scanty harem outfit complete with a diamond in her navel. In place of a traditional English tea, Joanna is treated to a sensual feast of Middle Eastern fare and succulent fruits.

> "God, I love decadence!" [Diana] sighed rapturously and this set Joanna to laughing. "Well, don't you?"
> "I do not know, I have never witnessed decadence, let alone indulged in it before."
> "You poor, deprived creature," Diana said with a look of sympathy. "It is a good thing that we have met so that I may instruct you in the proper way to conduct life."

"Decadence is of some importance in your scheme of things, is it?" Joanna inquired.

"Of paramount importance," Diana affirmed, dropping another strawberry into her mouth.

"I see." Joanna smiled. "You must disapprove of me very much, then. I'm not at all decadent you know."

"For an intelligent woman you do not know yourself at all."

"I know that I am not at all like you."

"On the contrary, you are very much like me. That is what you find so terrifying. 'Sisters we are, yea twins we be, Yet deadly feud ['twixt] thee and me.'"

"And what, praytell, do you mean by that cryptic quote?"

"Only that it seems to me that we are forever defending ourselves from the pleasure of each other's company," Diana said.

"You wore that atrocious costume," Joanna said.

"And you couldn't see the fun of it," Diana retorted.

"You take a perverse delight in shocking people," Joanna contended as Molly watched this interchange with great interest.

"Of course I do," Diana cheerfully agreed. "It's great fun."

"I do not like shocking people," Joanna declared self-righteously.

"That is because you have never done it before. I daresay you would enjoy yourself immensely if you but tried it once."

Joanna gave it up and began to laugh. "You are incorrigible."

"Of course I am, but I'm right," Diana replied. "Have a strawberry." To her surprise Joanna found herself opening her mouth which Diana promptly filled with a fat strawberry. (64-65)

This is not only one of the best duels of wit in the novel, but illustrates a conventional wooing in regency romance. The experienced lover—which, in the case of heterosexual romance is always the hero—challenges the conventions of propriety in which the inexperienced lover—the heterosexual heroine—has been drilled all her life. The latter realizes that she has always secretly questioned these notions and although excited by the discovery of a kindred spirit, feels that her safe place in society is threatened.

I must also acknowledge the related convention of unsatisfactory partners. The heroine is pressured into this form of verbal intercourse with a partner who is, as the saying goes, not up to her weight. In Heyer's *Venetia*,[3] the heroine is confronted by a singularly dull suitor, whose lack of wit protects him from feeling the veracity of Venetia's refusal of his proposal. He is further protected by Venetia's kind-heartedness and sense of propriety while Martin's Lord Humphrey does not fare so well:

Diana's relief at Mr. Garfield's departure was shortlived, for she quickly found herself trapped near the main door of the Drawing Room by the amazingly persistent Lord Franklin Humphrey.

"You have been sorely missed, Lady March," he declared without preamble. "I think it a barbaric custom to separate the men from such charming company as yours after dinner, don't you?"

"I have always found the company of women immeasurably preferable to that of men," Diana bluntly replied.

Lord Humphrey smiled at her. "Now you are teasing me.... Ah, Lady March, you are too clever to reveal your real desires. Mustn't let men swell up with their own importance, eh? I commend you. Women gushing about one's manly features can be quite wearying."

"Had I known that, I would have been a geyser of praise," Diana replied.

But the remark apparently went over her tormentor's head. "You are a delight, Lady March," he declared.

"And you, my lord, are amazingly obtuse."

Lord Humphrey began to laugh. "What will you say next?"

"I doubt if you would like to hear it."

"Any gentleman would be eager to hear the opinion of so lovely a lady."

"Your eyes deceive you, my lord," Diana said frostily. "I am remarkably plain. It is my fortune that is handsome."

"...You see that I have been caught by your beauty and you seek to punish me for such presumptuousness. Alas I am but a humble moth caught by your brilliant flame. Do with me as you will."

With a cheerful smile into Lord Humphrey's unappetizing face, Diana calmly poured her glass of wine over Lord Humphrey's pulsating abdomen. (45-46)

A recent trend in regency romances is to question not only the restrictive roles of women but to criticize the narrow values of a shallow society where one's worth is judged by the fashion of the day. In *A Lady's Point of View,* the heroine is exiled from the London season for giving the cut direct to the famous Beau Brummel. This cardinal sin occurs by virtue of her extreme near-sightedness. The unwritten law that no physical defect be revealed if a young lady is to be considered marriageable denies the heroine in question the use of a lorgnette. The romance is loaded with damning views of a society which would make poor vision a necessity to avoid a worse fate—spinsterhood[4]—but the novel ends with the requisite marriage (in this case a double marriage) and the tacit understanding that the couple will partake of the entertainments of the *ton.*

As the romance progresses the verbal duel is abandoned. This is, in part, because it is an superficial form of intercourse, which becomes an obstacle to the deepening friendship. On the other hand, this friendship is somewhat threatening to at least one of the parties involved. This usually results in one partner attempting to turn aside the the verbal sallies of the other, to discover the true feelings of the other, who contrariwise attempts to defend herself by her wit.

In addition, the more grueling romances, of which *Pembroke Park* is one, contain a great deal of tortured misunderstanding, as one of the parties believes that she or he has mistook the friendship of the other for true love, and/or a great deal of similarly tortuous dialogue along the "get-away-from-me-you-don't-know-what-you-do-to-me-you're-in-danger!!!!!" line. I suspect that this is symbolic of the inadequacy of language to express deeper emotion, and the breakdown of communication which results when language, in the form of the conventional duel of wits, is the only socially acceptable form of personal intercourse.

Pembroke Park is the regency romance turned on its ear, complete with its forthcoming socially acceptable lord-lady wedding. As Martin uses comedy to a greater extent than tragedy, it is through the aforementioned wedding or, in this case, weddings that she both acknowledges conventions and joyously tosses them to the wind. The weddings are to allow Lady March and Lady Sinclair[5] and Geoffrey Hunt-Stevens and Richard Sinclair to continue their respective exclusive gay relationships safely in England. To remove any specter of romantic interest within the marriages, Martin comically renders her characters incapable of deciding who is to marry whom.

"...We could draw straws."
"Blindman's Bluff," Diana countered. "Whichever one we catch we marry."
"We could toss a coin," Joanna said.
"Never!" Diana insisted. "I'll not call heads for any man."

NOTES

1. It is a bit unclear as to whether the male homosexual is undesirable to the hero, the heroine, the narrator, or the reader.
2. Russ's words originally appeared in *Women's Review of Books*, 3 (11): 6.
3. An unusual romance indeed. The rakish Hero knows that he is not worthy to kiss the satin slipper of Venetia, and will not ask her to marry him because doing so would drag her down to his level. Refusing to stand by and let him sacrifice the happiness of both by such misguided chivalry, Venetia threatens to go and live with her mother if he will not marry her. As her mother is a notorious divorcee who exists on the fringes of British society—when she is not in Paris, which is so much more tolerant of such things—only by virtue of her second husband's immense fortune, our Hero instead chooses to accept our Heroine's proposal of marriage. The romance ends with Venetia telling her fiancé that if he intends, in the future, to hold any such orgies at the manor as those which made his youth notorious, she expects to participate fully.
4. Shades of Dorothy Parker.

5. I'm using titles because the similarity of "Diana" and "Joanna" is quite confusing, especially in oral presentation.

WORKS CITED

Aiken, Joan. "Regency Romance Romp," in *Writing and Selling the Romance Novel*, Sylvia Burack, editor. Boston: The Writer, Inc., 1983.

Atwood, Margaret. *Lady Oracle*. New York: Ballantine Books, 1987.

Diamond, Jacqueline. *A Lady's Point of View*. Toronto: Harlequin, November 1989.

Martin, Michelle. *Pembroke Park*. Tallahassee, FL: The Naiad Press, 1986.

Mussell, Kay. *Fantasy and Reconciliation: Contemporary Formulas of Women's Romance Fiction*. Contributions to Women's Studies, Number 46. Westport, CT and London: Greenwood Press, 1984.

Thurston, Carol. *The Romance Revolution: Erotic Novels for Women and the Quest for a New Sexual Identity*.

Zimmerman, Bonnie. *The Safe Sea of Women: Lesbian Fiction 1969-1989*. Boston: Beacon Press, 1990.

WORKS CONSULTED

Barnhart, Helene Schellenberg. *Writing Romance Fiction--For Love and Money*. Edited by Susan Whittlesey Wolf. Cincinnati, OH: Writer's Digest Books, 1983.

Frenier, Mariam Darce. *Good-bye Heathcliff: Changing Heroes, Heroines, Roles, and Values in Women's Category Romances*. Contributions in Women's Studies, Number 94. New York and London: Greenwood Press, 1988.

Heath, Sandra. *The Wrong Miss Richmond*. New York: Signet, 1989.

Heyer, Georgette. *Regency Buck*. London: Heinemann, 1935.

____. *The Talisman Ring*. London: Heinemann, 1936.

____. *An Infamous Army*. London: Heinemann, 1937.

____. *The Spanish Bride*. London: Heinemann, 1940.

____. *The Corinthian*. London: Heinemann, 1940.

____. *Faro's Daughter*. London: Heinemann, 1941.

____. *Friday's Child*. London: Heinemann, 1944.

____. *The Reluctant Widow*. London: Heinemann, 1946.

____. *The Foundling*. London: Heinemann, 1948.

____. *Arabella*. London: Heinemann, 1949.

____. *The Grand Sophy*. London: Heinemann, 1950.

____. *The Quiet Gentleman*. London: Heinemann, 1951.

____. *Cotillion*. London: Heinemann, 1953.

____. *The Toll-Gate*. London: Heinemann, 1954.

____. *Bath Tangle*. London: Heinemann, 1955.

____. *Sprig Muslin*. London: Heinemann, 1956.

____. *April Lady*. London: Heinemann, 1957.

____. *Sylvester: or The Wicked Uncle*. London: Heinemann, 1957.

___. *Venetia*. London: Heinemann,1958.

___. *The Unknown Ajax*. London: Heinemann,1959.

___. *A Civil Contract*. London: Heinemann,1961.

___. *The Nonesuch*. London: Heinemann,1962.

___. *False Colours*. London: Bodley Head,1963.

___. *Frederica*. Bodley Head,1965.

___. *Black Sheep*. Bodley Head,1966.

___. *Cousin Kate*. Bodley Head,1968.

___. *Charity Girl*. Bodley Head,1970.

___. *Lady of Quality*. Bodley Head,1972.

Law, Elizabeth. *Double Deception*. New York: Zebra Books, November 1989.

Miner, Madonne M. *Insatiable Appetites: Twentieth-century American Women's Bestsellers*. Contributions is Women's Studies, Number 48. Westport, CT: Greenwood Press, 1984.

Radway, Janice A. *Reading the Romance: Women, Patriarchy and Popular Literature*. Chapel Hill, NC and London: University of North Carolina Press, 1984.

Smith, Joan. *Lover's Quarrels*. New York: Fawcett Crest, 1989.

13

Louise Erdrich as Nanapush

SHARON MANYBEADS BOWERS

Louise Erdrich understands well her Chippewa heritage and writes about it in her third novel, *Tracks*. She says in a *New York Times Book Review* that "...in the light of enormous loss (she) must tell the stories of contemporary invasions while protecting and celebrating the cores of cultures left in the wake of the catastrophe."

Although feelings of desolation and helplessness of the characters of this novel are evident as a result of raging epidemics; "bureaucrats sinking their barbed pens into the lives of Indians"; and lumber companies ravaging their forests; it is the act of storytelling that makes survival possible.[1] Alternately narrated by Nanapush, a witty elder of the Chippewa tribe and Pauline, a bitter Canadian Chippewa who centers on images of death, the story is one of survival. As Nanapush says after battling consumption, "I got well by talking. Death could not get a word in edgewise, grew discouraged, and traveled on."[2] His works demonstrate the thin line between tragedy and comedy. The trick is how the story is told.

The narrative technique reveals the structure of the plot that sets forward the oppositional strands of twentieth-century Chippewa existence. Old man Nanapush embodies Chippewa trickster hero and powerful spirit, Nanabozho. According to oral tradition, Nanabozho was one of the first humans on the earth, a super trickster who dreamed with different forms and languages, spoke the same tongue as the plants and animals.[3]

Some might call Nanapush a liar, but his lies and truths are tied and committed to ways that have served and survived the centuries' generations.

Pauline is also called a liar. Nanapush calls her the "crow of the reservation." Her lies and truths are tied and committed to a baroque and austere mission-house Catholicism. Nanapush's narrative style is interspersed with Pauline's to create a narrative combat—his lies, her lies—as the non-Indian world inserts its road into Indian lands, sinks its sawteeth into Indian timber, and poisons Chippewa souls with printing ink. At the center of this cultural biformity is Fleur Pillager, the mother of Lulu to whom old man Nanapush tells his versions of the truth. Fleur stands against both worlds, Chippewa and white, cursing them each in turn, and working fabulous revenge when her times come. She gets no chance at narration, but her vision disallows any romanticizing of either side.

One of the central themes developed successfully in this novel is the humorous exchanges that are familiar, welcome, and expected in most Indian homes. One of my Chippewa friends says that her family in Minnesota refers to *Love Medicine* as that "funny book" and *Tracks* as that "other funny book." Part of the humor is in the treatment of the three romantically linked couples, Margaret and Nanapush, Eli and Fleur, and Pauline and Napoleon. The gender humor that develops as a result of these pairings is a combination of teasing, one of the familiar Indian social patterns, slapstick and burlesque. The humor that evolves gives us a chance to enjoy the less serious side of the characters. At the same time the characters become more fully developed as we see them attempt to make sense out of absurd situations.

A basic framework of characters reveals: that old man Nanapush was seduced by a bald-headed Margaret who insisted on having her way; Eli fell in love with a wild woman of the woods who dabbled in old medicine ways and witchery; and Pauline insisted on becoming a bride of Christ after her encounter with Napoleon and childbearing. In each instance, the patriarchal image of man suffers in favor of wiley women of power who are resourceful, ambitious, and relentless. Thus, the preconceived notion of romance is turned upside down and a burlesque comedy unfolds.

One of the trademarks of a cultural trickster hero, such as Nanabozho, is that he is often the one that gets tricked. Old man Nanapush doesn't admit that Margaret Rushes Bear tricked him into seeking her as a partner, that is part of his discretion as a storyteller giving his version of the truth to young, impressionable Lulu. My point here is the humorous approach to a Romeo who is toothless and bald and a Juliet who is "thin on top, plump as a turnip below, with a face like a round molasses cake and gray" braids that looked like they were slipping off her head.[4] This is only part of the senior citizen version of a familiar plot—virile, handsome man desires sensuous, fatally attractive member of the opposite sex.

Margaret determinedly "set her trapline" for old man Nanapush around her kitchen table with good, strong coffee, plenty of gaulette, warm berry pudding and began wooing him with teasing remarks about his manhood. She not only encouraged him with her food, she resisted him at the same time with her insinuations, mocking his name. This is the same man that was told by his father, "Nanapush. That's what you'll be called. Because it's got to do with trickery and living in the bush. Because it's got to do with something a girl can't resist. The first Nanapush stole fire. You will steal hearts."[5] He had satisfied three wives and was feeling the infirmity of old age creeping up on him when Margaret Rushes Bear burst in on him and called him an "old man, two wrinkled berries and a twig."[6] This form of gender humor left his tongue tingling for the last word and sparked an interest at the same time. She kept the topic of sex open and continued taunting him with her sharp tongue, "In the old days even the white-haired ones could do more than talk." And in the same scene, "You'll die hard, you'll stick up through the dirt."[7] Nanapush rallied with his own gender humor telling Lulu, "Some mothers swell up on the power of giving life, so much that the harbor the notion they can shrink their children back to seeds. Margaret was one of those,"[8] he told Lulu. If this is a way of stating that Margaret was a busybody, it is also a statement of women's exceptional maternal instincts and their power. It is a subtle approach to cultural conditioning where the mature Chippewa man is entitled to complete respect from women and children. The respect goes both ways according to the traditional Indian view on child rearing. This is an important point to consider in view of the fact Lulu has just returned from harsh years at a federal boarding school where she had been mistreated and subjected to an entirely foreign value system. This reveals a glimpse of crucial social and educational changes Chippewa people were forced to tolerate on a widely increasing scale at this point in their history.

Another instance of role reversals occurs when Nanapush is the nurturer, saving Fleur from her near fatal bout with consumption. He also comes to the rescue of Lulu who had suffered from exposure and severely frostbitten feet. Nanapush gave Margaret the credit for this last performance as a healer; she had instructed him what to do and left abruptly on her own mission. He then struggled to overcome Lulu's resistance and also the medical doctor's intervention and eventually won the exhaustive battle relying entirely on his native intelligence.

Nanapush is up to his tricks on lampooning the Catholics with his antics with Father Damien and Pauline. He pulls the wool over Father Damien's eyes with the information he supplies for Lulu's official birth record. He gives his own last name to get even with Margaret for jeering at his abilities as a healthy functioning male. Father Damien's character is at risk when Nanapush gets finished with him; Father Damien appears as a bumbling drone carrying out orders by mail.

The bear motif appears in several places including the slapstick comedy scenes between Eli who is determined to court Fleur and Nanapush who he asked for the old-time way to make a woman love him. Nanapush said the thing he found about women is that you have to use every instinct to confuse. This is the essence of his bear story and the advice he finally gave Eli, "Look here, it's like you're on a log in a stream. Along comes this bear. She jumps on. Don't let her dig in her claws."[9] This is an example of how the small story works efficiently to convey a picture image, or vision, something that will stay in place rather than be lost in the plain language of "how to" instructions. This leaves a wider margin of interpretation, or how to maintain the vision. It's also a subtle way to connect the characteristics of a bear with a woman, a Rushes Bear woman. It is no mistake, then, that Nanapush chooses the bear image for both Eli and himself.

Nanapush pulls out all the stops with Pauline when she comes to visit on a mission to save souls dressed in her habit, wearing her shoes on the wrong feet to remind herself of Christ's suffering. Nanapush lifted up her habit with his cane and said to his audience, "God is turning this woman into a duck...."[10] By this time had had noticed Pauline restricted herself to a prescribed time to visit the outhouse—sundown. As a true trickster, he fixed Pauline a pot of strong sassafras tea mixed with plenty of sugar—a rare treat—while he told a long story that involved a flood, a girl, and a sticking-out thing. According the an agreement, when the flood waters receded and the sticking-up thing was exposed, the two coupled until their parts smoked. Nine months later a child of the flood, a water child was born. At this point, to the delight of the rest of his audience, Nanapush took out a rubber safety, or condom, from his vest and slowly filled it with tea as he explained how the child of the flood grew and grew. Thus, Nanapush successfully inundated Pauline with water symbols until she was forced to make for the door in a crouching run to relieve herself well ahead of sundown. Here is where we see the storyteller interact with his audience. Pauline's reaction is different from that of Margaret, Lulu, and Fleur who are egging Nanapush on. The storyteller is framed within the larger story and gets yet another reaction from an audience outside the novel.

In this lesson, Nanapush's hospitality and storytelling were designed as a trap to undermine Pauline's mission to save souls by her honest efforts. Nanapush made sense out of nonsense without direct confrontation. He chose a rather titillating subject for a novice and used very graphic language in a legitimate way. The sticking-out thing is a valid Indian name/description like "woman-who-brings-back-horses." Tricky Nanapush leaves room for interpretation or gap-filling by his audience. He tricked Pauline, only because she was tricking herself wearing her shoes on the wrong feet and walking like a duck. He seduces Pauline, the rest of his audience, Margaret, Lulu, and Fleur who are roaring at the tricks, and the readers as well.

This form of indirect teasing, ribaldry and teaching through storytelling did not quench Pauline's intense desire to set terribly hard limits for herself as a penitente. She picked up right where she left off and put burrs in the armpits of her dress and screwgrass in her stockings and nettles in her neckband. Although this involves a description of devices to inflict pain and discomfort, the burlesque of her previous water scene with Nanapush breaks the rhythm of her story and allows us to see her in a new light. The alliteration makes it more comical than morbid to think of screwgrass in her stockings and nettles in her neckband. This is also part of the mockery of the Catholic values and the adverse effects its teachings has on some of its followers.

For example, later, Pauline stood naked in a sinking canoe, laughing convulsively in the middle of winter defying Mishepeshu, the water man. Water spirits have from the earliest possible times played an important role in the lives of Chippewas. On many of the rivers and lakes, eddies form and reform on the surface as if some Monster Spirit lurks in these mysterious depths. Among the prime spirits which the Chippewa attribute to the water are mermen/mermaids, horned serpents, Mishepehsu (Water Lynx), and the Ma-ma-qui-sha-wok or Little-People-in-the-Rocks. Little People would be helpful if the Chippewa performed the proper ritual to appease them. When Chippewa travel over large expanses of water, they offer up tobacco to the Little People.[1] Margaret Rushes Bear did this when Nanapush rode her across the lake in his leaky canoe. Perhaps this was Pauline's intentional error since she failed to ascribe to Chippewa ways.

She wanted to be pure Canadian, like her grandfather. Later, in her maddened frenzy on shore, she only imagined it was Mishepeshu she had crushed and destroyed. Finally she came to recognize the human shape of Napoleon Morrissey, father of their daughter, Marie, and drug his body off to the woods before she rolled in the mud and covered herself with sticks and leaves for her journey back to the convent. But, despite logic, she convinced herself that she had not sinned. She had, instead slain the water monster. Thus, she revealed with even conviction the events of one day of her life that fired her religious zeal to become the demoniac Leopolda we first found in *Love Medicine*.

In order to put this kind of intense drama into perspective, it helps to look at it with comical relief, as a hilarious episode of a behind-the-scene report on the Catholic conquest in Indian country.

There is a tradition of humor in all great societies of the world. A society without humor is probably neither great nor healthy. The Indians and European cultures have clowns, stand-up comedy, cartoons, jokes, theater and films to lighten things up. The Rio Grande Pueblo culture has its "Delight Makers." To this day visitors at a Zuni public dance can't avoid the tribal clown circulating among onlookers, sometimes making jest at the most unpredictable moments. Thus humor is infectious, the sign of a healthy community.[12] Margaret teases Nanapush and he teases back. Margaret, Fleur, and Lulu were all rocking with laughter when Nanapush was entertaining Pauline in her convent habit with a rubber safety. Humor is the social sanction to look at things differently.

Clowning is a way of making a point and opening the heart to laughter. The Hopi clowns are the ones that wear body paint in wide white and black stripes and very little else. The white paint is in honor of the daylight, and the black paint is in honor of the night. Their headdress is an elaborate twin-spired sculpture of cornhusks which makes them look very funny. The clown chief leads his long line of clowns over the adobe housetops to decide how to get down the ladder to the plaza where the people are gathered and waiting. He usually picks the most difficult way, hands first and snaking around the ladder instead of a straight descent. The rest follow and it is a funny scene. The Hopi clowns have a saying, "If but one person smiles, let that smile bring all good things for us. Let it be a blessing for the people." For the smile is sacred.

The backwards approach seems to work on several levels in *Tracks*. The characters are familiar from *Love Medicine,* yet we see them at a much younger age. The star romantic couple isn't the youngest or most virile couple; Margaret and old Nanapush take top honors for persistence, resistance, and insistence. Nanapush is going backwards in time for Lulu, telling her the story of Chippewa history before she was born. The way in which he tells it, with zesty imagination and humor make it lively and entertaining.

The business of a trickster is to take her work very seriously. It is to find a way to change the rhythm, to find a way to look at things different-ly. If it works, and just one person smiles as a result, that smile is a blessing for all the people. Louise Erdrich is a Nanapush for our time.

NOTES

1. *Booklist,* July 1988, page 1754.
2. Erdrich, Louise. *Tracks.* New York: Harper and Row, 1980, 46.
3. Asikinack, William. "Anishinabe (Ojibway) Legends Through Anishinabe Eyes." *Contemporary Native American Cultural Issues.* Thomas E. Schirer, editor. Sault Ste. Marie: Lake Superior University Press, 1988.
4. Erdrich, Louise (1989). *Tracks.* New York: Harper and Row, 47.
5. Ibid., 33.
6. Ibid., 48.
7. Ibid., 53.
8. Ibid., 55.
9. Ibid., 46.
10. Ibid., 146.
11. Asikinack, William. "Anishinabe (Ojibway) Legends Through Anishinabe Eyes." *Contemporary Native American Cultural Issues.* Thomas E. Schirer, editor. Sault Ste. Marie: Lake Superior University Press, 1988, 8.
12. "AISES News." *Winds of Change,* Winter, 1990. 74.

14

Confirming the Place of "The Other": Gender and Ethnic Identity in Maxine Hong Kingston's *The Woman Warrior*

KHANI BEGUM

The personal quest motif appears frequently in the literature of occidental societies, but rarely surfaces in that of oriental cultures, where integration with the community and family takes precedence over individuation of self. Maxine Hong Kingston's *The Woman Warrior: A Memoir of a Girlhood Among Ghosts,* analyzed by most critics as a quest for identity,[1] is perceived also as "oriental," exotic, and mysterious because it expresses the Chinese American[2] experience. Even when critics evaluate its literariness within the tradition of American literature, they cannot resist marginalizing it. Kingston's narrative, on the one hand, lends itself to analysis as a quest narrative precisely because it is concerned with questions of self-definition and identity. On the other hand, it resists categorization as individual autobiography because it concurrently interweaves myth, fiction, and reality to create its own unique tapestry of form. It refutes facile distinctions of form that place it as representative of

143

either occidental or oriental literature. While Kingston's memoir is not strictly autobiographical (its subtitle, "Memoirs of a Girlhood Among Ghosts," indicates ambiguity of both form and content), it still deals with a journey or quest. More specifically, it explores the quest of a unique and *particular* self, one that is female and one whose experience of growing up is both Chinese and American. Caught between two cultures and the product of both, Kingston's protagonist Maxine, in order to find her authentic self, must negotiate the contradictions between her two worlds before discovering and valorizing her individual cultural uniqueness and otherness from each.

Kingston's and/or her protagonist Maxine's quest for identity actually occurs on three levels, those of gender, ethnicity, and nationality. It involves confronting her Otherness—first, as a woman in patriarchal society (both Chinese and American societies being patriarchal in structure); secondly, as a member of an ethnic minority in America; and finally, as an English speaking (and writing) American within a "real Chinese"[3] family ("my parents did not understand English" [WW 165]). It is only through painfully confronting, acknowledging, and validating her Otherness at all three levels that she discovers her true individual self and its connections with and place within community and family. It is as a daughter of another disenfranchized Chinese woman in American society, Brave Orchid, that she journeys toward self actualization. Bonding with her mother while at the same time tearing herself apart from her, Maxine re-evaluates her relationships with her mother, Chinese American culture, and America. The mother/daughter relationship with both its bonds and its tensions becomes crucial to her search for ethnic and gender identity.

Employing feminist psychoanalytic approaches drawn from Luce Irigaray concurrently with Gayatri Spivak's notions about the disempowerment of minority cultures, I wish to explore issues of 'Otherness' and notions of Subjectivity from a Marxist/psychoanalytic perspective in *The Woman Warrior*. While Irigaray, claiming that any theory of the Subject has been appropriated by the "masculine" (*Speculum* 133), defines empowerment for women in terms of an essential feminine or as "the sex which is not one," Spivak opposes the essentialist position by emphasizing Marxist views grounded in Third World experience that concentrate on exploitation. Spivak's argument is deconstructive rather than psychoanalytical. She develops the experience of the female body as the object of male censorship and exploitation. Pointing out that any understanding of the 'subaltern classes' (Third World and/or Asiatic societies) in terms of their adjustment to European models is destructive, she sees the political project as being that of allowing the subaltern to speak. This translates to feminist issues as well, for women too function as a subaltern class that has been defined and silenced by the dominant culture, which in most cases is both male and white.

Paralleling and contrasting the tasks of the historian and the teacher, Spivak says:

> A historian confronts a text of counter insurgency or gendering where the subaltern has been represented. He unravels the text to assign a new subject-position to the subaltern, gendered or otherwise.

> A teacher of literature confronts a sympathetic text where the gendered subaltern has been represented. She unravels the text to make visible the assignment of subject-positions. (Spivak 241)

In examining texts like Kingston's, texts that reflect a subaltern culture's struggle for recognition and empowerment amidst or adjacent to a dominant culture, the critic is both historian and teacher, for he/she must unravel the text to both assign new subject-positions as well as make visible the assignment of existing ones. Despite the fact that over the last decade or so Maxine Hong Kingston's place appears to have been established within the American literary canon,[4] too many American as well as Chinese American critics, reviewers, and readers continue to perceive Kingston's *The Woman Warrior* in terms of marginal experience because it represents for them an experience that *appears* marginal from *their* own subject-positions. Kingston, maintaining that it is an experience shared by many Chinese Americans and because the Chinese American is a *type of American,* wants it to be considered within mainstream American literature. With the exception of a few progressive curriculums, however, her books more often continue to be taught in multi-cultural, ethnic literature, or women's studies courses rather than alongside works by mainstream American writers like Thomas Pynchon, Saul Bellow, and such. As long as this is the case, the critic and teacher cannot ignore the subalternity of her texts; instead, they must begin by recognizing these texts as reflecting varieties of subaltern experience and then proceed to illuminate not only their uniqueness and Otherness but also their bonds with and roots within the dominant cultural experience.

The first step toward self-actualization and identity requires a facility with language and the power to speak. All oppressed and disenfranchised societies and groups have achieved their goal of freedom and recognition only after they articulated their situation and defined themselves. Spivak finds that the disempowerment of minority cultures is often achieved by the dominant culture through the denial of language or the power to speak out. By silencing the Subaltern, the dominant group maintains power. Irigaray too writes about the need for woman to speak in her own tongue or tongues and not become, like the Pythia, a vehicle for patriarchal opinion. Two Asian American writers, Frank Chin and Jeffrey Paul Chan, voice their anger over what they consider the castration of Chinese American males through the denial of a "legitimate mother tongue." They perceive the erasure of the Chinese American male's manhood as resulting from the concept of dual personality; being both Chinese and American, the "Chinese-American is never completely accepted by either the Chinese from China or the white Americans. Considered a foreigner and an alien by American society, he is expected to be at home in the Chinese language, while the "real Chinese" refuse him acceptance as Chinese because his birthplace is the U.S.

> The concept of dual personality successfully deprives the Chinese American of all authority over language and thus a means of codifying, communicating, and legitimizing his experience. Because he is a foreigner, English is not his native tongue. Because he was born in the U.S., Chinese is not his native tongue. Chinese from China, "real Chinese," make the Chinese American aware of his lack of authority over Chinese, and the white American doesn't recognize the Chinese American's brand of English as a language, even a minority language, but as faulty English, an "accent."...the development of Chinese American English has been prevented, much less recognized. The denial of language is the denial of culture.
>
> ("Racist Love" 76)

Finding deprivation of language to be a contributing factor "to the lack of a recognized style of Asian-American cultural integrity...and the lack of a recognized style of Asian American manhood," Chin and Chan claim: "On the simplest level, a man in any culture speaks for himself. Without a language of his own, he is no longer a man" ("Racist Love" 76-77).

Chin and Chan, perceiving this denial of language as affecting essentially Chinese males, consider the literary success of Chinese American women authors as yet another form of emasculation of the Chinese American male: "The mere fact that four of the five American-born Chinese-American writers [Jade Snow Wong, Diana Chang, Virginia Lee, Betty Lee Sung, Pardee Lowe] are women reinforces this aspect of the stereotype [stereotype of the Asian male as completely devoid of manhood]" ("Racist Love" 68). While their point that the deprivation of language contributes to the Chinese American male's crisis of identity is a valid one, their implication that it devastates only Chinese American males is disturbing. Such gender differentiation over the effects of language deprivation apparently arises out of Chin's and Chan's conviction that literary creativity belongs in the domain of men.[5] This bears out Irigaray's claim that any theory of the Subject has been appropriated by the "masculine." To perceive the Chinese American woman's (only relative) publishing success as emasculating, indicates that the Chinese American male is assuming a gender exclusive claim on creative subjectivity. And, he in turn, by denying the Chinese American female the right to creative subjectivity and identity as co-subaltern, relegates her to a doubly subaltern position. Moreover, in most oriental cultures, women are expected to remain silent and are discouraged from voicing their opinions. In fact, silence in women is considered a virtue reflecting shyness and inner beauty, qualities considered embodiments of femininity.

For Kingston, the importance of speech, of being able to express oneself to others in a common language is crucial in asserting one's subject-position. Its significance becomes almost overwhelming in the scene where Maxine in the sixth grade, both verbally and physically harasses the "quiet" Chinese girl to get her to talk: "If you don't talk, you can't have a personality.... You've got to let people know you have a personality and a brain" (180). The violence with which Maxine attacks the girl, pinching her cheeks and screaming at her, is motivated by her own fear of losing identity, and it is directed as much at herself as it is at the quiet Chinese girl, who stands for every Chinese girl in America. Unlike the Japanese kids, who "were noisy and tough" (166), Maxine, like other Chinese girls, finds talking agonizing: "It was when I found out I had to talk that school became a misery, that the silence became a misery. I did not speak and felt bad each time that I did not speak" (166). She soon realizes the connection between silence and being Chinese: "The other Chinese girls did not talk either, so I knew the silence had to do with being a Chinese girl" (166). Recognizing the subalternity of her Chinese American and gender positions, she painfully confronts her Otherness in American society. Even though Maxine herself has "a terrible time talking" (165) and burns with embarrassment when she hears her own voice splinter and sound like "bones rubbing jagged against one another" (169), she valiantly tries to overcome her shyness.

The conflict here is between her Chinese sense of female identity, which requires women to be shy and voiceless, and her American identity which insists that without a voice you have no personality. "Sometimes I hated the ghosts for not letting us talk; sometimes I hated the secrecy of the Chinese" (183). Maxine recalls the first time she became silent and her disgust at the sound of her own voice.

> When I went to kindergarten and had to speak English for the first time, I became silent. A dumbness—a shame—still cracks my voice in two, even when I want to say "hello" casually, or ask an easy question.... A telephone call makes my throat bleed and takes up that day's courage. It spoils my day with self-disgust when I hear my broken voice skittering out into the open. (165)

She perseveres in making herself talk because she knows that she must talk to get a job, make a living, and "speak up in front of the boss"—in short to survive in America. She recalls that her silence was thickest during the three school years when she covered her school paintings with black paint (165) and for the first year spoke to no one at school. Evidently the conflicts and contradictions of her two worlds that have been tearing Maxine apart throughout her childhood, finally erupt in her venomous outburst inside the girl's washroom. Her paintings, covered over with black paint, are the external evidence of the young Maxine's schizophrenic condition. Hiding her paintings with black paint points to a desire to conform to the codes of at least one of her worlds and a wish to end the conflict going on within herself. The black paint serves as a shade or curtain pulled over the person she is becoming, and thereby silencing whatever personality her paintings may be trying to express.

Paul John Eakin points out that the encounter with the quiet Chinese girl represents the making of the self and even though Maxine fails to make the girl speak, she succeeds in voicing herself with awesome power (Eakin 269). After this experience, Maxine spends the "next eighteen months sick in bed with a mysterious illness" (181-182). Her attempt to negotiate between her Chinese Otherness and the need to have a personality takes this physical toll, and when she returns to school she has "to figure out again how to talk" (182). Torn between the need to be a Chinese woman, and hence silent, and an inborn desire for personal autonomy, it is Maxine's *American* self that surfaces in the washroom incident allowing her to acknowledge that speech and language are instruments of power.

Kingston's memoir begins with an example of another silenced woman, namely the story of No Name Woman, the aunt who was shunned by family and community for committing adultery and who eventually drowned herself and her newborn child in the family well. No Name Woman's narrative is meaningful at all three levels of gender, ethnicity, and nationality within the context of Kingston's own experience. As Eakin suggests, the retelling of this tale makes Kingston's narrative a

> ...symbolic analogue of not only the aunt's initial defiance of tradition in search for a private space in which individuality could dwell "secret and apart," but also of the aunt's subsequent plea for the observance of tradition in the endless search of her ghost for the place and recognition of a name.
>
> (Eakin 258-259)

Even though No Name Woman's battle occurred in China, it parallels Maxine's situation symbolically. For Maxine too is seeking a private space where she can dwell as an individual—as a Chinese American woman. Like No Name Woman, who is an alien in her community because of her nonconmformity, Maxine, who also is Other and outcaste in her family through the fact of having been born in America and for having established bonds with her environment, an otherwise alien culture, must find her own private place and identity. No Name Woman's Otherness and alienation stems from the rape or act of sexual indiscretion (Maxine wonders whether her aunt was victim or rebel), which in either case makes her a *pariah* by virtue of the stain of immorality it implies and because her "aunt crossed boundaries not delineated in space" (8). Since the traditional definition of what it means to be a Chinese woman categorically rejects anyone marked with a 'scarlet letter,' so to speak, Maxine's aunt has no other identity except that of outcaste and no recognizable place within the traditional family structure. Unlike Maxine's, her choices are limited. She chooses to die with one last bid for identity by drowning herself in the family well. This becomes an act of protest, of "speaking out" and it forces the oppressor to take notice, even if it is only by way of forbidding further mention of her name and story.

The fact that No Name Woman's suicide is actually an act of vengeance—by drowning herself and her child in the family well she effectively pollutes their water supply—indicates that she re-assigns her own subaltern position from that of female victim, one whose body has been exploited by the patriarchal culture,[6] to that of active Subject. Rather than allow the males to appropriate all subject-positions,[7] woman (No Name Woman through her suicide and Maxine through her reportage of the forbidden tale) re-appropriates for herself the subject-position. Actually No Name Woman is both victim and victor, for she in turn victimizes the entire family—men and women—by temporarily denying them drinking water.

Her own victimization and subsequent act of vengeance continue to haunt the family. The men declare that her story never be told, but it is passed on to the next generation of women by another subaltern, Brave Orchid. Though the tale is told the young Maxine as a warning, it only succeeds in empowering her, for it is not only a cautionary tale about the victimization of those who defy tradition, but also about their strength and the power of protest. By spreading the story to the next generation, Brave Orchid re-assigns subject-positions for both No Name Woman and herself, involuntarily empowering herself and Maxine. She exacts her own vengeance by repeating the forbidden tale and, as the storyteller, assumes subjectivity for herself. Her's too is an act of insurgence against the will of the patriarchy. The tale, instead of warning Maxine into compliance with patriarchal wishes, motivates her to defiance by reiterating what she has begun to realize, namely the subalternity of woman's existence in patriarchal culture. Her resistance, resembling her mother's act of insurgence, takes Brave Orchid's "talk story" a step further. She begins her memoir with No Name Woman's story, and inscribing it as historical record, she re-assigns subject-positions for both No Name Woman and herself. By making it a part of her own memoir, she also succeeds in empowering future genera-tions of women in her family.

Loss of a name implies loss of identity, of familial continuity, and even personality. The story of No Name Woman echoes the struggle of all Chinese Americans in establishing their right to be counted as Americans in the face of Chinese Exclusion Acts, deportations, and laws denying them citizenship. They all have been, in a sense, 'No Name Persons.' Many had to change their names either to avoid deportation or to facilitate the processing of immigration papers. Maxine notices "The Chinese I know hide their names; sojourners take new names when their lives change and guard their real names with silence" (5). Margaret Miller too points out that often in Chinese culture children are not aware of their parents' and grandparents' names, as it is the position occupied by each family member within the family unit that takes precedence over their individuation as personali-ties (Miller 16). In the case of immigrant families the real names were often not disclosed in order to keep children from inadvertently giving away any secrets about illegal immigrant relatives. Many Chinese Americans often had several different names for different purposes, and identity was often flexible—a Chinese name for use amongst the Chinese community and an American name for immigration purposes.

In *The Woman Warrior*, when the rumor goes around that the U.S. Immigration authorities have set up headquarters in San Francisco, parents warn their children:

> Lie to Americans. Tell them you were born during the San Francisco earthquake. Tell them your birth certificate and your parents were burned up in the fire. (184)

Just as No Name Woman is denied identity within her Chinese community, Kingston is denied identity as an American writer by some critics within the literary community. Speaking of the reviews about her book, Kingston finds the "exotic-inscrutable-mysterious-oriental reviewing" ("Cultural Misreadings" 56) offensive. She feels that to say Chinese Americans are inscrutable, mysterious, and exotic "denies us our common humanness, because it says that we are so different from a regular human being that we are by our nature intrinsically unknowable" and "to call a people exotic freezes us into the position of being always alien" (57). She also objects to the ignorance about her nationality displayed in most of these reviews:

> Another bothersome characteristic of the reviews is the ignorance of the fact that I am an American. I am an American writer, who like other American writers, wants to write the great American novel. *The Woman Warrior* is an American book. Yet many reviewers do not see the American-ness of it, nor the fact of my own American-ness." (57-58).

They do not see its American-ness or recognize Kingston as an American writer because of the subject-position from which they read the book, and because of the positions they assign it as a representation of a marginal or subaltern experience and Kingston as a Chinese-American writer (Chinese-American with the hyphen).[8] They thus classify both her and the representations in her work as subaltern material. Even as Kingston attempts to establish her identity as a young Chinese woman growing up in America, she is denied her national identity by those reviewers who orientalize her work by praising it for its "strange and brooding atmosphere inscrutably foreign, oriental" ("Cultural Misreadings" 56). Kingston, reacting to such praise with, "How dare they call their ignorance our inscrutability" (56), finds that even those critics who perceive it as mainstream American literature (for example, Michael T. Molloy), criticize her for stepping out of the "exotic" role (57). Spivak's point, that in approaching works of cultural history one needs to be conscious of the assignment of subject-positions, applies also to the critical apparatus brought into play, which too employs its own set of subject-positions. On the one hand, critics who see Kingston's work as oriental, inscrutable, and foreign, do so because they have already assigned themselves a subject-position and Kingston and her work a subaltern one. On the other hand, Kingston's annoyance with such reviews indicates that, perceiving herself as a type of American, she assigns herself and her work subject-positions. Thus the dilineation of what is true and real and what is imagined and illusory changes constantly depending upon what subject-positions are being assigned and adopted by author, reader, and critic.

Within Kingston's narrative too subject-positions are always shifting. The demarkation between the real and the illusory or the mythic is never clear, and the reader is continually forced to examine the assignment and re-assignment of subject-positions within the text. The subtitle, "Memoirs of a Girlhood Among Ghosts," emphasizes the shifting ambiguity of narrative form and content. While the work proposes to be autobiographical, the word "memoir" allows it to take liberties with the objective factuality and chronology of events. The use of the word "ghosts" throws into question the objective reality of the characters, who are being represented intermittently through memory and the imagined recreations of reality and myth by the author.

The other "ghost" features in the narrative belong to Maxine's dreams and also originate from her mother's "talk story." They are the tales of the woman warrior, Fa Mu Lan and the epic poet, T'sai Yen. The stories of these two mythic characters run contrary to the reality of women's lives in Chinese culture, as both Fa Mu Lan and T'sai Yen are heroic figures who not only forge their individual destinies and personalities, but also locate themselves within familial and communal bonds. Maxine finally pulls together her differences from the ethnic community, her family, and American society and draws her connections with these mythic characters by insisting that she too can have a place within the ancestry of her Chinese family and still remain an individual in both her American-ness and her Chinese-ness.

The mother/daughter relationship, crucial for Kingston's final self actualization, directs the movement of the entire narrative. Kingston, having been raised in America, derives her experience and understanding of China and its culture through her parents, with her mother functioning as the primary source of information about her cultural heritage. As females and as members of subaltern classes, women of ethnic minorities find their valuation limited by the dominant culture as well as by the patriarchal structure of their own ethnic society. Maxine's early recognition of these limitations almost devastates and silences her. For example, the onset of the eighteen month mysterious illness results as the consequence of her inner conflict over confronting the quiet Chinese girl—an act of insurgence defying the patriarchy's silencing of woman. Instead of being silenced either by suicide, as in the case of No Name Woman, or by madness, as in the case of Moon Orchid, Maxine recovers from her illness and learns to talk again. Maxine establishes both her connection with and her distance from her mother by itemizing all the things she feels the need to tell Brave Orchid. Listing her grievances in this way allows Maxine to recognize the powerful role language plays in the oppressed individual's quest for identity.

Language finally allows Kingston to establish her identity as neither specifically Chinese nor specifically American, but rather as a Chinese American Woman. She owes her empowerment to her mother, who taught her the art of "talking story" and who also cut her frenum when she was little to allow her to speak in many tongues. As with the other tales in the narrative, where the distinction between reality and fiction is obscured continually, this tale too is fraught with ambiguity. Uncertain whether her mother cut her frenum to allow her to speak or to silence her, Maxine examining her frenum in the mirror, wonders if the whole incident isn't yet another "talk story." Nevertheless, inspite or because of the cut frenum, Maxine learns to speak with power and transcribes her mother's stories in a language foreign to their origins. Thus, by recreating these Chinese tales in English and paralleling them with her own story, she makes them her own; she makes them representative of her individual Chinese American identity. By speaking out about the truths forbidden her as a woman of Chinese culture, she empowers herself. Her mother's transgression of patriarchal ways through "talking story" the unspeakable and the forbidden, is taken beyond the oral tradition by Maxine who speaks these forbidden truths and myths out on paper.

Through the act of writing she understands and defines exactly who she is, someone that society, both Chinese and American, has not yet defined accurately—a Chinese American, whose experiences, while sometimes common with those of the Chinese, the Americans, and the men among whom she has grown up, differ greatly from all three groups to make her a unique individual, a Chinese American woman.

She belongs to the true subaltern class, one that frequently has been silenced not only by the dominant culture, the dominant sex, and the males of her subaltern class, but also has been made invisible. Spivak's political project, that of allowing the subaltern power to speak, is played out in this narrative of a young woman, who as a member of a subaltern class, inherits both the limitations and the tools for her survival from her mother and learns the lesson of speaking out. To speak out and define herself and her rightful place, she, of necessity, has to distance herself from her mother. Realizing her separateness and Otherness from men, from the Chinese, and from the Americans, she affirms her individual identity only by confirming her Otherness at all these three levels.

Despite her attempt to pull away from her mother, Maxine is more like Brave Orchid than she is willing to admit while growing up. Brave Orchid, despite patriarchal limitations imposed upon her, became an individual who exorcised ghosts, delivered babies, immigrated to America, worked the family laundry, and raised a family in a foreign country. The grown-up Maxine finally recognizes the great debt she owes her mother and her own instinctive connection with her before closing her narrative with the story of T'sai Yen: "Here is a story my mother told me, not when I was young, but recently, when I told her I also talk story. The beginning is hers, the ending mine" (206). It is impossible to distinguish where Brave Orchid's story ends and Maxine's version begins, for Maxine intertwines the stories and thus connects herself back with her beginnings. She, like her mother, also "talks stories"—only hers are written ones. Following in her mother's footsteps, she too is a pioneer who has exorcised her own ghosts and broken bonds of silence. Despite their differences, and possibly because of them, they are both engaged in a similar quest for individuation, for self, and for identity as woman, as Chinese, and as American. The evolution of Maxine's identity holds larger significance for all Asian Americans who, as the editors of *Aiiieeeee! An Anthology of Asian American Writers* explain, have been separated by geography, culture, and history from their land of origin (vii). As a result, the identities they will carve out for themselves will reflect cultures and sensibilities that are distinctly not Chinese, Japanese, Indian, Korean, or white American, but that are distinctly original and unique.

NOTES

1. See analyses by Jeanne Barker-Nunn ("Telling the Mother's Story: History and Connection in the Autobiographies of Maxine Hong Kingston and Kim Chernin" in *Women's Studies* 1987 14[1]:55-63), Patricia Lin Blinde ("The Icicle in the Desert: Perspective and Form in the Works of two Chinese-American Women Writers" in *Melus* Fall 1979 6[3]:51-71), Paul John Eakin (*Fictions in Autobiography: Studies in the Art of Self-Invention.* New Jersey: Princeton UP, 1985, 255-275), Suzanne Juhasz ("Maxine Hong Kinston: Narrative Technique and Female Identity" in *Contemporary American Women Writers: Narrative Strategies,* eds. Catherine Rainwater and William J. Scheick. Lexington: UP of Kentucky, 1985, 173-189), Margaret Miller ("Threads of Identity in Maxine Hong Kingston's *The Woman Warrior* in *Biography* Winter 1983, 13-33), Victoria Myers ("The Significant Fictivity of Maxine Hong Kingston's *The Woman Warrior*" in *Biography* Spring 1982, 9[2]:112-125), Veronica Wong ("Reality and Fantasy: The Chinese-American Woman's Quest for Identity" in *Melus* Fall 1985 12[3]:23-31), among others.

2. Throughout this essay I use the adjectival form, "Chinese American," rather than the hyphenated form, "Chinese-American," which is used only when quoting from another source. See also note 8 for Kingston's preference of the adjectival form over the compound noun.

3. Frank Chin and Jeffrey Paul Chan, in their essay, "Racist Love," analyze the unique condition of the "Chinese-American" as one who must struggle for acceptance and identity not only in white society, but also among the "real Chinese"—Chinese from China. The "Chinese-American," by virtue of having been born in America, is not considered native Chinese by the "real Chinese."

4. Receipt of the National Book Critics Circle Award 1976), the American Book Award (1980), and inclusion in *The Norton Anthology of Literature by Women* and in the *Columbia Literary History of the United States* all seem to prove Kingston's acceptance within the American Literary canon.

5. Elaine Kim too notes Frank Chin's argument regarding Asian American men being threatened by "the comparatively large number of Asian American women writers" and finds that they feel threatened because "Chin, Chan, and others have concluded that manliness means 'agressiveness, creativity, individuality, just being taken seriously,' while femininity means 'lacking daring, originality, aggressiveness, assertiveness, vitality'" (198). She also chides Chin and Chan for objecting to "Kingston's attempts to delineate her experiences from the point of view of a Chinese American woman" and for perceiving Kingston as trying to "cash in" on a "feminist fad."

6. Maxine wonders if No Name Woman's adultery was voluntary and whether the man responsible joined in with the rest of the villagers in shunning her; she also wonders whether the treatment meted out to her aunt would have differed had she given birth to a baby boy.

7. In *Speculum of the Other Woman* Irigaray points out that since any theory of the subject has been appropriated by the "masculine," woman is denied subjectivity. And, when woman submits to such a theory, she is "subjecting herself to objectivization in discourse—by being 'female'" (133).

8. Kingston, contrasting the terms Chinese American and Chinese-American, prefers the adjectival form over the compound noun: "And lately, I have been thinking that we ought to leave out the hyphen in 'Chinese-American,' because the hyphen gives the words on either side equal weight, as if linking two nouns. It looks as if a Chinese-American has double citizenship, which is impossible in today's world. Without the hyphen,...a Chinese American is a type of American" ("Cultural Misreadings" 60).

WORKS CITED

Chin, Frank, Jeffrey Paul Chan et al., eds. *Aiiieeeee! An Anthology of Asian-American Writers.* Washington D. C.: Howard UP, 1974.

Chin, Frank and Jeffrey Paul Chan. "Racist Love." *Seeing through Shuck.* Ed. Richard Kostelanetz. New York: Ballantine Books, 1972, 65-79.

Eakin, Paul John. *Fictions in Autobiography: Studies in the Art of Self-Invention.* New Jersey: Princeton UP, 1985.

Irigaray, Luce. *The Speculum of the Other Woman.* Ithaca: Cornell UP, 1985.

Kim, Elaine H. "Chinatown Cowboys and Warrior Women." *Asian American Literature: An Introduction to the Writings and their Social Context.* Philadelphia: Temple UP, 1982.

Kingston, Maxine Hong. "Cultural Misreadings by American Reviewers." *Asian and Western Writers in Dialogue: New Cultural Identities.* Ed. Guy Amirthanayagam. London: Macmillan P, 1982, 55-65.

____. *The Woman Warrior: Memoirs of a Girlhood Among Ghosts.* New York: Vintage Books, 1989.

Miller, Margaret. "Threads of Identity in Maxine Hong Kingston's *The Woman Warrior.*" *Biography* Winter 1983, 13-33.

Spivak, Gayatri Chakravorty. *In Other Worlds: Essays in Cultural Politics.* New York: Routledge, 1988.

—15—

Feminist Humorist of the 1920s: The "Little Insurrections" of Florence Guy Seabury

THOMAS GRANT

When the urbanization of America finally evolved into a self-consciously modern urban culture in the 1920s, centered in New York City, its resident humorists were mostly men, transplants from the country, who worked on the new magazine created specifically to celebrate metropolitan pleasures and opportunities, the *New Yorker*. Under founding editor, Harold Ross, these men, such as Robert Benchley and James Thurber, created the comic hero that readers of the magazine have come to love over the years—the neurotic "little man" who dreams of great conquests, only to fall victim to speeding cabs, gaping potholes, overbearing bosses— and, of course, nagging wives. That the "little man's" greatest nemesis was woman herself, best immortalized by the formidable Mrs. Ulgine Barrows in Thurber's story, "The Catbird Seat," shouldn't surprise us since Ross's operation on West 43rd Street was, by all accounts, an all-male preserve crowded with often-married, neurotic writers and artists with a deep, abiding distrust of, and in a few cases contempt for, women, particularly bright and liberated ones. This "jittery crew," as Thurber called them, was captained by a self-confessed prude, a misogynist, a homophobe and even a racist—Harold Ross, himself (1). Perhaps the misogynist streak down the back of *New Yorker* humor was provoked, if only indirectly, by women's push for political empowerment that followed the passage of the nineteenth amendment in 1920. Whatever the motive, the battle of the sexes, what Gilbert and Gubar have called the leitmotif of literary modernism, provoked by male perceptions of usurpation by self-possessed females, became the dominant comic mode in the magazine. The battle yielded a high casualty rate, including the cuckolded Leopold Bloom, the eunuch Jake Barnes, the paralyzed Clifford Chatterly, the castrated Joe Christmas—a company of maimed, victimized men to which one should add Thurber's meek and chinless dreamer, Walter Mitty (2).

When women wits entered the battle of the sexes, you would naturally assume they would fight on the side of their gender. However, the most celebrated woman humorists of the period—Dorothy Parker and Anita Loos—were rather comfortably entrenched in the enemy camp. Although Parker was one of the few women Ross hired for his new magazine, she contributed stories and poems in which the vain and vacuous men are seldom as intolerable as the women—sappy, obsequious and self-destructive. "Mrs. Parker," as she insisted on being known, always said she preferred the company of men and earned their praise by hurling her well-publicized barbs not at men but at *other women*. "You know," she once said of the amorous behavior of an accomplished contemporary, "that woman speaks 18 languages? And she can't say 'No' in any of them" (3). The gentlemen who prefer blondes may be, according to Anita Loos, dumb and dithering sugardaddies, but her heroine—Lorelei Lee—is no better: a conniving gold-digger who merely trades lucratively on male vanities. "I really think that American gentlemen are the best of all," swoons Lorelei, "because kissing your hand may make you feel very good but a diamond and safire bracelet lasts forever" (4). Loos herself, like Parker, became the darling of another male preserve, Hollywood, and parlayed her connections into a lucrative career writing screen romances that celebrated traditional gender stereotypes. Both writers mocked "little men" and the women who capitulated to their whims; but neither was able or willing to question the system of gender inequality they served.

While the battle of the sexes waged, other women wits were busy, however, chiding both the combatants and mocking the gender war itself. These were the radical feminists who were politically active in the suffrage movement during its most successful phase (1905-1915), and who, after the return to prosperity following the World War, continued to attack satirically gender inequalities in books of humor, in the women's column in urban newspapers and in essays in the more liberal cosmopolitan literary weeklies. Since they hoped to overturn traditional assumptions about gender, they perfected role-reversal or "What If" humor that comically dethroned men and elevated the "weaker sex," in order to separate readers gently from comfortable but self-serving attitudes and thus expose male hegemony as the absurd folly it is. Unlike the *New Yorker* humorists, they were not interested in settling scores, but in abolishing competition altogether and replacing it with cooperation between the genders, to the benefit of society as a whole (5). All of these feminist humorists were widely read in their day but are now completely forgotten. They include Josephine Dodge Daskim Bacon, Alice Duer Miller, and Helen Rowland. The least known of this "lost generation" was Florence Guy Woolston Seabury (1881-1951). During the 1920s, she published elegant and pithy essays in the more progressive magazines of the day in which she wittily dissected changing gender relations in urban America and in so doing fully realized the satirical possibilities of the polemical essay now written by feminists like Gloria Steinem, Barbara Ehrenreich and Anne Wilson Schaef.

Unlike the *New Yorker* wits of the period, Florence Woolston was not a provincial who was content with being easily amused by the tolerable discomforts of urban life. Instead, she was a New Yorker who was steeped in the harsher inequities of class-bound urban America. Biographical details are scarce, but she was a graduate of Columbia and the New York School of Social Work, and she worked in the settlement house movement on the lower East Side in the early part of this century. In 1912, she became editor of the radical monthly, *The Woman Voter,* the official organ of the Woman's Suffrage Party and a member of "Heterodoxy," a kind of consciousness-raising group based in Greenwich Village, far from the *New Yorker's* New York, for "unorthodox women," according to Mabel Dodge Luhan, a member, "that is to say, women who did things and did them openly." Clubmembers totaled about 110 and included heterosexual and lesbian feminists from all walks of life, many of whom met for lunch every two weeks to exchange ideas and to entertain one another. "All the Heterodox women," said Luhan, "were fine, daring, rather joyous and independent women" (6). Leftist journalist Randolph Bourne was even more effusive:

> They shock you constantly....They have an amazing combination of wisdom and youthfulness, of humor and ability, an innocence and self-reliance, which

absolutely belies everything you read in the story-books or any other description of womankind. They are of course all self-supporting and independent, and they enjoy the adventure of life; the full, reliant, audacious way in which they go about makes you wonder if the new woman isn't to be a very splendid sort of person. (7)

Members included nearly all the most celebrated women of the times, such as Agnes de Mille, Crystal Eastman, Zona Gale, Charlotte Perkins Gilman, Susan Glaspell and Fannie Hurst.

Florence Guy Woolston was apparently one of the more obscure members of Heterodoxy—and seemed destined to remain so. In a photo album dedicated to founder Marie Jennie Howe, in which members paid tribute to her leadership beneath their photographs, Seabury's is notable for its self-effacement:

Writing a sentiment for your album is like being asked to make a confession of love in public. I know it is done in the best Heterodite circles, but early Victorian hangovers make me prefer a quaint corner in which to tell you what you know already—the name Marie's spelled deep in my life.

F. Seabury (8)

Her only known contribution to the club's entertainment, at least in print, is an accomplished parody of *The Family* (1906) by noted anthropologist and Heterodox clubmember Elsie Clewe Parsons, called "Marriage Customs and Taboo Among the Early Heterodites," published in *Scientific Monthly* (1919), complete with mock etymologies and mock footnotes. Just as the academic style of the new social science was congealing into jargon, Seabury mimics it expertly to dissect this "tribe of women living on the Island of Manhattan": "The early Heterodites are generally housed in caves, piled perpendicularly. A cross section would resemble a honey-comb—(Huinigcamb)." One paragraph summarizes "marriage customs":

Three types of sex relationships may be observed, practiced by those who call themselves monotonists, varietists and resistants. Most of the monotonists were mated young and by pressure of habit and circumstance have remain mated. The varietists have never been ceremonially mated but have preferred a succession of matings. The resistants have not mated at all. These classes are not at all arbitrary. Some monotonists have practiced variety secretly. Some varietists would like to become monotonists because the marriage union label is useful in some lines of professional work. Many of the monotonists wear rings to show that they have passed through the ceremonial and are nominally the exclusive possession of some male. The scientific observer, however, should not be led astray by outward totems because I have discovered several instances of ring wearing which are deceptive—rings not having been given by the ceremonial mate. Some of the varietists distinguish themselves by short hair, but again, this is not an infallible sign for one or two varietists wear switches or even transformations. (9)

Sometime in the late teens, Florence Guy Woolston met and married David Seabury, a psychologist who became well known and influential until well in the 1950s for his many books on modern applied psychology. Like many of the active feminists, she became interested in the Gestalt psychology, pioneered by Carl Jung, which was more sympathetic to woman's psychology and to healing conflicts between the genders than was its competitors, the new Freudianism and Behaviorism (10). Later, she taught the new science at Briarcliff Junior College—but for how long is not known. In the early 1920s, she began to contribute to *The Nation* and *Harper's,* generally high-brow magazines representing a liberal Eastern metropolitan point of view, and *The New Republic,* a more liberal weekly, begun in 1914, that professed to be carrying the torch of Progressivism after the movement itself flickered out in the aftermath of the World War. *The New Republic* was dedicated to extended political analysis, reasonableness and a muted wit. "*The New Republic* Idea," according to spiritual father and first editor, Herbert Croly, was "less to inform and entertain its readers than to start little insurrections in the realm of their convictions" (11). Florence Seabury fulfilled Croly's mission more wittily than most. Typically, her essays are framed as mock psychological case studies of the modern American male who is caricatured as the befuddled and beleaguered breadwinner stripped of his traditional dominance and thus unable to cope with his wife, who has become, inexplicably to him, independent and modern. Her bumblers resemble Thurber's, but they are objects of mockery rather than empathy. Perry Winship, the delicatessen husband of an essay so titled (*TNR,* April 25, 1923) is reduced to living, quips the narrator, "from can to mouth" (12), jostling crowds in grocery lines to bring to his apartment "his share of the canned tongue and chicken wings," while his wife, Ethel, is busy as a professional chemist—and pondering what went wrong:

All women, he believed, are domestic at heart and if the desire for cooking and dish washing has been unnaturally suppressed, marriage will miraculously unfold it. (p. 32)

The reversal of gender roles subverts Perry's assumptions about true womanhood learned in childhood:

Perry keeps a little flower under his mother's picture on the chiffonier. After all, she was his ideal of the true and womanly. Never in her busy life did she permit her husband or any of her four sons to eat food prepared or cooked out of the sacred precincts of the home kitchen. Perry told Ethel recently that he doubts if he can maintain his morale much longer on canned salmon, tuna fish, bologna sausage, frankfurters, cold ham and potato salad. (p. 35)

Clearly, a major cause of man's resistance to gender equality is the treasonable truth: his own dependence on women—since the cradle. In the "case" of Arnold Hutchins in another essay, "The Sheltered Sex" (*TNR,* April 4, 1923), Seabury dispels man's delusion of independence:

Before his marriage Mrs. Hutchins, Senior, mothered him intensively, and when she passed him on to Ann, it was a sacred trust. Outwardly, he was a big, robust man, with a powerful voice, but his mother regarded him as a delicate orchid or a fragile lily. Ann had a talent for music, and was hoping for a modest career even after marriage, but the job of shielding Arnold from the disturbing contacts of life has occupied all her time and effort in the last twenty years. (pp. 44-45)

The workplace, like the home, is built on the theory of masculine protection:

In every well-regulated office a cordon of women employees vie with each other to keep the outside world from permeating the inner sanctum. A young girl answers the telephone and prevents access of any but the acceptable; a woman secretary is always on duty as buffer and custodian of the sacred presence; feminine stenographers, bookkeepers and file clerks carry on the drab routine, while "he" sits majestically in an inner chamber. (p. 49)

Since men are excluded from the only primal activity experienced by women, childbearing, they must insist on a male God to affirm their superiority, their divinity. Thus are men trapped in what Seabury calls "The Masculine Dilemma" (*Nation,* Nov. 12, 1924):

a curious paradox that while men are treated as gods, as superior beings to be worshipped and obeyed at the same time they are regarded as children whose womankind direct and sustain them. Who does not know the secret councils of the kitchen cabinet where a man's nearest female relatives get together to plan his conduct? The mother-heart and the wifely love, the sister's discernment and the daughter's sagacity are a compass to guide the perpetual small boy, the incurable child, to a harbor of safety. (p. 266)

By contrast, women live in the real world, enduring, quips the narrator, "with a baby in one arm and a husband in the other" (p. 51).

Seabury's indictments are of course familiar ones today; but they are so suavely and succinctly phrased that one hardly feels the knock-out punch. As these examples indicate, She maintains the restrained pose of the clinical psychologist, which, together with her command of scientific method, gives added authority to her stinging mockery. The modern American male not only *has* a "case" of the jitters, as well he should in the face of woman's legitimate threat to his autonomy, but he *is* a "case"—the gender in dire need of therapy and cure. Typically, Seabury's mock case studies resolve on a conciliatory note, in favor of rescuing men from their enslavement to outmoded traditions. Clearly, Seabury's main charge is the central one of feminists, before and since: a "patriarchal system" (p. 154) that encourages double standards to flourish, to the detriment ultimately of both genders. In an essay called "Albertism" (*TNR,* Dec. 14, 1921), Seabury argues that being a Prince Consort rather than King could be liberating for men rather than humiliating:

Deft, capable and tender, they are sometimes much more understanding than women, yet ignoring the fact that the sense of nurture is human and not masculine or feminine, we patronizingly regard these great gifts as something unworthy of a man. (p. 232)

Under a new realignment of duties, Albertism,

a man with domestic inclinations will not have to slink along through life with the apologetic air of a man in a woman's club. (p. 227)

Seabury's call for true gender equality reveals the influence of Jung's theory of transcendence, in which marital harmony is achieved by a synthesis of opposites, anima (masculine) and animus (feminine) so that gender itself, except in a biological sense, is abolished (13). One of the professional advocates of this new social ideal, what Jungian therapists of the period called "companionate marriage" (14), was David Seabury, whose 1924 book, *Unmasking Our Minds,* was dedicated to his wife. He called his Centralism, and its aim was "full liberation and wise direction of the deeper and finer forces of the nature by the principle of their affirmative emphasis, in place of the archaic method of accentuating and controlling evils" (15).

While the sensible, conciliating voice of feminist social scientist dominates her many essays, another, harsher voice at times penetrates the veneer of genial humor, that of the radical socialist. If men persist in keeping women submissive to their power and privilege, their delusions are fed by the new agent of industrial capitalism, consumerism. In "Journals for Gentlemen" (*TNR*, Feb. 22, 1922), she critiques men's fashion:

> They are not permitted to be beautiful. We do not even allow them to make the best of whatever nature has given them, unless they are matinee heroes or moving-picture players. The rigid attitude which allies masculine beauty with weakness and any deviation from the standards of ugly apparel as eccentric or vainglorious has created a passion for similarity in dress. Men's clothes stamped like so many Ford parts are an identical combination of monotonous cylinders. (p. 151)

She also attacks popular fiction, fashion magazines and advertising. "This is," she says, "concededly a period of up-keep" (p. 157). She could, of course, be surveying our own time, especially when she describes the arrival of the man's fashion magazine:

> A beauty editor could wage a crusade for cosmetics, offering prizes for pictures of men before and after they turned their attention to this important matter. Timely special articles by famous actors and opera singers would prove a valuable feature. Barrymore on "The Use and Abuse of Hair Dye": Valentino on "The When and the Where of Rouge." (p. 159)

Nor is Seabury soft on women who follow fashions, the latest political ones, from child labor to better housing, or social ones, from Freudianism to Free Thought—but without conviction or commitment. In "Gustatory Evolution" (*TNR*, May 31, 1922), Seabury sardonically mocks fellow leftists encased in their ideological shells and thus unable to adapt in swiftly changing times. Radicals are crustaceans that come in three varieties:

> hard-shelled orthodox "Reds" with a theology as set as an old-fashioned Puritan; mottled, red and white soft-shelled theorists, crawling constantly toward mere liberalism, and last, and most prevalent—the gustatory radicals—that host of pale, pink thinkers who have eaten their way from conservation through years of public dinners. (*TNR*, p. 17)

Jasmine Jewett is one of the last, a liberated WASP wife of a Wall Street banker who has supped lightly at the endless banquet of social causes and now longs for a second coming of free speech. Meanwhile, says the author,

> she is dining for culture. She has joined a society which feeds celebrities and makes them all tell the story of their lives in ten minutes.... At other times, she hears speeches on Disarmament, Psychic Phenomena and Relativity. But being a

gustatory isn't what it used to be. Where once, they ate for anarchy with wine, now it's water for general information. (*TNR*, p. 18)

In "The Professional Understander" (*TNR*, Jan. 25, 1922), Seabury sheds the mask of the genial wit altogether to attack male amateur psychologists who presume to understand women best and parlay this bogus authority into advice for profit:

The P.U. is as different from the ordinary amateur man who merely thinks he knows all about women as the waxed-mustached Paris dressmaker is from the husband whose thumbs button up his wife's waist. The P.U. is an efficiency expert on the subject of women. There is nothing hidden that shall not be revealed—to him. (p. 190)

Women themselves are willing accomplices in this power play. Both conspire to make counselling itself just another commodity that sells:

Whatever happens, women must be serial-indexed and card-catalogued. Understanding women pays. (p. 198)

If the Heterodox clubmembers were as buoyant and playful as Randolph Bourne thought in the 1910s, their good humor was doubtless inspired by part by rising expectations for the suffrage cause. For many, however, laughter turned to dismay and then disillusionment and bitterness when the vote failed to produce concrete and permanent social and material improvements for women. By the mid 1920s, the Socialist cause had been swept aside by the "Back to Prosperity" parade stage-managed under the reign of three reactionary Republican administrations. By the late 1920s real and lasting improvements in gender relations became even less likely, and vanished utterly in the Great Depression, not to be reclaimed until the mid 1960s (16). Seabury herself remained optimistic and conciliatory, in her essays at least, but she left the magazine scene by the end of the decade. In the mid 1930s, she resurfaced as a professional psychologist with her own book on modern applied therapy, *Love is a Challenge* (1935), a learned text with a preface by her husband. The book is remarkably jargon-free and lively, but the gifted comic storyteller is replaced by the clinical social scientist, perhaps a persona better suited to decidedly less cheerful times. In this, "Our Phallic Age," says Seabury

In place of the understanding of human contacts we load young people with don'ts of behavior. Even worse, we bequeath them a set of ancient patterns of emotion, equipping them with stereotypes which belong to other days, encouraging a romanticism which wars with reality.

Egotism is the most conspicuous blockage to love, she concludes, as have the classical satirists since Aristophanes, observing that: "we think about ourselves so much because we know ourselves so little" (17).

In a recent interview, columnist Ellen Goodman, explained what she does in a column by using her hands to form a small oval space in front of her and then twisting the imaginary issue slowly:

> This is the way people are looking at it.... Let's turn it around and look at it another way. And to the degree you can make people turn it around and look at it another way every time, and make them think of something a little different-ly...that is the reaction I want people to have. (18)

Although Seabury was more ideologically feminist than is Goodman, she was an astute and penetrating social observer who was practicing the same method—shifting our perspective on an issue, in order to make us rethink comfortable and self-serving beliefs—and make the discovery of refreshing truths seem not only morally correct but eminently reasonable. Thus, her "little insurrections started in people's convictions," to recall Croly's mission for *New Republic* essayists, like the gently subversive writings of her contemporary radical feminists, provided a healthy antidote to the vengeful humor of James Thurber, the self-lacerating wit of Dorothy Parker, not to mention the vitriolic diatribes of H.L. Mencken. Whatever influence, if any, she had among readers of the *New Republic* and *The Nation* is not known, since she was shadowed by the liberal luminaries of the period, such as Walter Lippmann, Lewis Mumford, Edmund Wilson and Margaret Sanger. Yet she can be called one of the mothers of the contemporary feminist essay, who, along with the other lost wits of early twentieth-century feminism, deserves in this persistent "Phallic Age" to be re-discovered.

NOTES

1. *The Years with Ross* (Boston: Little, Brown, 1957), p. 87. Chroniclers of the *New Yorker* story, of course, abound, but for a candid and apparently accurate account of the magazine's undisguised misogyny, see Brendall Gill, *Here at the New Yorker* (New York: Random House, 1975).
2. Sandra M. Gilbert and Susan Gubar, *No Man's Land: The Place of the Woman Writer in the Twentieth Century,* Volume 1: "The War of the Words" (New Haven: Yale University Press), Chapter 1.

3. Quoted in Thomas Grant, "Dorothy Parker," *American Humorists*, Part 2, ed. Stanley Trachtenberg (Detroit: Gale, 1982), p. 370.

4. Anita Loos, *Gentlemen Prefer Blondes: The Illuminating Diary of a Professional Lady,* (New York: Liveright, 1925), p. 100. See also Grant, "Anita Loos," *American Humorists*, Part 1, ed. Trachtenberg, pp. 283-291.

5. The distinctively conciliatory nature of women's humor is ably examined by Nancy A. Walker, *A Very Serious Thing: Women's Humor and American Culture* (Minneapolis: University of Minnesota Press, 1988).

6. *Intimate Memoirs* (New York: Harcourt, Brace, 1936), III, 143-144.

7. Quoted in Nancy Cott, *The Grounding of Modern Feminism* (New Haven: Yale University Press, 1987), pp. 34-35.

8. Irwin Inez Haynes Collection, "Heterodoxy to Marie," Schlesinger Library, Radcliffe College.

9. Reprinted from *Scientific Monthly* (November, 1919) in Judith Schwarz, *Radical Feminists of Heterodoxy in Greenwich Village* (Lebanon, NH: New Victoria Publishers, 1982), Appendix B.

10. Demaris S. Wehr, *Jung and Feminism* (Boston: Beacon Press, 1987), Chapter 1.

11. Quoted in David Seideman, *The New Republic: A Voice of Modern Liberalism* (New York: Praeger, 1986), p. 68.

12. Reprinted in *The Delicatessen Husband and Other Essays* (New York: Harcourt, Brace, 1926), p. 30. Page references hereafter cited in the text.

13. *Jung and Feminism,* p. 46.

14. Cott, p. 156.

15. (Harcourt, Brace, 1924), xxxi.

16. See various essays in "Women in the Modern World," *Annals of the American Academy of Political and Social Sciences,* CXLIII (May, 1929).

17. (New York: Whittlesey House, 1936), p. 8.

18. Quoted in Neil A. Grauer, *Wits and Sages* (Baltimore: Johns Hopkins University Press, 1984), p. 164.

16

Irony and Ambiguity in Grace King's "Monsieur Motte"

ZITA Z. DRESNER

Born in 1851, the same year as Kate Chopin (or in 1852 or 1853—the sources vary), Grace King gained a reputation as a southern writer of fiction at the end of the Reconstruction period, but unlike Chopin, she has, until very recently, received relatively little critical attention, especially from feminist scholars, and she has not been included in anthologies of American writers, even those compiled by female editors. A selection of her writings, *Grace King of New Orleans,* edited and introduced by Robert Bush, was published in 1973; and two biographies—one by David Kirby, for Twayne (1980) and one by Robert Bush for LSU Press (1983)—have appeared. Despite the fact that both her biographers claim to see a feminist slant in her work, only Anne Goodwyn Jones, in *Tomorrow Is Another Day* (LSU Press, 1981), devoted critical attention to her work prior to her treatment in two recent publications that reflect the current interest in race and gender studies: Helen Taylor's *Gender, Race, and Region in the Writings of Grace King, Ruth McEnery Stuart, and Kate Chopin* (LSU Press, 1989) and Anna Shannon Elfenbein's *Women on the Color Line* (UP of Virginia, 1989).

One reason for King's neglect may well be her sense of herself as an apologist for and defender of the South. Robert Bush writes that "she was never a New South author with a fully conciliatory national spirit" and that, throughout her life, she kept bright her memories of the sufferings of New Orleans' residents under Union occupation and her sense of the humiliations undergone by her family and friends under Reconstruction (5). Consequently, he argues, she could not accept reconciliation with the North or relinquish her allegiance to the upper-class Louisiana whites who sought to reestablish their political power. Moreover, her attitude toward blacks seems typical of her social class and time period: patronizing and paternalistic. In fact, anyone who has ever read anything about Grace King, if asked to recall one thing about her, would probably repeat the point made in all sources that the impetus for her writing was to refute George W. Cable's critical portrait of Louisiana Creoles and "his preference for colored people over white and...quadroons over the Creoles" (King qtd. in Bush 8), by presenting portraits of Creoles as *she* knew them and of positive relationships between the races. Because her attitudes, whatever her intent, were based on a belief in white superiority, those critics and scholars who have been involved in reclaiming and promoting the work of women writers—who have argued that these writers were relegated to minor status, or misinterpreted or ignored, because of gender or gender/race discrimination—may be discomforted, if not outrightly offended, by at least some aspects of King's treatment of black characters.

A second possible reason why King's work has remained in relative obscurity may be its specificity. As the title of her second book, *Tales of a Time and Place,* suggests, King's fiction is rooted in the regionalism that inspired the vogue of local-color literature in the 1880s and 1890s, the decades in which her work appeared in *Harper's* and *Century* magazines. As the popularity of such literature faded after the turn of the century, so did King's reputation and general interest in her work. Further, as Joan Myers Weimer points out in "Women Artists as Exiles in the Fiction of Constance Fenimore Woolson" (*Legacy* Fall 1986: 3-15), the work of writers like Woolson, Mary E. Wilkins Freeman, Sarah Orne Jewett, and Kate Chopin was trivialized and derogated by the dismissive labels of "local color" or "regional" writing applied to it by male critics. However, while these women have had their fiction re-evaluated and recognized for its universality and artistry, King, by and large, has not. As suggested earlier, her tendency to focus on the upper class of Creole society, her view of blacks, and her concern with the negative effects of Reconstruction on the white patricians of the Old South, whose social positions and material wealth were lost with the Confederate cause, may simply provide too great a barrier for critics to overcome before being able to sympathize with her characters and/or perceive her purpose as anything but racist propaganda.

Despite these factors, those who have grappled with her life and work find her fiction intriguing for a number of reasons. First, King, like other American women who began writing after the Civil War, was a realist who rejected sentimentality for irony and was among the first American women writers of fiction who, as Weimer avers, "saw themselves not just as professionals but as artists...competing with male writers not just for readers but for laurels" (3). In fact, King envisioned herself as something of a social historian as well as a serious fiction writer, infusing her stories with historical fact and describing, with great perceptiveness, both her own time and the history of New Orleans and its environs.

Second, the central emphasis throughout King's fiction is on portraying the concerns and problems of women, on exploring the nature of women's lives, and on depicting the feelings and experiences of women, especially as these cut across the lines of class and race. That King consciously wrote from a female point of view is clearly expressed in her three page introduction to *Balcony Stories* (1892), which evokes a tone and setting for this third collection of stories that is evident as well in her previous work: "There is much life passed on the balcony in a country where the summer unrolls in six moon-lengths.... And in that country the women love to sit and talk together of summer nights, on balconies, in their vague, loose, white garments...with their sleeping children within easy hearing.... Experiences, reminiscences, episodes picked up as only women know how to pick them up from other women's lives—or other women's destinies, as they prefer to call them—and told as only women know how to relate them...." In addition to their female-centered consciousness and voice, her stories also focus mainly on female characters: particularly older women, often spinsters and widows, girls on the brink of womanhood, and black servants. In dealing with the political, social, and economic effects of the war and Reconstruction on the lives of their characters, the stories celebrate female strength and resilience in the face of disaster or loss and the enduring force of the bonds of affection between women.

Perhaps the most compelling reason for reexamining King's fiction, however, is that her use of irony in treating the collapse of the old regime and the reversals in social position and material wealth that followed the Civil War gives her stories a special flavor—a mix of sympathy and humor that often forces the reader to draw his/her own conclusions about an ambiguous character or situation. Indeed, as Helen Taylor asserts, King's "heavy use of irony" is instrumental in exposing "the ambivalences and anxieties of southern women of her time and place" concerning gender, class, and race relations; and these inconsistencies are provocative enough, in themselves, to warrant for King's work further critical attention ("The Case of Grace King," *The Southern Review* Fall 1982: 700-702). Moreover, it is King's irony that commentators on King have mentioned most frequently and used most consistently to support or refute interpretations of King's views on gender and race. However, it seems to me that the irony in King's fiction serves more to underscore than to reduce the ambivalences, creating ambiguities (in William Empson's use of the term) of meaning and purpose in King's work. According to Empson, ambiguity stems from the reader's response, which depends upon the social contexts of discourse that the reader brings to the work, and "gives room for alternative reactions to the same piece of language" (Eagleton 52-53). Indeed, as the following discussion of "Monsieur Motte," King's first published story, argues, it is the interplay of ironies—those intended by King, those seemingly unintended by King but expressed by the text of the story, and those perceived by the reader who brings to the text a set of values and beliefs about gender and sex different from those professed by King—that results in the ambiguities, or *aporia* (irresolvable moments), that enhance the interest in King's fiction for the contemporary reader. These ambiguities, moreover, derive from the contradictions encoded in the texts of King's fiction by her conscious and subconscious use of opposing systems of signification that reflect her own ambivalence about the ideologies of class, race, and gender prevalent in her time and place.

Supposedly written by King on a dare from Richard Gilder, editor of *Century Magazine,* to provide a truer picture of Creoles than Cable did, "Monsieur Motte" is set in the Institute St. Denis, an aristocratic French Creole school for girls in New Orleans, similar to the one King, herself, attended. The story focuses on the relationship between Marie Modeste, a student at the school who is about to graduate, and Marcelite, a quadroon hairdresser, who has been supporting Marie since she was a small child by pretending that she, Marcelite, was the servant of a nonexistent uncle of Marie's, named M. Motte. The complication of the plot, which provides the context for character development, is that Marie's graduation will require her to leave the school where she has been boarding since the age of four. Since she, as well as her classmates and the school's headmistress, Madame Lareveillere, expect that she will go to live with her uncle,

Marcelite is finally forced to admit her deception and reveal that M. Motte does not exist. The dilemma of what to do with Marie after Marcelite's revelation is resolved by Mme. Lareveillere's decision to take Marie in; for once Marcelite proves that Marie is the daughter of Marcelite's former owners and, therefore, white, there is no question of Marie's living with Marcelite despite her support of and devotion to the girl for thirteen years.

As this brief synopsis suggests, the story raises significant questions central to its meaning: How is the reader supposed to respond to Marcelite? to Marie? to the relationship between them? For the contemporary reader who has been reared on the concept of racial equality rather than inequality, King's portrayal of the characters' unquestioning acceptance of a racist caste system—a system that makes Marcelite's sacrifices appear shameful, almost criminal—could well evoke indignation at both Marcelite and Marie, who have imbibed, and at Madame, whose school has inculcated, white society's belief in Negro inferiority. For this reader, the irony on which the story turns, that M. Motte does not exist, becomes not just incongruous but almost irrelevant, because the purpose for which he was created is unacceptable, a racist conceit. This reader would find it impossible to acknowledge King's premise that a black woman would, first of all, devote herself and her life entirely to bringing up a white child, especially the child of those to whom she was enslaved, and, more important, would educate that child in the same way her slave-owner parents would have, thereby ensuring that the girl would end up rejecting, if not biting, the hand that fed her. On the other hand, King's intentions are still ambiguous and her ironies unresolved even if one accepts King's premises about Marcelite. This is because the character herself represents the duality inherent in King's statement to her mentor, Charles Dudley Warner, about the creation of Marcelite: "Great instances of devotion were found among even the worst treated slaves; I love to dwell on this, what I would call, holy passion of the Negro women, for it serves to cancel those other grosser ones, with which they are really victimised by their blood" (Bush, 14). Because King is unable to provide a plausible bridge between the two extremely divergent aspects of character that she seeks to use to define Marcelite—because, in a sense, the the meaning of the signified (Marcellite) is entangled in various chains of conflicting signifiers—the narrative evokes reader responses and interpretations that contradict each other, adding another layer of irony and/or ambiguity to the story.

One problem King faces in her conceptualization of Marcelite is that, in order to illustrate the power of the black woman's love for the white child,

Marcelite is depicted throughout most of the story as a commanding and heroic figure—strong, resourceful, independent, and proud. Although at the bottom of the southern social scale, as a woman and a black, she possesses the courage and imagination to fabricate a mask for herself of those at the top, the patrician white male M. Motte, in order to provide Marie with the education and material goods that only such an individual could afford. As hairdresser to the headmistress, faculty, and students of the Institut St. Denis, as well as to other society women, she is economically independent and socially indispensable, drawing power from other women's dependence on her abilities to make them attractive—the most important goal in their lives, because their attractiveness to a large degree determines and maintains their social and economic position. Marcelite's power gives her the self-confidence and air of defiance we witness upon her entrance into the story, when Jeanne, the white gatekeeper of the school, refuses to open the big gate for her to enter the grounds because, King writes, "She [Jeanne] was maintaining her own in a quarrel begun years ago; a quarrel involving complex questions of the privileges of order and the distinctions of race; a quarrel in which hostilities were continued, year by year, with no interruption of courtesy or mitigation of truce" (17). Marcelite, however, unintimidated by Jeanne's hostility, threatens to ring "Madame's bell," forcing Jeanne to back down and open the gate to avoid a reprimand that would "quickly reverse their relative positons by a bonus to Marcelite" (18). Finally, in addition to her pride, Marcelite, as self-appointed guardian to Marie, is shown to exhibit a deep devotion to and selfless love for the white child that are undeniably impressive and redemptive, however incomprehensible or unacceptable they may appear to some, or even most, readers.

Because of these strong, positive qualities, as Anne Goodwyn Jones points out, it is Marcelite who, ironically, best and most fully "embodies the ideal that King adumbrated" in her depiction of the major female characters in the story. "But Marcelite is black," Jones continues. "How can a white southern woman put her authorial voice into a black woman?" (104). How, indeed? One possible answer to this question is that King does not in fact do so. Helen Taylor supports this response by arguing that King never forgets that Marcelite is black, making constant references full of contempt to that blackness and having Marcelite express self-hate for it (57). Jones, on the other hand, suggests that the dilemma may be resolved by seeing the narrator as one who "associates Marcelite's behavior with that of all women" who are oppressed (104) and by positing, therefore, "that King's emotional identification went strongly into the creation of

Marcelite, for she represents in the extreme the condition of the white southern woman" (105). The difficulty with Jones's interpretation, however, is that it does not, as Jones herself admits, account for the story's ending, which, in Jones's words "must see the alien civilization as black, not male" (105).

In fact, viewing King's narrative voice as identified with Marcelite seems to make the conclusion even more ambiguous—and the meaning more elusive—than it might appear to the reader who acknowledges King's racist assumptions. For they at least *do* account for two possible readings. First, if one takes King's statement to Warner seriously, then the strength of Marcelite's character and devotion to Marie can be read as further valorizing the white woman who inspires such qualities in the black woman. Second, implicit acceptance of the South's racist caste system makes plausible the impossibility of Marie going to live with Marcelite without Marie becoming an outcast and eschewing the future for which Marcelite has striven to prepare her. Thus, although it may appear to many readers either incongruous or a gross miscarriage of justice that Marcelite's place as surrogate mother to Marie is usurped by Mme. Lareveillere simply because Marcelite is black and Madame, white, the story's ending reinforces the ideology that the best chance for happiness for those living within the racist social system of the post-bellum South is adherence to that system. That none of the characters would be better off or happier for bucking that system is an irony discernable only to the reader who views King's sympathy as lying primarily with Marcelite and who, consequently, infers that the apparent discrepancy between Marcelite's sacrifices and rewards is intended by King to call into question the institutions and values that foster such an injustice. I personally cannot read such intentions into the narrative, agreeing with Helen Taylor that "King's southern apologist and orthodox racial lines" (33) infuse all of her work. However, because the relationship between Marie and Marcelite leads to an impasse of resolvability, an *aporia,* the text of "Monsieur Motte" may be read as both racist and nonracist, or as a dialogue between the social ideology that King consciously accepted and conflicting, perhaps subconscious, feelings about gender and race derived from her personal experiences as a southern woman whose patrician upbringing had included being served by black slaves and servants.

Like much of King's subsequent work, "Monsieur Motte" opens itself to these varied, often conflicting perceptions of how irony is inscribed and meant to function in the narrative as an indicator of meaning, mainly because of the ambiguities evident in the depiction of her female characters—white as well as black. As stated earlier, Marcelite's positive qualities dominate much of the story, thus evoking for her from the reader enormous empathy and admiration. There is also no doubt that, when Monsieur Goupilleau, Madame's friend and adviser, exclaims at the close of the story, "They say, Eugenie, that the days of heroism are past, and they laugh at our romance" (King 103), the word "heroism" alludes at least in part, if not wholly, to the sacrifices of Marcelite for Marie. Since Marcelite is given an heroic dimension by King, readers may well find it difficult to simultaneously experience her character as the degraded, primitive, savage, helpless individual that King would have her race make her. How can the Marcelite of the beginning of the story—self-contained, defiant, and in control of herself and her environment—be reconciled with the Marcelite who appears at the end—a "panting, tottering, bedraggled wretch," with her clothes torn, her skin scratched and bleeding, groveling at the feet of the petit-bourgeois Monsieur Goupilleau, calling him "Master" and flagellating herself with the word "nigger"?

Even if one accepts King's conception of the double nature of black women and her premise that what empower and ennoble Marcelite are her love for Marie and her adoption of the *persona* of M. Motte, the discrepancies in King's depiction of Marcelite seem to resist fusion. This occurs because, as Elfenbein suggests, "the role she [Marcelite], along with everyone else, assumes that she, as a Negro, must play,...[is] a role too small for the person she has become" (103). And the role is too small because King, in her desire to illustrate the transforming effects on black women of their "holy passion" for white women, created a character who, ironically (though probably unintentionally so) is *not* contained by the parameters of racist ideology that the narrative attempts to construct for her.

It appears to me that there are two main reasons for this "failure" on King's part to circumscribe what Marcelite's characterization signifies. The first has to do with the fact that the mask of M. Motte, while presented as both weapon and shield for Marcelite, is actually neither. King wrote in a transitional passage between the original "Monsieur Motte" and the story that became Part II of *Monsieur Motte* that "unmasked, stripped of disguise," Marcelite loses "her nerve and audacity" and is reduced to playing the "part of a faithful servant" when "as Monsieur Motte, what could she not do?" While it is true that Marcelite's fabrication of M. Motte allowed her to become a covert surrogate mother for Marie, overtly she presented herself only as his and Marie's "faithful servant." Since she never pretended to *be* M. Motte, Marcelite did not, by creating him,

liberate herself from the constraints of racism or gain for herself opportunities that she would not otherwise have enjoyed—except for the "opportunity" to maintain a relationship with Marie in which she, Marcelite,
continued to do what slaves had always been expected to do: physically
take care of and economically provide for their masters. In addition, as
Elfenbein argues, the fictional existence of M. Motte masks "the racism
and sexism that infect their [Marie and Marcelite's] relationship" and
"prevent both women from confronting the ironies and similarities of their
constrained roles" (101).

Even more significant, Marcelite's power and independence in the world
derive not from her position as M. Motte's emissary but from her talents
as a hairdresser and her knowledge of and taste in fashion—qualities
indispensable to women both outside and inside the walls of the Institute
St. Denis, whose value depends upon the appearance they present in
society. The despair of the faculty and students at Marcelite's failure to
appear before the graduation ceremonies to prepare their coiffures, attests
to the irony of their dependence on her *as Marcelite* to make them
acceptable to the "larger world governed by powerful white men [such as
M. Motte was believed to be] who profit from the class and caste
prejudices instilled in women" in places like the Institute St. Denis
(Elfenbein 101-102). For it is Marcelite—described by the narrator to be
precariously prone to reverting to the primitive, bestial behavior of her
race—who has the power to prevent the "white ladies" from looking in
public like the savages and beasts they envision themselves to be (King
65-73), who can transform their appearances with combs and curlers,
hairpieces and make-up. Consequently, the mask of M. Motte is a double
deception that hides Marcelite's "heroism" from others but also masks
from her and from the reader the true source of her power: herself.

The second major reason why Marcelite appears to the reader as larger
than King intended is that the other characters are so much less "heroic"—
more dependent, selfish, and cowardly—than she. Perhaps most obvious,
Marie as the heroine of the story has little commanding about her. In
contrast to Marcelite, who is physically and emotionally robust, Marie is
weak: sickly looking, small for her age, self-absorbed, and introverted—an
ironically successful product of an unhealthily narrow environment. Like
her classmates, she passively accepts whatever the school, as an extension
of society, teaches her about her role as a white southern woman of good
family, and she takes without question and as her due both the beautiful,
expensive clothes that Marcelite brings her, supposed gifts from her uncle,
M. Motte, and the adoring affection that Marcelite lavishes upon her.

In some ways, she does depart from the norm typified by her pampered, genteel classmates. She is the only one of the girls who does not put her hair in curlers for graduation and thus the only one not dependent upon Marcelite to fix her hair; and having boarded at the school continuously since the age of three, she has had to learn to cope with isolation and with detachment from the real world in ways that the other girls have not. In addition, she does experience a degree of maturation and recognition when she is forced to face the realities of her life: first, that she has no uncle to live with and to provide for her entrance into society and her dowry; and, second, at the end of the narrative, that Marcelite can no longer protect her because the revelation of her, a black woman's, secret support has irrevocably changed their relationship. During Marie's "dark night of the soul," when she spends the night all alone in the school dormitory (following M. Motte's failure to come to her graduation and take her home, as all the other girls' parents had done), Marie's maturation is signified by the sudden awareness King attributes to her that women are as vulnerable and powerless in society as orphans.

However, King does not mention any similar realizations that Marie has about race. Marie does not, for instance, recognize the incongruity that Elfenbein notes: that no matter what Marcelite gives, she can never, as a black woman, be worth the value to Marie of M. Motte, even as an invisible presence (102). Rather, it is Marcelite who, we later learn, when hiding that night in Marie's room and listening to Marie's despairing words, realizes that she can no longer comfort Marie because the truth about her [Marcelite's] role in Marie's life, given the prevailing ideas about race, is cause for alienation rather than cohesion between them.

While the reader may experience this situation as sadly ironic, there is no irony in Marie's assertion that she will go to live with Marcelite, despite Marcelite's response that Marie cannot "live with a nigger." Rather, King makes it clear that both Marcelite and Mme. Lareveillere understand Marie's words as a sign of desperation, of surrender to the despair she had felt in the dormitory when she sensed that all hope for the future had to be abandoned. Consequently, I do not agree with Robert Bush's reading of Marie's acquiescence to circumstance as comparable to Huckleberry Finn's "All right, then, I'll *go* to hell" in shedding light on the injustice of the caste system (97). For Marie, to live with Marcelite is not rebelling against a racist social order but is giving into a kind of death wish that may stem in part from Marie's fear that she isn't white, as Marcelite suggests when, in response to Marie's "I want to live with you; I am not too good for that," Marcelite exclaims, "What! You don't think you ain't white! Oh, God! Strike me dead!" (100-101). Indeed, once Marcelite proves that Marie, in fact, is white and Mme. Lareveillere and M. Goupilleau then agree to be surrogate parents to her, Marie does not repeat her request to live with Marcelite or relate to Marcelite in any other way within the remaining lines of the story. Further, as mentioned earlier, it is Goupilleau, the white male, not Marie or Madame, who makes the concluding statement about heroism. Consequently, depending upon the extent of a reader's sympathy with or hostility toward King's expressed purpose and premise in constructing "Monsieur Motte," the "smallness" of Marie's character makes the enormity of Marcelite's devotion appear exaggerated, unrealistic, or, at least, ambiguous. Moreover, Marie's lack of recognition of the ironies and ideologies that mediate her relationship with Marcelite support Helen Taylor's point that "the female bonding Kirby sees as central to King's work rarely occurs between white and black women except in controlled circumstances, and in some cases it is violently rejected" (42).

Like Marie, Mme. Lareveillere, as Jones points out, is posited against a "typical" white southern woman, but in Madame, as in Marie, "independence, growth, insight, and strength are mitigated..." (103). The reason, Helen Taylor suggests, may be that King, "while admiring assertiveness and strength in women and cultivating those qualities herself,... retained the ambivalences and anxieties of southern women of her time and place..." (41). On the one hand, Madame reveals some qualities atypical of the valorized portrayal of the southern white woman and similar to those of Marcelite. The widow of an old aristocrat whose profligacy left her with the necessity of earning her own living, Madame demonstrates a degree of self-sufficiency and independence in supporting herself as headmistress of the Institute St. Denis. However, she perpetuates an education that has little relevance to the girls' lives and that encourages a traditional Creole notion of woman's place and role that leaves them vulnerable to the disappointments and exploitation that she experienced in her own marriage. Like the girls she serves, she also had, in her youth, romantic fantasies about men and marriage; and like Marie and her friends, she does not question M. Motte's failure to have any personal relationship with Marie during the entire time he has supposedly supported her stay in the school. To Madame, M. Motte, like most men she has known, is forgiven for and accepted as being too involved in his own interests and pleasures to do anything more for Marie than what duty strictly demands—even to write a letter or pay a visit to her. Thus King uses Madame in part, as she uses the girls, to point out the ironic contrast between women's romantic illusions about men and the realities of a system that leaves women in marriage with no authority over the money and property they or their husbands bring to the union and with little alternative to suffering in silence any vices, abuses, and infidelities their spouses may enjoy. Nevertheless, at the end of the narrative, unable to cope with the consequences of Marcelite's revelation that there is no M. Motte and that she, Marcelite, has in fact been Marie's sole support, Madame capitulates her position to a man, turning to M. Goupilleau, a notary public and "confidential adviser," to solve the problems.

Another major discrepancy appears in Madame's depiction. Although she, like Marcelite, is alone in the world, playing a male role not only in supporting herself economically but also in being the head of a large "family" of teachers and students, she is, like other women of her class, a victim of female vanity. Moreover, King treats with obvious ironic relish both Madame's dependence upon servants, like Marcelite, to take care of her personal needs and her dependence on flattering the vanity of the parents of her wealthiest students to assure her own survival. When Marcelite fails to show up on graduation day, Madame becomes ludicrous in her helplessness to prepare her own toilette—"How terrible it is," the narrator comments, "not to be able to comb one's own hair!" (67)—and she ends up, like her colleagues and students, looking *a la sauvagesse.* King's irony is no less overt in her treatment of Madame the day before graduation, busily awarding prizes by consulting two lists: the names of those who received the highest grades and the "list whose columns carried decimals instead of good and bad marks for lessons." As King comments, "No one but a schoolmistress knows the mental effort requisite for the working out of an equation which sets good and bad scholars against good and bad pay. Why could not the rich girls study more, or the poor less?" (44-45).

Madame also contrasts with Marcelite in that, until she is told of Marie's night alone in the dormitory following the graduation ceremonies and has Marie brought to her, she has never taken any personal interest in her students, had any emotional relationship with any of them, experienced any of the maternal love that Marcelite has felt for Marie. While Marie's desolation is represented in the text as revealing to Madame her own emotional isolation and Marie's need for comfort as perhaps arousing some dormant maternal instincts in Madame, it is primarily her own need for emotional connection that inspires her decision to be "a mother" to Marie. That decision, even more importantly, provides an excuse for her to form with M. Goupilleau, who agrees to be "a father" to Marie, the relationship

Madame desires—a relationship that will satisfy her need for affectionate support without requiring her to take the risk of making any emotional or legal commitment to M. Goupilleau, whom she considers socially inferior but who, as a man, would automatically have power over her. That Marcelite's heroism may have also inspired her decision to give Marie the home that Marcelite, because of race, is not permitted to give may be inferred by some readers but is not substantiated in the text. Thus, Madame also appears as a "smaller" character than Marcelite in her belief in the importance of style over substance and appearance over reality, in her reliance on flattery and artifice, and in her inability or refusal to handle the situation created by Marcelite's invention of M. Motte. Thus, she belies Marcelite's and the students' (as well as the reader's) initial image of her as a strong, reliable, and worldly individual. Her need to turn to a man to tell her what to do when she faces a crisis further undermines her credibility as an independent female character and provides another significant contrast with Marcelite, who pretends to be dependent on a man (M. Motte) but is actually independent.

Whether King intended to make this point of contrast or to use it to encode a feminist subtext is certainly debatable. After all, Marcelite also defers to M. Goupilleau in the end, agreeing to tell him (and only him) the truth about her relationship with Marie, confirming in her request that Marie and Madame leave the room before she speaks, that power and authority are vested only in the white male. On the other hand, King's description of Goupilleau as an anti-romantic figure—middle class, slight of build, with poetic (feminine) features and disposition—implies a criticism of the traditionally macho, egotistical, irresponsible, aristocratic Creole male of Madame's previous experience and creates a contrasting masculine ideal more suitable for Madame, and women generally, to trust and depend upon in the changing, destabilized social and economic environment of post-bellum New Orleans.

The second major area of debate concerns the location of meaning in a discourse about race characterized by a chain of contradictory signifiers distributed around the female characters and the relationships between them. Thus, the fact that Madame may be treated with more overt irony by King than is Marcelite does not lead me to support Elfenbein's conclusion that, in juxtaposing Madame and Marcelite as role models for Marie, King's "sympathy rests with Marcelite" (94). On the contrary, Marcellite appears to me as less fully realized in human terms by the text than is Madame—as more ambiguous because more objectified. Although the *reader's* sympathy may nevertheless rest with Marcelite to varying degrees, there is no indication that King perceives any incongruity in Marcelite's exclusion at the end of the story from what Jones calls "the pseudo family of white folks" (104): Madame and Goupilleau replacing Marcelite and "M. Motte" as surrogate parents for Marie. Moreover, as Taylor notes, instead of celebrating the bonds among the story's female characters, the ending can be read as simply a "crude attempt at a sentimental closure appropriate to southern fiction of the period" (60)—a closure that effectively separates Marcelite, as a black woman, from her "bebe" and from the world that now claims Marie while at the same time denying Marcelite a tragic dimension by seeming to "reward" her with continued access to Marie so long as she reassumes the subservient, degraded role of servant prescribed for her by white society.

Referring to the assumed role of Cable's work in motivating King's writing, Taylor asserts, "King's early work (especially *Monsieur Motte*) is an example of work produced (in [Julia] Kristeva's words) 'in the complex movement of a simultaneous affirmation and negation of another text'" (46). In this sense, a convincing reading of King can perhaps occur only within a system wherein King's narrative functions as a text in relation to Cable and to other larger cultural texts of which "Monsieur Motte" is but one sign. But even within such a context, I would suggest that the ambiguities, the irresolvabilities of "Monsieur Motte" remain because much of the irony of "Monsieur Motte" stems from King's perhaps unconscious attempt to simultaneously affirm and negate both the racism that separates Marcelite from Marie and the sexism that encourages male egotism and female dependence but also promotes the *status quo*—the social and economic stability of the pre-war South that King and her class had lost. This duality of purpose results in the encoding of inter-racial bonding as both ennobling and taboo, making closure indeterminate and leaving a series of intepretations among which the reader must mediate to extract some sort of meaning. This very indeterminacy, however, enlarges the narrative, just as it enlarges Marcelite. Consequently, the value of "Monsieur Motte," and of King's subsequent work, may reside in its ability to evoke conflicting responses and present multilayers of irony and ambiguity that compel us, as readers, to confront within ourselves and our environment questions about race, class, and gender that we might otherwise ignore.

WORKS CITED

Bush, Robert. *Grace King*. LSU Press, 1983.

___, ed. *Grace King of New Orleans*. LSU Press, 1983.

Elfenbein, Anna Shannon. *Women on the Color Line*. UP of Virginia, 1989.

Jones, Anne Goodwyn. *Tomorrow Is Another Day*. LSU Press, 1981.

King, Grace. *Monsieur Motte*. New York: Armstrong, 1888.

Kirby, David. *Grace King*. Boston: Twayne, 1980.

Taylor, Helen. "The Case of Grace King." *The Southern Review* 18.4 (1982): 685-702.

___. *Gender, Race, and Region in the Writings of Grace King, Ruth McEnery Stuart, and Kate Chopin*. LSU Press, 1989.

17

Violence and Comedy in the Works of Flannery O'Connor

MARK WALTERS

Flannery O'Connor is not often read from a feminist perspective. This is not surprising; she herself made clear that she was largely concerned with spiritual matters, with the "demonstration of God's mystery at work in the world." Understandably, then, much O'Connor criticism has centered on the metaphysical implications of her fiction. But certainly that fiction should be addressed within contexts other than those she herself deliberately articulated, and certainly the effects on her art of her being female, female in a patriarchal South, merit attention. I believe, in fact, that looking at O'Connor's work from a feminist perspective can add much to the ongoing discussion of its most significant and mystifying element, i.e., the relationship between violence and comedy.

For O'Connor, or any American woman, to make comedy was and is in itself an act of defiance. Humor, of course, has long been connected to rebellion or, at the very least, irreverence. But for the female writer this rebellion seems three-fold: she typically debunks a certain convention, as would any male humorist; in the very process of debunking, she revolts against traditional expectations of female passivity; and by engaging in comedy, she calls into question the long-standing American belief that women are not and should not be funny.

As Alfred Habegger suggests in his study of 19th-century writers, because women were perceived as saints, they could not indulge in comedy and still maintain that particular illusion; to be funny was to be unladylike (141). Obviously, one effect of making women saints, making them "ladies," is to deny them sexuality, to keep them "little girls" forever. Habegger asserts that this attitude still exists; and I believe that it is one conflict point from which we might read O'Connor's humor.

In a 1955 letter to her editor, Catherine Carver, O'Connor writes:

> I have just got through talking to one of our honorable regional (with a vengeance) bodies.... After my talk, one lady shook my hand and said 'That was such a nice dispensation you gave us, honey.' Another said, 'What's wrong with your leg, sugar?' I'll be real glad when I get too old for them to sugar me. (*Letters* 120)

Because O'Connor was not only aware of but seemingly perturbed by the Milledgeville community's seeing her as the eternal child (she was thirty years old at the time of this letter), one function of her humor may have been to assert her adulthood, and in turn, her sexuality. Comedy may have allowed her to become something other than a saint. Moreover, it is significant that those whom O'Connor perceived as most culpable in the maintenance of that saint/child illusion were the ladies of the community themselves.

Habegger also asserts that "American humor has been the literature...of bad boys defying a civilization seen as feminine" (119). Certainly, if this is true, a woman is forced to identify against herself while reading American comedy (cf. Judith Fetterley's *The Resisting Reader*). But to begin practicing that art, to begin writing, necessarily entails not just identification against the self, but an attack on that self. Whether the writer's protagonist is male or female, the convention being defied is, in American humor, feminine. Naturally this places the woman humorist in a quandary: to relinquish her art is to confirm women's exclusion from comedy and to exercise it is to rebel against her "self."

But this is in fact a quandary only if the female humorist buys into the notion that women are to be equated with civilizing forces. If she does not buy into this, then she becomes a kind of resisting writer, either depicting the forces to be rebelled against as unmistakably masculine or, alternately, manifesting them in grotesquely ladylike figures who are then killed off.

It is perhaps more than coincidence that the Southern ladies of Milledge-ville—ladies for whom propriety assumed great importance—were among the most disapproving critics of O'Connor's work, and that such ladies repeatedly meet violent (and comic) ends in that work.

I want to assert, though, that O'Connor was more than a little ambivalent about killing off such ladies, that she could never detach herself completely from them, and that this simultaneous sympathy and repulsion for the women about whom she grew up informed and darkened her comedy. In support of this reading, I want to look particularly at O'Connor's treatment of mother-daughter relationships in her work and at her own relationship with her mother, Regina O'Connor. I also want to suggest how this ambivalence leads into her usurpation of the mother-in-law joke and, further, how such a joke inevitably becomes an attack on the self.

Louise Westling has noted the mother-daughter patterns in O'Connor's short stories and has pointed to the recurrent "hardworking widow who supports and cares for her large, physically marred girl" (510). That the mother is representative of patriarchal values—she is, most often, a "lady"—and that the daughter is just as often disagreeable and defiant, but unable or unwilling to relinquish entirely the mother-daughter bond, is significant. A daughter's ambivalence toward her mother marks these stories and, as I will point out, O'Connor's personal letters.

A number of critics have suggested that a specific strain of humor—the mother-in-law joke—arose from men's perception of the strong mother-daughter bond. The humor of these jokes rests most often upon the doing of violence to the mother-in-law, who is equated with civilizing forces. It is especially helpful to look at this particular kind of comedy with regard to O'Connor because, unlike humor in general, it explicitly demands that female bonding which critics have often overlooked in her fiction. Seeing that O'Connor exercised a darker and more complex variation of the mother-in-law joke while not denying the bond on which it rested, clarifies the possibility that her violent comedy arose from ambivalent concerns inseparable from her femaleness.

Loxley F. Nichols has traced the humor of many of O'Connor's personal letters to a playful conflict between the writer and her mother, a conflict that, she suggests, at times became uneasy and more clearly angry (28). For instance, O'Connor writes:

> The other day she [Regina] asked me why I didn't try to write something that people like instead of the kind of thing I do write. Do you think, she said, that you

are really using the talent God gave you when you don't write something that a lot,
a LOT, of people like? This always leaves me shaking and speechless, raises my
bloodpressure 140 degrees, etc. All I can say is, if you have to ask, you'll never
know. (*Letters* 326)

Obviously, Regina was a lady for whom decorum was primary.
O'Connor, on the other hand, was the daughter who was at once repressed
by and dependent upon her. On a larger level, with Regina as representative of the female community of Milledgeville, O'Connor is again "sugar,"
the eternal child whose mother is likewise an eternal innocent in the
patriarchy that sees them both as saints. But O'Connor could never
completely extricate herself from the ladylike idea which held her in check;
in fact, Nichols argues convincingly that O'Connor's letters indicate that
she was "more like Regina than she realized or cared to admit" (25). And
so like those male humorists who write mother-in-law jokes in response to
the threat of female bonding to their own primacy and control, O'Connor's
own sense of her relationship to her mother(s) may have contributed to her
version of the same joke.

In "Greenleaf," for instance, O'Connor describes Mrs. May in terms
which establish her as the conventional mother-in-law figure, this despite
the fact that her only children—two sons—remain unmarried. We first see
her standing at her bedroom window: "Green rubber curlers sprouted
neatly over her forehead and her face beneath them was smooth as
concrete with an egg-white paste that drew the wrinkles out while she
slept" (311). O'Connor further plays out the lines of the joke by setting
Mrs. May up as that oppressive and civilizing force against which is pitted
the easygoing male, Mr. Greenleaf, her hired-hand, who is responsible for
her land and livestock—that to which she is most closely bound—and so
is representative of the persecuted son-in-law in this daughterless story.
Appropriately, Mrs. May sees Greenleaf as lazy and irresponsible, as "too
shiftless to go out and look for another job" (313). Mrs. May will of
course get her come-uppance, violently.

But what distinguishes O'Connor's joke from the masculine version and
what suggests that she was not extricating herself completely from that
mother figure is that she restricts the point of view to Mrs. May, giving
us the sense that—despite the irony of the narrative—the males are indeed
outsiders. O'Connor also depicts the males closest to Mrs. May—her
sons—as decidedly unsympathetic and, further, in the habit of addressing
their mother in the very sorts of terms against which O'Connor herself
bristled: "sweetheart" and "sugarpie." Finally, by not providing Mrs. May

with a literal daughter, O'Connor allows her to assume a version of that role herself: Mrs. May is at once matriarchal protectress and wooed maiden, a grotesque representative of the very bond upon which the mother-in-law joke rests. Her would-be lover is the bull who stands beneath her bedroom window, "gaunt and long-legged...chewing calmly like an uncouth country suitor" (312).

Despite at first portraying the bull as an awkward and naive country youth—traditionally the least threatening of a girl's suitors—O'Connor begins to make clear that something is in fact to be feared and that that something is unmistakably masculine, Dionysian, sexual. Still beneath Mrs. May's bedroom window: "The bull lowered his head and shook it and the wreath slipped down to the base of his horns where it looked like a menacing prickly crown. She had closed the blind then; in a few seconds she heard him move off heavily" (312). But what is just darkly hinted at in the early stages of the story is realized at the conclusion: the bull, that ostensibly bumbling youth who calls for his sweetheart beneath her bedroom window, meets Mrs. May on his own turf, so to speak, and brutally consummates their relationship:

> [Mrs. May] stared at the violent black streak bounding toward her as if she had no sense of distance, as if she could not decide at once what his intention was, and the bull had buried his head in her lap, like a wild tormented lover, before her expression changed. One of his horns sank until it pierced her heart and the other curved around her side and held her in an unbreakable grip. (333)

O'Connor has, at this point, played out the mother-in-law joke: the aggressive matriarch has been dispatched forcefully before the representative son-in-law—Mr. Greenleaf—can arrive to help. The persecuted male has indirectly (here, through the bull) reasserted his dominance and ruptured the mother-daughter bond without relinquishing the appearance of being likeable and easygoing.

But O'Connor also plays out this joke from a decidedly feminine perspective. She merges the matriarchal identity with that of the pursued daughter, and she strips the country youth of his guileless appearance, depicting his ultimate conquest in frightening and sexual terms. O'Connor thus rewrites one version of the marriage myth.

But perhaps most significant, overall, is that O'Connor does in fact kill Mrs. May. Through her story she is able to overthrow the well-bred lady to whom she could only respond with frustrated silence in her actual life. But because she could not seem to separate herself entirely from that ladylike idea, those ladylike figures, O'Connor would seem to be killing a part of herself in these stories, a necessary consequence of such ambivalence. To get at this issue more precisely, it is helpful to consider the theme of female self-hatred.

Ellen Moers suggests that "the savagery of girlhood," the themes of "self-hatred" and "the impetus to self-destruction," account for the persistence of the Modern Female Gothic (107). She attributes these themes to "the female's compulsion to visualize the self," to consider whether or not she is pretty. Moers concerns herself with the way this compulsion is expressed in Southern women writers' depiction of "freaks," and she calls attention to Freud's study, "The Uncanny," as a means of getting at the base of Southern Gothic horror.

Moers, however, does not do as much with Freud's work as she might to connect it to the Southern writer's creation of the "grotesque." Freud asserted that the uncanny exists "when repressed infantile complexes have been revived by some impression, or when primitive beliefs we have surmounted seem once more to be confirmed" (157). Elements making up the uncanny can include fears of castration, penetration, and being devoured. (Significantly, not only is Mrs. May in "Greenleaf" penetrated, but at the beginning of the story she dreams of being eaten by the bull.) Especially important to our discussion of O'Connor, though, is a point made by Claire Katz, that the "grotesque" results from the "admixture of the uncanny and the comic" (59). In other words, we might see the "grotesque" as the striking manifestation of the meeting between fear and the desire to revolt against or overthrow that fear. Moers makes a similar point, but she neglects to mention the comic, an omission that results in a one-sided reading of the Female Gothic, the dark side only.

We might, however, make use of Moers' thesis that the employment of the grotesque signals a "self-hating self," a response to the patriarchal emphasis on beauty that women have adopted and maintained with rigor.

Hulga is the name that Joy Hopewell, in "Good Country People," assumes to mark her ugliness. She goes clomping about on her wooden leg, wearing a "six-year-old skirt and yellow sweat shirt with a faded cowboy on a horse embossed on it," and, according to her mother, she has "never danced a step or had any normal good times" (274). She is, according to traditional feminine standards, a freak; and she must be, according to Moers' thesis, an expression of O'Connor's self-hate. But this is the point at which I want to leave Moers and suggest a way in which we might read a concluding scene in the story as a comic display of anger directed away from the self.

With the arrival of Manley Pointer, we are set up for another version of the naive country suitor unmasked and, consequently, another rewriting of the marriage myth. Pointer, the young Bible salesman, after portraying himself as an innocent, sexually seduces Hulga in order to steal her wooden leg.

Louise Westling argues that in this seduction scene, O'Connor is providing "the profound symbolic material...for an understanding of rape" (519). But what Westling fails to account for is O'Connor's use of the grotesque, her merging of the uncanny and the comic, and how this allows her and Hulga to triumph over Manley Pointer.

Nichols, again with reference to the personal letters, shows that "even on those occasions when O'Connor appears not to have the upper hand, when laughter is seemingly provoked at her expense, a closer look reveals that she is still in control, still manipulating the scene" (21). She cites O'Connor's recordings of a number of exchanges in which Regina is allowed the last word, a last word whose absurdity is amplified by O'Connor's own silence. A review of the concluding lines of dialogue in most of O'Connor's short stories will, I contend, demonstrate the same strategy.

At the conclusion of the Manley-Hulga seduction scene, a scene in which two elements of the uncanny—penetration and castration—are enacted, O'Connor grants Manley the final and most obviously ridiculous line: "'you ain't so smart. I been believing in nothing ever since I was born'" (291). In other words, O'Connor turns her wit on the violator, rebels against him, by allowing him to speak and Hulga to remain silent.

But O'Connor does not end the story with that scene. She takes us back to those representative ladies, Mrs. Hopewell and Mrs. Freeman, and, in the final comic indictment of that group's passivity, blindness, and resulting complicity in at least one version of the marriage myth, gives them, respectively, the following lines: "'[Manley] was so simple...but I guess the world would be better off if we were all that simple.'" And "'Some can't be that simple...I know I never could'" (291).

Certainly O'Connor's choosing to conclude with "the lady" as comic target suggests her own understanding of what oppressive force needed first to be overturned in the struggle for freedom, just as her earlier allowing of Joy/Hulga to be as easily duped suggests how close she was to the limitations of that oppressive force. In this proximity to and distance from her subject matter we find the roots of that ambivalence which gave rise to her humor. We see the comic writer's necessary denial of and bonding with the Lady within herself, a process which provokes her art and makes it uniquely female.

WORKS CITED

Fetterley, Judith. *The Resisting Reader: A Feminist Approach to American Fiction.* Bloomington: Indiana UP, 1978.

Freud, Sigmund. "The Uncanny." *On Creativity and the Unconscious.* Ed. Benjamin Nelson. New York: Harper, 1958. 157.

Habegger, Alfred. *Gender, Fantasy, and Realism in American Literature.* New York: Columbia UP, 1982.

Katz, Claire. "Flannery O'Connor's Rage of Vision." *American Literature: A Journal of Literary History, Criticism, and Bibliography* 46.1 (March 1974): 54-67.

Nichols, Loxley F. "Flannery O'Connor's 'Intellectual Vaudeville': Masks of Mother and Daughter." *Studies in the Literary Imagination* 20.2 (Fall 1987): 15-30.

Moers, Ellen. *Literary Women: The Great Writers.* 1976. New York: Oxford UP, 1985.

O'Connor, Flannery. "Good Country People." *Flannery O'Connor: The Complete Stories.* New York: Farrar, 1978, 271-91.

____. "Greenleaf." *Flannery O'Connor: The Complete Stories.* New York: Farrar, 1978, 311-34.

____. *Letters of Flannery O'Connor: The Habit of Being.* Ed. Sally Fitzgerald. New York: Farrar, 1979.

Westling, Louise. "Flannery O'Connor's Mothers and Daughters." *Twentieth-Century Literature: A Scholarly and Critical Journal* 24.2 (Winter 1978): 510-22.

—18—

Laughter as Feminine Power in _The Color Purple_ and _A Question of Silence_

JUDY ELSLEY

In the end, the changed life for women will be marked, I feel certain, by laughter. It is the unfailing key to a new kind of life. In films, novels, plays, stories, it is the laughter of women together that is the revealing sign, the spontaneous recognition of insight and love and freedom.

(Carolyn Heilbrun, _Writing A Woman's Life._ 129)

I intend exploring laughter as a mark of the changed lives of women in a novel and a movie. In both the novel, _The Color Purple,_ and the movie, _A Question of Silence,_ laughter acts as a catalyst in women's journey to self-empowerment. In both cases, the women laugh when they bond with each other, and that bonding gives them sufficient strength and support to set themselves free of an oppressive society.

Celie's life in _The Color Purple_ does not give her much to laugh about. The first laugh she records is shared with Sofia in an incident that begins when Harpo asks Celie for advice in trying to control his powerful wife. Celie suggests the treatment she has received from Mr.---: "Beat her. I say" (43). When Sofia discovers Celie's betrayal, she storms over to her house to confront her. Celie apologizes, the two women reconcile with each other, and Celie begins to speak her truth for the first time as Sofia listens sympathetically:

> Well, sometime Mr.--- git on me pretty hard. I have to talk to Old Maker. But he my husband. I shrug my shoulders. This life soon be over, I say. Heaven last all ways.
>
> You ought to bash Mr.--- head open, she say. Think about heaven later.
>
> Not much funny to me. That funny. I laugh. Then us both laugh so hard us flop down on the step. (47)

That laughter signifies Celie's new born challenge to the power of a patriarchal system that up until then has formed the context of her life. As Luce Irigaray says, "Isn't laughter the first form of liberation from a secular oppression?" (163). By questioning the authority of men in her life, Celie begins the process of claiming her own power. Laughter is the vehicle by which she moves through that process.

Celie's journey to self-empowerment is sealed in the activity which follows that initial laughter: "Let's make quilt pieces out of these messed up curtains, she say. And I run git my pattern book"(47). As Celie puts the pieces of fabric together in a quilt pattern significantly named "Sister's Choice," she also begins to gather up the fragments of her life.

But she works on neither her fabric nor her life alone. The laughter Celie shares with Sofia, and later with other women, is a sign of the bond developing between the women which gives Celie the strength to make her challenge to the patriarchy. Paradoxically, autonomy for Celie comes through bonding with other women. As Audre Lorde says, "For women, the need and desire to nurture each other is not pathological but redemptive, and it is within that knowledge that our real power is rediscovered" (98).

Celie and Sofia begin their quilt-making process by cutting up fabric to create their pattern. That rending has the effect of creating space between the pieces, a liminal, undefined place of creative freedom for these quilters from which they can create the pattern of their choice. In "The Laugh of the Medusa," Helene Cixous describes the need for "everywoman" to make such a space for herself in order to create herself: "woman has never had her turn to speak...the space that can serve as a springboard for subversive thought" (311). Celie and Sofia speak their truths to one another as they quilt. They create a space that serves as a springboard for the subversive thought of no longer acquiescing to the men in their lives. Their quilting leads to their bonding; their bonding to a support of one another; the support to a growing sense of their own individual strength.

The laughter in that first quilting scene ripples through the novel as the women bond with each other and thus find the strength to move towards greater personal autonomy. More than merely comedic, this laughter erupts at the most serious moments in the story, particularly when Celie takes successive steps towards self-respect and autonomy. For example, Shug and Celie laugh together when Shug encourages Celie to look at her genitals for the first time. This represents an important moment for Celie because, with the help of another woman, she is coming to a sense of herself sexually:

> She say, What, too shame even to go off and look at yourself? And you look so cute too, she say, laughing...
>
> You come with me while I look, I say.
>
> And us run off to my room like two little prankish girls.
>
> You guard the door, I say.
>
> She giggle. Okay, she say. Nobody coming. Coast clear.(79)

Celie's most significant step towards autonomy comes with her declaration of independence from Mr.---. At this point of crisis, the women sitting around the family dinner table support her, completely baffling the men with their laughter:

> Shug look at me and us giggle. Then us laugh sure nuff. Then Squeak start to laugh. Then Sofia. All us laugh and laugh.
>
> Shug say, Ain't they something? Us say um *hum*, and slap the table, wipe the water from our eyes.
>
> Harpo look at Squeak. Shut up Squeak, he say. It bad luck for women to laugh at men.
>
> She say, Okay. She sit up straight, suck in her breath, try to press her face together.
>
> He look at Sofia. She look at him and laugh in his face. I already had my bad luck, she say. I had enough to keep me laughing the rest of my life. (182)

The women are not so much laughing *at* the men as expressing in laughter their own bonding and their individual release from a system that has held them captive for so long. Refusing to be commodities of exchange among men any longer, the women shift, in effect, from object to subject.

The laughter marks an understanding between the women that does not need expression in words. This wordless bonding perplexes the men because it effectively excludes them. As Carolyn Heilbrun says, "Women laugh together only in freedom, in the recognition of independence and female bonding"(129). Some things are so serious that laughter is the best response, and Celie's declaration of independence is one of them.

These women are disrupting the patriarchal world with their laughter to make room for themselves. Although writing about the nature of the novel rather than about women, Bakhtin describes that disruptive power of laughter as "a vital factor in laying down that prerequisite for fearlessness without which it would be impossible to approach the world realistically" (23). Judy Little extends the idea of comedic inversion from temporary disruption to a vehicle for effecting permanent changes in a woman's life:

> Comedy in which the liminal elements are never resolved, comedy which implies, or perhaps even advocates, a permanently inverted world, a radical reordering of social structures, a real rather than temporary and merely playful redefinition of sex identity, a relentless mocking of truths otherwise taken to be self-evident or even sacred—such comedy can well be called subversive, revolutionary, or renegade. (Little 2)

Celie's laughter around the dinner table demonstrates Little's theory as she begins to make permanent changes in her life.

Laughter as feminine power is explored in the very different cultural context of Marleen Gorris' Dutch film, *A Question of Silence,* made in 1983. The movie, much darker in tone than Alice Walker's life-affirming novel, revolves around three ordinary women who are arrested for murdering the owner of a clothes store. The women do not know each other, but all three freely admit to the crime. Janine de Bos, a renowned psychologist, is brought on to the case to determine whether the women are sane enough to stand trial.

As we watch her interviewing the women, we see Janine frustrated at every point. Annie chatters and laughs but won't address the questions she's asked; Andrea fields back questions or gives enigmatic answers, and most disturbing of all, Christine remains completely silent. The three women seem to bond with each other in an unspoken understanding of why they committed the murder.

That understanding is based on the common context of the women's lives. All three are trapped in a patriarchal culture, oppressed by the men in their lives: Christine, the housewife with harried husband and noisy children reverts to silence because no one listens to her; Andrea is a frustrated secretary who, negated professionally, distrusts and questions the system; and Annie, a waitress who daily serves blue collar workers cracking sexist jokes, spurns men by refusing to them seriously.

The murder, which the women never explain, is an act of reclamation. It begins when one woman deliberately shoplifts a garment. The store owner upbraids her, but she takes another piece of clothing, slowly, deliberately, openly. The other two women who just happen to be in the store at the same time, surround the man, stuffing clothes slowly, challengingly, into their bags. The male shop owner becomes a symbol of all men and their oppressive hold over the women's lives, down to the very clothes they wear. The women are taking back what is theirs in a scene that turns stealing into a silent ritual. The shop owner senses the gravity of the situation, but like a terrified rabbit, he is frozen in place. The women murder him with the same slow, deliberate, ritualistic movements that they employ to steal the clothes. Although the murder is shocking, the viewer remains sympathetic to the women as Gorris gradually reveals the difficulties of their lives in a series of flashbacks.

After the crime, the women find themselves in the even greater patriarchal grip of the prison. Shots of the building reveal a tall, white, sterile, modern building—an architectural phallus. Inside, men monitor the building through a network of t.v. scanners. Men also operate the electronic locks that allow the women to move through the building. The three women, who have been metaphorically incarcerated by the patriarchy all their lives, are now literally under the watchful eye of Big Brother.

The men in the movie stand well outside the unspoken understanding that binds the women to each other. They are convinced that the women are mad. The detective on the case tells Janine, "it's an open and shut case—they didn't deny anything." Her husband, a lawyer, comments, "It's obvious. These women are completely deranged." To recognize their sanity would be too threatening. But the more Janine puzzles over the case, the more she realizes that the three women are not mad: "I can't reach those three very ordinary women; I meet them all the time. They're so normal." As she grows into this realization, she finds herself shifting from attachment to the patriarchal order that has supported her professionally, and simultaneously distancing herself from her husband. The closer she becomes to the women, the further she moves from the familiar rational world of men in which she normally operates.

The film ends with the trial. The court represents the most heavily controlled male domain yet. The rules have been made by men, and most of the principal actors in this legal drama are male: the judge, the prosecutor, the witnesses and the pathologist all speak up. The women are defined only in terms of their external labels—their names and addresses. The climax of the film, which takes place in the court room, is a graphic example of the power of feminine laughter. The prosecutor begins to make his argument. He describes the women as indulging in the "harmless feminine past-time" of buying clothes. By trivializing clothes shopping he shows how little he understands the defendants. As he goes on to condemn the senseless brutality of a murder he cannot understand, one of the defendants begins to laugh. Her laugh is infectious, rippling through the courtroom. The other two defendants laugh, followed by the female spectators of the trial, some of whom were also unidentified observers in the boutique when the murder took place. Finally, even Janine, the psychologist, laughs. Like the final court scene in *Alice's Adventures in Wonderland,* the house of cards comes tumbling down as patriarchal authority is lost. The judge cannot keep control of his courtroom, proceedings come to a halt, and the three defendants are led away, still laughing.

Their laughter in court is the only time in the film that the women demonstrate any power within a society that has entrapped them. In the end, they are likely to be "sentenced"—torn from the safety of silence by the power of the verbal constructs of the patriarchy—so their temporary victory remains ambiguous. But for the time being, as the film closes, Gorris shows the one way these women can come to power: through laughter.

Why is their laughter so disturbing, so powerful, so disruptive? First, the women wordlessly bond together. Their laughter brings defendants, psychologist and the silent witnesses of the crime into understanding and sympathy with each other. As a result of that bonding, the women gain the strength to resist and exclude the ruling male order. They refuse to be intimidated, to be controlled, to be shaped by the patriarchy any longer.

The women's laughter in Marleen Gorris' film works in the same way as Celie's laughter. In both cases, women's laughter dissipates the power of an oppressive culture; it brings the women closer together; and most important of all, their laughter expresses the women's growing sense of autonomy.

WORKS CITED

Bakhtin, M.M. *The Dialogic Imagination.* Austin: University of Texas Press, 1981.

Cixous, Helene. "The Laugh of the Medusa." *Critical Theory Since 1965.* ed. Hazard Adams and Leroy Searle. Tallahassee: University of Florida Press, 1986. 309-321.

Gorris, Marleen. *A Question of Silence,* 1983.

Heilbrun, Carolyn. *Writing A Woman's Life.* New York: Norton, 1988.

Irigaray, Luce. *This Sex Which is Not One.* Ithaca: Cornell University Press, 1985.

Little, Judy. *Comedy and the Woman Writer: Woolf, Spark, and Feminism.* Lincoln: University of Nebraska Press, 1983.

Lorde, Audre. "The Master's Tools Will Never Dismantle the Master's House." *This Bridge Called My Back: Radical Writings By Women of Color.* ed. Cherrie Moraga and Gloria Anzaldua. Watertown, Mass: Persephone Press, 1981. 98-101.

Walker, Alice. *The Color Purple.* New York: Washington Square Press, 1982.

19

The Goblin Ha-Ha:
Hidden Smiles and
Open Laughter
in *Jane Eyre*

ROBIN JONES

The association of laughter with Charlotte Bronte's *Jane Eyre* seems an incongruous endeavour at first. Readers do not respond with hilarity to the novel. The plot, theme, or characterization hardly fulfills any requirements of comedy or humor. Nonetheless, laughter is found within the text, most notably in the goblin "ha-ha" of Bertha Mason Rochester, the "mad-woman in the attic."[1] While critical reaction to Bertha has been stimulating and far-reaching, there has been a definite neglect in an analysis of this particular action of Bertha's.[2] The laugh of a woman has been problematic to consider, manipulated as it is by traditional theories of humor, comedy, and laughter. But the act of laughter is very revealing of social construction. Exploring why and how women in the novel laugh or don't laugh reveals cultural mores and attitudes about women. Laughter for women in *Jane Eyre* is a response to a patriarchical construct but can also be seen as an expression of self (specifically in regards to sexuality) and is a tool with which knowledge of women's experience is passed on, from woman to woman, through smiles, snickers, giggles and roars of laughter.

I

What is the importance of laughter, what does it mean? Traditional critical analysis of laughter largely depends upon Aristotle's notion of the incongruous or Freud's works with jokes, wherein humor is based upon aggression. According to these two definitions, we laugh when we are confronted with things that do not fit into our normal scheme of things or when we, to assert our own superiority, want to identify others as laughable. Women have been a butt of jokes for centuries. They are funny because they do not fit into the norm of a patriarchal society, i.e., they are not men. And in their cultural roles as nurturers, they are the repositories of aggression, not the instigators. Laughter in women is unexpected because the incongruous or the marginal aren't expected to laugh at the dominating force, nor is humorous aggression appreciated in women. Women learn early on the minimal expectations of laughter for their gender.

Jane Eyre is a creation of her social world, and within her we see the constructional devices of who laughs, how and why. Her abused childhood at Gateshead allows for no laughter and its infrequent smiles are subdued or hidden. Her tenuous relationship with the servant Bessie is the only occurrence of a lighter mode. There is no laughter at Gateshead, but we do see the potential in Jane for a capacity for humor, if only in self-defense. Taunted and abused by her cousin John, Jane awaits the blow that she knows will soon fall, musing on "the disgusting and 3 ugly appearance of him who would presently deal it" (42).[3]

Jane can't laugh at John as he no doubt laughs at her, but privately she can regard *him* as incongruous and as worthy to be laughed at. She knows the dangers of letting her inner musings out, on purpose or inadvertently, for John guesses her thoughts and hurls a book at her. At Gateshead, Jane realizes the potential for punishment in releasing her own emotions and begins the process of disassociating from her inner self and creating an appropriate and non-threatening public self.

At Lowood School, Jane continues this process. Here she learns how *not* to laugh or smile. She watches her role model Maria Temple hide a smile as the school principal, Mr. Brockelhurst, chides students for their vanity in growing curly hair: "Miss Temple passed her handerchief over her lips, as if to smooth away the involuntary smile that curled them..." (96).

Brockelhurst cuts their hair off, effectively reminding them of their powerlessness as children and women in a patriarchy. The scene has its humor in ironic absurdity, for in their own turn, the Brockelhurst family is richly and ornately over-dressed. But Miss Temple's hidden smiles are a social education for Jane. Women do not show amusement towards men. Clearly, such amusement may threaten a dominant hierarchical structure which establishes what Judith Newton defines as "domininant-subordinate roles of parent-child and husband-wife" (116).

The roles in Newton's social structure parallel the structure which determines who may laugh and who may not. Parents and husbands may laugh at children and wives, but when the children and wives turn around and laugh themselves, the structure becomes uneven and unsteady. Definitive roles such as woman, wife, or mother become unclear if the performer changes attitude. Thus other roles—such as man, husband,and father—must control the attributes of social construction to maintain the clarity and stability of all roles.

Jane's roles in Thornfield Hall are at first those of a woman and a teacher within particular definitions of womanhood and a specific class structure. Her place within the social hierarchy is determined by her position as governess. Charlotte Bronte's own experiences as a governess informed her of the tribulations of gentile poverty coupled with social humiliation. Within the hegemonic structure of social class, it is the aristocracy who determine popular behavior; they are the "makers of manners." The treatment metted out to Jane by the Ingrams and before, by the Reeds, reflects the attitude of the rich towards the poor, the beautiful towards the plain, the upper class towards the working class. Blanche Ingram epitimizes the disdainful attitude of the superior to the inferior with her laugh: "She laughed continually; her laugh was satirical, and so was the habitual expression of her arched and haughty lip" (202).

Blanche, as part of the upper class, can laugh at Jane, the working-class governess, small and plain. Jane is the incongruous in Blanche's world of power and beauty, yet as another woman possibly competing for the attention of Edward Rochester, Jane is also a recipient of aggression. Blanche has a rather "masculine" sense of laughter in light of this situation, for she aggressively marginalizes Jane as a governess and negates her very gender. When Jane comes searching for Edward as he and Blanche play billiards, Blanche recognizes her presence: "'Does that *person* want you?'" (251, emphasis mine).

But we can see Blanche's laughter falling into the more "feminine" traits that Jane has learned as well. Blanche laughs to put others in their place, but she also laughs in a way that reflects her standing as a woman in a patriarchy. She and other women in the novel laugh, not when it moves them, as much as when it is appropriate. They respond to the social codes of the situation. It is appropriate for Blanche and other young women of the party at Thornfield to giggle as part of a flirtation with young men, but it is done as a response to these gentlemen, not to any real humor. Following the games of charades in which Edward and Blanche are "married," he chides her: " 'Well, whatever I am remember you are my wife; we are married an hour since, in the presence of all these witness.' She giggled and her colour rose" (214). Edward subtly reminds Blanche of his power and position in their social estate. He has the capacity to be many things while she has only one ultimate role to fulfill, that of a wife. Blanche's giggle responds to the hope of a marriage and manipulates and is manipulated by her need for an identity, that of a wife. She can only giggle; words are inappropriate for her at this moment as too forward yet encouragement is necessary. This laugh, false and coercive as the charade (which heralds the future first failed attempt of marriage between Jane and Edward), is heard from other women in the party. When Edward disguises himself as a fortune-telling gypsy, the young women collapse into "blushes, ejaculations, tremors, and titters..." as the gentlemen of the party surge around in curiosity (223). The women use laughter to call attention to themselves specifically from men, when propriety does not allow the use of language. The attention of the men in the party will further the women's identity in a society where a sense of self worth comes from masculine sources.

While this type of laugh is one manner of expression for women, another type is seen in Jane. Not an avid giggler, Jane continues to hide her smiles and in her subservient role as a governess, she perpetuates the system of appropriate humorous or humored responses. When Adele begs for a flower for her "toilette" Jane responds:

> I took a rose from a vase and fastened it in her sash. She signed a sign of ineffable satisfaction, as if her cup of happiness were now full. I turned my face away to conceal a smile I could not suppress: there was something ludicrous as well as painful in the little Parisienne's earnest and innate devotion to matters of dress. (200)

Jane is well aware of Adele's origins, the illegitimate offspring of Edward and his French mistress. Adele's devotion to outward dress reflects the importance of appearances, especially women's, to establish a sense of identity. Women's appearance is geared towards male approval, as we see when Edward tries to dress Jane as he would have her—a "second Danae with the golden shower falling daily around" (297) rather than her own inclinations as a "plain Quakerish governess" (287). While Jane is able to confront and stop Edward from changing *her* appearance, she is unable to recognize with Adele, the influence of the same system of male appropriation of female appearance and in hiding her smile, hides from herself the "painful" route Adele is approaching. Like Maria Temple, Jane has learned not to openly smile at things which might threaten what men like or say.

She has further learned to abide by definitions that men do like or control. Edward's control over her emotions, her appearance, and her very name (he often addresses her as Janet) extends to her ability to laugh:

> Do you never laugh, Miss Eyre? Don't trouble yourself to answer—I see you laugh rarely, but you can laugh very merrily; believe me, you are not naturally austere, any more than I am naturally viscious. The Lowood constraint still clings to you somewhat; controlling your features, muffling your voice, and restricting your limbs; and you fear in the presence of a man and a brother—or a father, or master, or what you will—to smile too gaily, speak too freely, or move too quickly...."
> (169-170)

Edward is the author of her text, her "physiognomy," with no need for her voice or her answer or her laugh. He identifies her, not as a separate individual in her own right, but in contrast to his own identity; she is "not naturally austere" just as he is not "naturally viscious." He points out those around whom a woman's identity is built: brother, father, master. Certainly we see these relationships within the Reed and Rivers families, whose structure and strength depends upon the men of the family, John Reed and St. John Rivers. John, "no one thwarted, much less punished" (47) and St. John's decisions guide those of his sisters, Mary and Diana. Jane's future rests on *her* master, either to retain her as governess, mistress, or a wife.

Not only her future, but her very identity is decided by men in the novel. John Reed calls her a "rat" (43) and Brockelhurst brands her as a "liar" in Lowood (98). While Maria Temple clears Jane of this later charge, it is important to note that it is done privately, within the school's world of women and not within the public eye of the male administrative domain. Edward defines Jane according to his peculiar notions regarding women. He sees her as an "elf," "a fairy," "sprite," or "changling," even a "salamander." Jane's identity within the Victorian world will depend upon her association with a man—as his sister, servant, or wife. And this will not always be an association of her choice. When confronting St. John's proposal of marriage, she attests to her willingness to be his sister, but he presses for and refuses anything but her becoming his wife.

Jane is nervous about becoming a wife. Bronte's own fear of sexuality and her awarness of the hazards of marriage for women may very well be the stimulus for Jane's hesitancy about wedding Edward: "There was no putting off the day that advanced—the bridal day" (303). Her identity as Jane Eyre, however trivial, will be completely subsumed under the title Mrs. Edward Rochester—"young Mrs. Rochester—Fairfax Rochester's girl- bride" (287). Jane's resistance to this role attests to her awareness of the difficulty and loss she will encounter with this new position. Before the marriage she resorts to a game of manipulation to prove Edward's devotion to Mrs. Fairfax and to calm her own fears that his passion will not overstep bounds of propriety. Her task is "not an easy one" and the strain is indicitive of the harder role of wife to come. If she must restrain her own feelings before marriage, how much more will be lost during marriage? Jane informs the readers: "I laughed in my sleeve at his menaces," (302) but is this only a sign of the lack of laughter yet to come?

II

Jane continues to hide her smiles. And just as hidden, Bertha, Edward's first wife, laughs from her attic chamber in Thornfield:

> ...the last sound I expected to hear in so still a region, a laugh, struck my ears. It was a curious laugh—distinct, formal, mirthless. (138)

This is the reader's first introduction to Bertha and her laugh, a laugh which Gail Griffin calls the "most eloquent utterance in the novel" (118). But it is critically unexamined and unresolved and even incorrectly identified as the laughter of Grace Poole. Yet is is the one vocal representation we have from Bertha, and the only thing of her own, besides her actions as reported by Jane of which to make meaning. What does Bertha's laughter mean and how is it similar or different from the laughter of the other women in the novel?

The very sound of her laugh, "distinct, formal, mirthless," sets her apart from the titters and giggles of the other women in the novel, but the fact that her laughter is still hidden aligns her with Jane, as a marginalized member of the already incongruous. Bertha is kept in a room

without a window, [where] burnt a fire, guarded by a high and strong fender, and
a lamp suspended from the ceiling by a chain. (321)

The room itself does not bode well for any sort of comic relief. There is
no window in this room, no natural light or chance of enlightenment. The
fire is guarded and deflected by a high and strong fender. Bertha is from
the tropics and may well be chilled by England's climate but what is more,
her own passion and emotion, her own fire within, is just as guarded and
deflected by the fender of societal constraints. And while a common
enough feature, the chain holding the lamp lends a sinister tone to an
already oppressive atmosphere. Just as Jane resented the imagery of
Edward attaching her to "'a chain like this (touching his watch-guard)'"
(299), the extreme of this situation, Bertha bound and stilled, can only
suggest the utter mirthlessness of a stagnant and angry condition (Rowe 8).

Bertha's laugh is unlike that of other women's for it goes beyond a
particular social context of appropriateness and calls attention to her physicality. Bertha's laughter qualifies her body, her materiality as opposed to any
need for male confirmation. Because Edward has denied her, has hidden her
away and refuses to acknowledge her as his wife, she does not have to rely
upon the ideological identity that Victorian society would have given her. Her
mother and father are dead. She can't be seen as her father's daughter and
indeed we see her identity as resting upon a patrilinear line potentially
subverted, if only negatively, when Edward claims Bertha is her mad
mother's daughter. All Bertha has left is her body, and this is reemphasized
by her garb when seen by Jane; "I know not what dress she had on; it was
white and straight; but whether gown, sheet, or shroud, I cannot tell" (311).
This garb is a far cry from the wrappings, drapings, and corsets used to
disguise the female body and its odors during Victorian times. Bertha's body
is revealed in its curves, bulges, and odors, and Jane's "Janian" response is
to deny the female body. When confronted with the sensuality or sexuality of
the human body, Jane "knows not" what is going on, either in her own
actions of striking John Reed (and one wonders where she struck him to make
him cry out "Rat, rat") or in potential behaviors leading to the sexual
intercourse expected in marriage.

The standard of behavior for women was one which Jane could fulfill by
hiding her emotions, her laughter, indeed her very self. Jane adheres to the
asexual Victorian model of a woman as we see when she confesses her love
for Edward:

'...it is my spirit that addresses your spirit; just as if both had passed through the
grave, and we stood at God's feet, equal—as we are!' (281)

Jane believes (or perhaps hopes) she and Edward can really only meet in the
abstract. Throughout the novel we sense her uneasiness about the meeting of
the flesh and it has been critically commented upon that it is only when
Rochester has been amutilated and crippled (perhaps emasculated) that their
fleshly marriage can be consumated. Bertha too seems very abstract. Reports
about her are confused and misleading, she is often spoken of as a ghost, but
this is done to hide the reality of her very material presence.

Just as Jane is defined by Edward through a system which sees her only
through her ability to fit to his mold, Bertha too is seen as appropriate or
inappropriate to Edward's needs. She is defined in opposition to his
ideological requirements of what a woman or wife should have: "modesty...benevolence...candour...refinement in her mind or manners" (333).
Instead Edward finds "her nature wholly alien...her tastes obnoxious" to his
(333). What exactly Bertha is like, we do not know, for she is defined in
terms of what she is not, nor do we hear from her ourselves.

Bertha does not speak, she is not privy to the language of the patriarchy.
She has not chosen not to speak, instead language has been appropriated from
her. Neither Jane nor the readers hear more than her laugh or her snarls.
What we hear are reports of her speech, by her husband and her brother.
Following a meeting and an attack between sister and brother, Richard Mason
tells Edward: "She sucked the blood; she said she'd drain my heart" (242).
Bertha is shut back up in her chamber during this scene and reports of her
language come from the men who control her life. Edward eventually tells
Jane tales of Bertha's "wolfish cries," adding parenthetically "since the
medical men had pronounced her mad, she had, of course, been shut up"
(335). And Bertha has been shut up, figuratively and linguistically. Such an
attack and such cries do not seem out of place in a strong willed person who
has been hastily married off for financial gain, but we could further
understand Bertha's frustration in being judged by contradictory standards that
depend upon one's class and gender. Bertha's characterization by Edward is
that of "intemperate" and "unchaste" (334), attitudes Edward himself will
assume with his relationship with Celine Varens. Bertha's laugh points out the
incongruous of a social system which perpetuates different standards of
behavior for men and women.

Bertha's body and her laugh are things from which Jane could learn as
Bertha's actions reflect her own experience as a sexual being, not an asexual
object. Bertha's laugh reiterates her own materiality and power, as a response

to an environment which she acknowledges as oppressive, unlike the laugh of other women who laugh to continue the conditions of oppression. Her laughter heralds acts of revolution and anger and reminds the society that tried to deny her that she does still exist.

Her laugh challenges the cultural models of her world, even as she physically tries to change these models, by fire and violence. Her attacks on Edward release the anger and passion that women were supposed to suppress. While Edward deplored her unchasteness, it may very well be that what he really was afraid of was a woman's appreciation of sex in a time when women's sexuality was inappropriate. Bertha was trapped in a societal construct which required sex from women but which did not let them enjoy it. According to Mikhail Bakhtin, "laughter demolishes fear and piety before an object" (23) and in this case, Bertha's laughter debunks the power of the patriarchy by laughing at it. She instead attempts to call attention to women's experiences of sexuality in this social construction with her laugh. Jane awakens one night to

> a demoniac laugh—low, suppressed and deep—uttered, as it seemed, at the very keyhole of my chamber door. (179)

Jane is in the process of falling in love with Edward Rochester. Bertha's laugh through the keyhole ironically warns Jane of the intrusion marriage will make on Jane's "keyhole," her symbol of female genitalia. Bertha's sexuality was punished by solitude and imprisonment, Jane's fear of sexuality may keep her safe from this fate, but leaves her open to others. Bertha's visit on the night Jane is to marry Edward hints of this, when she rips asunder the wedding veil Edward had purchased for Jane. This act, indicative perhaps of the sexual trauma women undergo upon first sexual intercourse, could be seen as a warning from one woman to another, heralded by the unexpected laugh of knowledge.

Bertha goes beyond warnings in her behavior to Edward. If his bedchamber is representative of a dominant force, Bertha's firing of it further demolishes societal structures and expectations. As Edward's wife, her main role would have been fulfilled upon this bed and how well she fit into it (or the role of a Victorian wife). But being unacceptable, she was completely marginalized, hidden and locked away. Bertha, in her own turn, rectifies matters by destroying the bed or the measuring rod of her adaptability.

Bertha's laugh and the acts of violence following subvert societal expectations of women as meek, quiet, or complaisant. Judith Wilt suggests that comedy (and I extend her idea to include laughter): "validates the body, celebrates fertility, offers the catharthis of anger" (177). Bertha has a body and she knows how to use it rather than let her body be used by others. But as a result, she is locked away. The anger heard in her laugh is evocative of her body and her materiality as a sexual being, not an asexual imp. Even when Jane attempts to dehumanize Bertha as a "vampire" or "goblin" (311), we are seeing the standard definition of womanhood skewed by emotion and passion. Bertha's laughter calls attention not to other people as incongruous or inferior but to herself as real and with potential for self identity.

Jane could have learned much from listening to this laugh. She yearns for just such a sense of self identity. She has often heard Bertha laugh, when she, Jane, was atop the roof of Thornfield, pondering her life. Jane reflects:

> Women are supposed to be very calm generally; but women feel just as men feel; they need exercise for their faculties...they suffer from too rigid a restrain, too absolute a stagnation.... It is thoughtless to condemn them, or laugh at them, if they seek to do more or learn more than custom has pronounced necessary for their sex. (141)

And here, Jane is interupted by that "goblin laughter," that "slow ha-ha." Is Bertha laughing at her? It seems quite likely, for Jane's musings, her feminist polemic, is hardly fulfilled by the end of the novel. From living in a potential utopian community of women, her cousins Mary and Diane, Jane ends up in Ferndean, a musty, dank mansion in which Edward Rochester had refused to let even Bertha reside. Here, living completely for her husband and her son, we see the last of Jane, marginalized again, even to the extent that the text of the novel ends with St. John Rivers, not with our familiar female protagonist. If Bertha had the gift of seeing the future, how could she but not laugh, comparing Jane's hopes with the final outcome?

Whether Jane learns from this laugh or not is questionable, but consider: Jane is trying to come to terms with the roles society forces her into versus her own notions of her identity. The novel's progression rests upon her exploration of relationships—with herself, Edward Rochester, the Reeds and Rivers. Her relationship with anyone depends upon how her role in society is accepted. Her conversation with Hannah at Moor House exemplifies this condition, when Jane berates Hannah for not seeing beyond Jane's lack of "brass": "Some of the best people that ever lived have been as destitute as I am; and if you are a Christian, you ought not to consider poverty a crime" (369). Nor should physical appearance, class, or intellect be considered a crime, but Jane has not escaped these role limitations. Her actions are still determined by public role versus private identity. Bertha, in her madness, allowed for no such distinctions between public roles and private identities and her death silences the laugh which attests to her resistance to conform to this opposition. Without Bertha's laugh, it is doubtful that Jane will attempt to change the system which creates yet castigates mistresses, governesses, and mad women. Jane does not acknowledge the economic and social situation which despises Blanche Ingram for seeking a rich husband but which forgives Edward being bamboozled into marrying a rich wife. She forgives Edward's sexuality but cannot accept her own.

Jane cannot see beyond surfaces though she has plenty of personal experiences in which she has been misjudged and mistreated because of appearances. Bertha's laughter would have called attention to the different levels of subterfuge within Thornfield, but Jane negates it, attributing it to Grace Poole. Neglecting the lessons of Bertha's laugh which call attention to her own materiality and the oppression of the patriarchical system of identification, Jane will end her life in Ferndean, no doubt happily, but one wonders with what kind of laughter? Will it be the laughter which creates separate identities of superiority and inferiority or will it be the wild and ringing laughter of a woman determined to live by her own standards, rather than society's?

Bertha's laugh is a tool for exploration and to make meaning within this novel. Her character is often difficult to deal with, we have so little of her history, indeed so little of *her.* But she deserves a more insightful look than usually given a "mad woman." Mad women do not conform to the norm and as such create potentials for change, albeit violent and incinerary. We cannot understand the mad woman in *Jane Eyre* or in other novels by shutting them away or locking them in attic chambers. We must listen to them, as individuals in their own right, to whatever utterance they have left. These are the women who can show us a different perspective of life, for themselves and for other characters. Blanche Ingram can not be viewed as the heartless gold-digger we originally think, when we see the dangerous potential for her too, to succumb to the restraints put upon a nervous and powerful temperament. Bertha's madness seems a marginal issue, but it is really a possible path any woman in the novel might have taken or might yet take. By tracing her laugh, we trace the experiences of her life, from which to learn and from which to make choices ourselves about mad women in attics.

NOTES

1. Susan Gilbert and Susan Gubar acknowledge Bertha in having titled their work on the woman writer and the nineteenth-century literary imagination after the phenomenon and

have included a insightful and critically important section on Bertha. See *The Madwoman in the Attic,* (New Haven: Yale University Press, 1979).

2. See Sandra M. Gilbert, "Plain Jane's Progress," *Signs,* 2 (1977), 779-804; Gail B. Griffin, "The Humanization of Edward Rochester," *Women and Literature,* 2 (1981), 118-129; Cara Kaplan, "Pandora's Box: Subjectivity, Class and Sexuality in Socialist Feminist Criticism," *Making a Difference: Feminist Literary Criticism,* (New York: Routledge, 1985), pp. 146-176; Jane Marcus, "Daughters of Anger/Material Girls: Con/Textualizing Feminist Criticism" *Last Laughs: Perspectives on Women and Comedy,* ed. Regina Barreca, (New York: Gordon and Breach, 1988), pp. 281-309; Helene Moglen, *Charlotte Bronte: The Self Conceived,* (New York: Norton, 1976), pp. 105-145; Adrienne Rich, *"Jane Eyre: The Temptations of a Motherless Woman,"* *MS,* (October, 1973), 68-107. Kaplan's and Marcus' informative essays both discuss Bertha in light of Virginia Woolf's criticism in *A Room of One's Own* but all three neglect a close examination of the central passage where Bertha is first introduced through her laugh.

3. Charlotte Bronte, *Jane Eyre,* ed. Q.D. Leavis, (London: Penguin, 1985), all subsequent page numbers refer to this edition.

WORKS CITED

Bakhtin, Mikhail. *The Dialogic Imagination.* Ed. Michael Holquist. Trans. Caryl Emerson and   Michael Holquist. Austin: University of Texas Press, 1981.

Bronte, Jane. *Jane Eyre.* London: Penguin, 1985.

Griffin, Gail B. "The Humanization of Edward Rochester," *Women and Literature,* ed. Janet
    Todd, Vol. 2 (1980), 118-129.

Newton, Judith Lowder. *Women, Power, and Subversion: Social Strategies in British Fiction,*
    1778-1860. Athens: University of Georgia Press, 1981.

Rowe, Margaret Moan. "Beyond Equality, Ideas and Images in *Jane Eyre, Ball State University Forum,* XXI, 4, (Autumn 1980), 5-9.

Wilt, Judith. "The Laughter of Maidens, the Cackle of Matriarchs: Notes on the Collision Between Comedy and Feminism," *Gender and the Literary Voice,* ed. Janet Todd. New York: Holmes & Meier Publishers, Inc., 1980.

20

The Art of Courting Women's Laughter

BETTE TALVACCHIA

The creation of simulacra of the human form is a practice that has been sanctioned as high cultural accomplishment ever since it became linked to theories of imitation of nature, idealization of form, and perfection of technical skill. When comments on this product of art get mixed with responses tied directly to the experience of viewing images of the body—responses to the erotic—a hybrid discourse results. The combination of reactions from the brain and the viscera leads, as do all discordant unions, to possibilities for humorous comment. If the channels for this humor are the mind and the pit of the stomach, its vehicle is the gaze. The process of looking at the human form elicits a sensual response; where this reaction might otherwise remain private and unadmitted, its verbalization can find social acceptability in the context of a discourse about art. Within this enfolding structure, a salacious observation can find a cultural cover.

Throughout the history of the creation of art, men have most often been the patrons who commission reproductions of the naked female body. Ownership of these objects has given the patron a privileged opportunity for eying the erotic, and beyond that, for controlling reaction to it. Possession of the object seen as erotic allows command of the situation in which it is viewed. In cases where the owner wished to use the object of art as a reference to the live female body, or as a vehicle for sexual raillery, a pronounced masculinist humor resulted, often with real women as the target of the joke. Two such instances from the courtly culture of France in the sixteenth century describe the mechanism of a particular kind of off-color art joke, in which the function of art in providing objects of delectation helped to form the setting for a special kind of *galanterie*. In particular, the traditional subject of the female nude presented the possibility of using these figures as props for erotic games in which the women were inadvertent players, or as a point of departure for suggestive conversations.

A letter that dates from the 1540s, written to the Duke of Ferrara by one of his agents at Fontainebleau, describes a scene where an ancient sculpture becomes an instrument for a masculinist *jeu d'esprit*.[1] King Francis I, in the company of his lover, the Duchess d'Étampes, went to inspect one of his commissions, a group of bronze sculptures that Primaticcio had cast from classical prototypes. The royal couple were accompanied by Cardinal d'Este, as well as by men and women of the court. A discussion about the sculptures ensued, during which the King directed Madame d'Étampes's attention to a statue of Venus. With the excuse of appraising an object of art, Francis spoke about the physical beauty of the female body in such a way as to provoke the discomfiture of his companion. For in pretending to discuss the merits of the statue, the King instead elaborated upon the physical attributes of Madame d'Étampes.

Here lies the crux of the King's joke: his lady is put in the embarrassing position of listening to an erotic discourse by her lover in the presence of others. If she responds in kind, it would be unseemly. If she pretends not to understand, she would show herself to be naive and unworldly, closed to the *frisson* of sensual arousal—a gaffe not to be committed at the court of Fontainebleau. The final irony of her situation is that the King could counter any rejoinder that Madame d'Étampes might make with a protestation that he was merely making observations about a work of art. Given these constraints, the behavior of Madame d'Étampes was less a spontaneous reaction than a clever and dutiful participation in the King's joke: we are told that she said nothing, but departed with a smile on her lips. A smile that implies an understanding of the joke, a good natured acceptance of the right of Francis to make his double entendre at her expense, and a knowing sophistication that acknowledges the atmosphere of charged connotations, yet responds with modesty by leaving the scene.

The scenario does not end with the withdrawal of Madame d'Étampes. The letter proceeds to say that all of the ladies left with the Duchess "to warm themselves up." Is this another joke, this time on the part of the observer, given that the ladies left the King's presence exactly because the climate was getting too hot? At any rate, Francis continued to deliberate about the other sculptures with the Cardinal, with whom he remained alone. Presumably the rest of the conversation unfolded more along the lines of connoisseurship, since lascivious comments on the part of the King would only hit their mark when aimed at his lover. Or, to be more precise, when aimed at his lady in the presence of others. The extended audience was crucial to this game of words, for erotic disquisition between lovers is compromising only when voyeurs are in attendance. The written letter perpetuates the incident and renews the joke, since the correspondent testifies to the other courtiers having witnessed the exchange. Finally, the Duke of Ferrara in his turn recreates the event as he reads the words of his correspondent.

The instances of voyeurism are renewed and compounded each time the letter is read or discussed. This began with the original recipient, and has continued with commentators from the more recent past. In his monograph on the Italian artist Primaticcio, published in 1900, Louis Dimier adds several interpretive nuances to the scene of the King's erotic conversation. As an art historian, Dimier presumably would have had a scholarly interest in the King's remarks about the statue of Venus, information that would have bearing on questions of patronage and reception of works of art. Instead, Dimier's discussion focuses on the libidinous nature of the jest, articulating details that do not exist in the original document, but which the commentator found to be lurking between the lines:

> These beautiful works [the copies of the ancient sculptures] served to decorate the gardens, in particular that of the Conciergerie, which soon became known as the garden of the Queen. But the details of their original placement is not known. A witness lets us see Francis I and the Duchess d'Étampes pay a visit to the sculptures when they were still novelties, in the company of the Cardinal of Ferrara and the Maréchal d'Annebaut. The King, who led Madame d'Étampes by the arm, stopped her in front of the Venus, whose beauties he commented upon, and remarked how she had a perfectly formed body. This was said in a certain tone of voice. The King's favored lady smiled and disengaged his arm to rejoin the other ladies in a room where they were warming themselves. The King remained with the Cardinal and continued his discussion on the merits of these figures.[2]

Dimier spices the tale to enhance the flavor. He provides a prologue to the story, and it consists of gestures. The King's physical contact with Madame d'Étampes is pointedly mentioned, and it is a gesture of domination as well as of affection. Francis is in full control of all movement, and he stops the Duchess in front of the statue. This alters the Ferrarese agent's more passive description that the King was holding Madame d'Étampes by the arm when he pointed out the statue to her. Dimier goes on to repeat the central motif of Francis's detailed colloquy on the perfection of the female body that he had before his eyes.

Then comes an addition. Just in case the King's witticism was so subtle as to escape the reader, Dimier specifies that the eulogy of the Venus was delivered in a particular tone of voice. This sentence is nothing less that a verbal nudge in the ribs, a gentlemanly rephrasing of the more vulgar "Get it?" The words that under other circumstances might have passed for formal analysis of a work of art are rendered lascivious by the innuendo of their inflection. The King's intonation and the presence of Madame d'Étampes signal that the discourse has as its real subject the object on the arm of Francis.

His alterations to the story's end follow the agenda set up by Dimier. As the smiling lady leaves, she cuts off the physical contact that Francis had established at the start of the encounter. "La favorite sourit et quitta le bras du roi" in order to join the rest of the women. The coquettish abandon-ment of her lover for the protection of her female companions who await her at a distance is a *mise en scéne* that modifies the more neutral original, where the Duchess simply entered with the other ladies into another room. Not only is Dimier's version more theatrical and sexier, but it presents the heroine as even more vulnerable. It isolates her as the only woman in a group of men, which was not the case according to the original letter.

Ironically, Dimier's art-historical knowledge serves only to introduce confusion about the setting, which is not open to doubt even in the most cursory reading of the letter. Dimier's reason for citing the document ostensibly is to speculate on the original disposition of Primaticcio's bronze casts, which eventually decorated the Queen's garden, later known as the Orangerie. The communication received by the Duke of Ferrara, however, makes no mention of a garden. Rather, the letter states that the statues had not quite been finished, and were "in a room," presumably where the work was progressing when the King and his entourage went to have a look. Dimier does not make reference to the site of the encounter contained in the sixteenth-century letter, and instead juxtaposes the later fact—the placement of the bronzes in the Orangerie—with the telling of his anecdote. Through their placement and sequence the reader connects the two discussions, and thus a garden setting is bequeathed to the proceedings. Although historically inaccurate, the change is rhetorically effective: a fiction worthy of, and perhaps more appropriate to, an erotic eulogy.

The key elements that combined to produce the King's prurient jest—a work of art, a woman as participant in and victim of the witticism, and an audience—are exactly the ones to be found in another courtly prank recounted only slightly later in the sixteenth century by Pierre de Bourdeille, the Duke of Brantôme. In his collection of racy but highly polished tales, *Les Dames Galantes,* Brantôme includes an elaborate narration of the merriment caused by a certain (nameless) gentleman who entertained his court by foisting erotic images upon his unsuspecting female guests while they were dining at his table.[3]

The story starts with a description of the vehicle of the jest, a goblet of considerable value, whose interior contained numerous figures composed with great skill[4]:

> This goblet was the pride of the prince's table,
> since, as I've said, it was very beautiful and
> artfully wrought, and pleasing to look at inside
> and out.

A justification for the story to be recounted is established. We are dealing with art, and thus have the basis for an acceptable discourse. This warrants the reader's sophisticated enjoyment of a topic that would otherwise be considered inappropriate. After the aesthetic value of the object that will carry the joke is established, the gender of the person on whom the trick will be played is stated. The joke will be gender specific, set in action "When he entertained the ladies and young women of the court", which the nobleman often did.

The nature of the raillery consisted in the fact that the chosen woman was served wine during the dinner from the special chalice whose finely executed decoration consisted of the coitus of beasts, as well as human couples engaged in the sex act. The woman's gradual awareness of the explicitly erotic images, revealed as she consumed her wine, became the butt of the joke. Any and all reactions on the lady's part were hilarious to her companions at the table; once targeted to be the performer of the farce the woman could not make the choice of non-participation. Thus Brantôme follows his description of the mechanisms of the joke with two long paragraphs that revel in the enumeration of all the different reactions that he (and/or others) witnessed.

Brantôme's obvious delight in the variations of the ladies' discomfort leads him to provide a kind of catalogue of basic reactions of the female guests. They indicate complete surprise by remaining speechless; they betray embarrassment by blushing; or they manifest a worldly reaction by exclaiming that they see obscene images, and will therefore not drink another drop. Similar to Madame d'Étampes's abandonment of the scene of her harassment, her counterpart would find the most sophisticated response to be disengagement. Brantôme, however, makes it clear that such a decisive negative reaction of possible dissenters would be ultimately punished, since in all events the banquet continued, and the ladies must drink or "die of thirst." Given the necessity of eventually slaking their thirst, the victims had two more alternatives, both of them risible. They could close their eyes while drinking, clumsily showing their modesty, or they could keep their eyes open, brazenly indicating that they had no shame.

So far, the audience (the prince and his other dinner guests) has merely observed. The laughing matter has been the stages of the victim's gradual discernment of the images as she innocently drinks her wine. The next phase involves interrogation. The prey must now verbalize the reasons for her amusing behavior, and must provide an apologia for whatever reaction she demonstrated. In his unfolding of this aspect of the game, the narrator slips into a revealing error. Although laughter was not listed as one of the female guests' reactions, it is now attributed to her when she is asked "What are you laughing about?"

Full of appreciation for the myriad possibilities for merriment introduced by the cross-examination of the not-guilty, Brantôme constructs another catalogue, this time a series of responses to the provocative demands of the witnesses/judges of the joke:

> "What's there to laugh about?"
> "Why didn't you close your eyes while drinking?"
> "What's better: looking or drinking?"
> "Did you get a rush from seeing this?"
> "Was the wine hot in that cup; did it get you hot?"
> "Which of the images would you like to have in your bedroom?"

The questions become more directed and increasingly risqué as the litany proceeds; the answers run the gamut from insolent to clever, from offensive to accommodating. One distinguishing trait obtains for all of the answers: they are all funny. This is posited by the nature of the game.

Brantôme makes clear the great success of the trick goblet as an evening's entertainment, in his judgment, both for the gentlemen and ladies gathered at dinner:

> In short, one hundred thousand railleries and small talk about the subject were exchanged among the gentlemen and ladies in this manner around the table; and, as I saw, this was a very pleasant game of banter, and something to experience....

And yet the universality of the sport is thrown into doubt by the conclusion of the above passage:

> ... but above all, in my opinion, the most and the best [fun] was to watch the innocent girls (or those who pretended to be so), and the women who were there for the first time, who, to keep a dispassionate demeanor, force out a half-hearted laugh, or restrain themselves and behave like hypocrites, as many women do.

Whether you join in the hearty laughter or hypocritically (says Brantôme) repress and withhold it, as the female victim of the joke you can not help but provide an amusing spectacle for your audience. Brantôme's minutely described scenario, however, never once entertains a crucial possibility: that you would not find it funny.

APPENDIX I

Letter to the Duke of Ferrara from Alfonso Calcagnino

Io essendo gia expedito di quanto havevo a fare per all'hora a Fontanableo, prima di partirmi volsi vedere certe bellissime statue di bronzo che ivi in una camera, S. M.ta Chr.ma facea fare, Et quali sono presso che finite et essendo io in detta Camera mi sopragiunse il Re chr.mo che a brazzo teniva Mad.ma d'Etampes con solo Il R.mo S.r Car.le Nostro seco, Mons.r d'Annibò, una sorella di detta Madama di etampes, et due damiselle, Dove stettero buon pezzo a ragionare, et S. M.ta mostrava alla predicta Madama d'etampes una Venere, come ella era di bel corpo perfettamente formata, la quale non disse altro, ma sorridendo intrò subito in una camera con le altre donne a scaldarsi, et il Re chr.mo resto col S.r Car.le al quanto a divisare di quelle figure, et poi con la predicta Mad.ma si come vennero, essendo, gia tardo sene ritornorno alle sue stanze. Altro non li diro per hora se non che in bona gratia di vostra ex.tia humilmente mi racomando: di Mellone alli 23 di xbre MDXXXXiij

Document transcribed and published by A. Venturi, *Archivio Storico dell'Arte* 2, 1889, 377-8.

APPENDIX II

Dimier's paraphrase of Calcagnino's letter

Ces beaux ouvrages servirent à orner les jardins, en particulier celui de la Conciergerie, qui prit bientôt le nom de jardin de la Reine. Mais on ne sait pas quel fut à l'origine le détail de leur distribution. Un témoin nous fait voir à cette époque Francois Ier et la duchesse d'Etampes les visitant dans leur nouveauté en compagnie du cardinal de Ferrare et du maréchal d'Annebaut. Le roi, qui donnait le bras à M.me d'Etampes, l'arrêta devant la Vénus, dont il lui fit remarquer les beautés, et comment elle avait le corps parfaitement bien fait. Cela était dit d'un certain ton. La favorite sourit et quitta le bras du roi pour rejoindre les autres dames dans une chambre où elles se chauffaient. Le roi resta avec le cardinal, se prolongeant à discourir sur le mérite de ces figures.

Louis Dimier. *Le Primatice.* (Paris: Leroux, 1900) 62-3.

APPENDIX III

Brantôme's account of the dinner parties.

J'ay cogneu un prince de par le monde qui fit bien mieux, car il achepta d'un orfevre une tres-belle coupe d'argent doré, comme pour un chef-d'oeuvre et grand speciauté, la mieux elabourée, gravée et sigillée qu'il estoit possible de voir, où estoyent taillées bien gentiment et subtillement au burin plusieurs figures de l'Aretin, de l'homme et de la femme, et ce au bas estage de la coupe, et au dessus et au haut plusieurs aussi de diverses manieres de cohabitations de bestes, là où j'appris la premiere fois (car j'ay veu souvent la dicte coupe et beu dedans, non sans rire) celle du lion et de la lionne, qui est tout contraire à celle des autres animaux, que n'avois jamais sceu, dont je m'en rapporte à ceux qui le scavent sans que je le die. Cette coupe estoit l'honneur du buffet de ce prince: car, comme j'ay dit, elle estoit tres-belle et riche d'art, et agreable à voir au dedans et au dehors.

Quand ce prince festinoit les dames et filles de la cour, comme souvent il les convioit, ses sommelliers ne failloyent jamais, par son commandement, de leur bailler à boire dedans; et celles qui ne l'avoyent jamais veue, ou en beuvant ou aprés, les unes demeuroyent estonnées et ne sçavoient que dire là-dessus; aucunes demeuroyent honteuses, et la couleur

leur sautoit au visage; aucunes s'entre-disoyent entr'elles: "Qu'est-ce que cela qui est gravé là dedans? Je croy que ce sont des sallauderies. Je n'y boys plus. J'aurois bien grand soif avant que j'y retournasse boire." Mais il falloit qu'elles beussent là, ou bien qu'elles esclatassent de soif; et, pour ce, aucunes fermoyent les yeux en beuvant, les autres, moins vergogneuses, point. Qui en avoyent ouy parler du mestier, tant dames que filles, se mettoyent à rire sous bourre; les autres en crevoyent tout à trac.

Les unes disoyent, quand on leur demandoit qu'elles avoyent à rire et ce qu'elles avoyent veu, qu'elles n'avoyent rien veu que des peintures, et que pour cela elles n'y lairroyent à boire une autre fois. Les autres disoyent: "Quant à moy, je n'y songe point à mal; la veue et la peinture ne souille point l'âme." Les unes disoyent: "Le bon vin est aussi bon leans qu'ailleurs." Les autres affermoyent qu'il y faisoit aussi bon boire qu'en une autre coupe, et que la soif s'y passoit aussi bien. Aux unes on faisoit la guerre pourquoy elles ne fermoyent les yeux en beuvant; elles respondoyent qu'elles vouloyent voir ce qu'elles beuvoyent, craignant que ce ne fust du vin, mais quelque medecine ou poison. Aux autres on demandoit à quoy elles prenoyent plus de plaisir, ou à voir, ou à boire; elles respondoyent: "A tout." Les unes disoyent: "Voilà de belles crotesques!" Les autres: "Voylà de plaisantes mommeries!" Les unes disoyent: "Voylà de beaux images!" Les autres: "Voylà de beaux miroirs!" Les unes disoyent: "L'orfevre estoit bien à loisir de s'amuser à faire ces fadezes!" Les autres disoyent: "Et vous, Monsieur, encore plus d'avoir achepté ce beau hanap." Aux unes on demandoit si elles sentoyent rien qui les picquast au mitant du corps pour cela; elles respondoyent que nulle de ces drolleries y avoit eu pouvoir pour les picquer. Aux autres on demandoit si elles n'avoyent point senty le vin chaut, et qu'il les eust eschauffées, encor que ce fust en hyver; elles respondoyent qu'elles n'avoyent garde, car elles avoyent beu bien froid, qui les avoit bien rafraischies. Aux unes on demandoit quelles images de toutes celles elles voudroyent tenir en leur lict; elles respondoient qu'elles ne se pouvoyent oster de là pour les y transporter.

Bref, cent mille brocards et sornettes sur ce sujet s'entre-donnoyent les gentilshommes et dames ainsi à table, comme j'ay veu, que c'estoit une tres-plaisante gausserie, et chose à voir et ouïr; mais surtout, à mon gré, le plus et le meilleur estoit à contempler ces filles innocentes, ou qui feignoyent l'estre, et autres dames nouvellement venues, à tenir leur mine froide, riante du bout du nez et des levres, ou à se contraindre et faire des hypocrites, comme plusieurs dames en faisoyent de mesme. Et notez que,

quand elles eussent deu mourir de soif, les sommelliers n'eussent osé
leur donner à boire en une autre coupe ny verre. Et, qui plus est,
juroyent aucunes, pour faire bon minois, qu'elles ne tourneroyent jamais
à ces festins; mais elles ne laissoyent pour cela à y tourner souvent, car
ce prince estoit tres-splendide et friand. D'autres disoyent, quand on les
convioit: "J'iray, mais en protestation qu'on ne nous baillera point à
boire dans la coupe"; et, quand elles y estoient, elles y beuvoient plus
que jamais. Enfin elles s'y avezarent si bien qu'elles ne firent plus de
scrupule d'y boire; et si firent bien mieux aucunes, qu'elles se servirent
de telles visions en temps et lieu; et, qui plus est, aucunes s'en des-
baucherent pour en faire l'essay: car toute personne d'esprit veut essayer
tout.

Voilà les effets de cette belle coupe si bien historiée. A quoy se faut
imaginer les autres discours, les songes, les mines et les paroles que
telles dames disoyent et faisoyent entre elles, à part ou en compagnie.

Brantôme (Pierre de Bourdeille). *Les Dames galantes.* (Paris: Editions
Garnier Freres, 1960) 27-9.

NOTES

1. For the text of this document see Appendix I.
2. For the original text see Appendix II.
3. For the original text see Appendix III.
4. The amorous figures were based upon those created by Giulio Romano, known as
   "I Modi". They were put into wide circulation around 1525 through prints engraved
   by Marcantonio Raimondi. Brantôme credits the figures in the goblet to Aretino,
   who wrote sonnets based on the prints. These were quickly published in editions
   together with the images, and widely known. For a general discussion of the
   imagery and the controversy surrounding its diffusion, see my essay and entries in
   the catalogue to the exhibition *Giulio Romano.* (Milan: Electa, 1989) 277ff.

21

The Ancestral Laughter of the Streets: Humor in Muriel Spark's Earlier Works

REGINA BARRECA

> It is known as a scrambler, because the connection is heavily jammed with jangling caterwauls to protect the conversation against eavesdropping; this harrowing noise all but prevents the speakers from hearing each other, but once the knack is mastered it is easy to hear the voice at the other end....(*Hothouse* 55)

Since she started writing in the early 1950s, Muriel Spark has received enormous critical attention. Evelyn Waugh called her first book "highly exhilarating" (*Spectator,* 22/2/1951) and her subsequent work "dazzling" (*Spectator,* 7/7/61). She has been called "the reasonable recorder of unreason" and likened, of course, to Jane Austen—"the Jane Austen of the surrealists," according to one critic (Hoyt 280).

223

Spark's work, like Elizabeth Bowen's, has a wide appeal and has spanned nearly forty years. David Lodge has called Spark "the most gifted and innovative British novelist of her generation, one of the very few who can claim to have extended and altered the possibilities of the form for other practitioners" (Lodge 1). Frank Kermode has said of Spark's novels that "some literate people dislike them, though not, so far as I know, for decent reasons."[1] The reasons some people dislike them may be more or less summed up by the following comments on Spark's works by Karl which appear in *The Contemporary English Novel:*

> [Spark's] novels...are so involved with the eccentric event and the odd personality that they have virtually no content. Miss Spark's novels are a sport, light to the point of froth. She can write about murder, betrayal, deception, and adultery as though these were the norms of a crazy-quilt society....(126)

Karl concludes by saying that she "lacks penetration." But, applying to Spark what another critic has concluded concerning Karl's remarks about Iris Murdoch: "Karl's misunderstanding...is so radical as to be helpful" (Kuehl 38). Peter Kemp has offered the following explanation for the perception of Spark's work by some critics—including but unfortunately not limited to Karl—as "lightweight": "books so entertaining, it is felt, must be proportionately trivial" (8). Updike, not surprisingly, has difficulties with Spark, though he admires what he calls the "ominous...witchcraft" of her work:

> The undercurrents of destruction [and] madness...are allowed to run unspoken, welling up here and there, as they do in life, with an unexpectedness that would be comic if we could laugh.[2]

Updike may seem sympathetic, but he *cannot laugh* and this is perhaps the most illustrative of the remarks made by male critics concerning comedic works by women writers. Women's writing, they claim, would be comic if "we" (sic) could laugh. It is my argument that *"we"* are indeed laughing. *"They,"* including Updike, are not.

For women writers, including Spark, undercurrents of destruction and unexpected wellsprings of madness are more a definition of women's comedy than an argument against it. These unspoken currents act like the jumbled text put through on the scrambler: they are there but difficult to perceive without initiation. However, Spark's subversive comedy, like the submerged text, is 'easy to hear' "once the knack is mastered," in other words, once the dislocating, encoded aspects of comedy can be perceived within the more conventional comedic context.

Spark deals with what Kermode rather neatly termed "a radically noncontingent reality" (131), and these aspects of her work as the "surrealist Jane Austen" have been discussed with more attention than the parallel aspects of Bowen's apparently more conservative fiction. V.B. Richmond, for example, writes that Spark's fiction "mirrors the uncertainty, confusion, infidelity, and violence that are ordinary characteristics of contemporary society" (106). In contrast, Faith Pullin claims that Spark's severe editing of her text "encourages the reader to suspend his belief, not his disbelief" (76). Quoting from *Loitering With Intent,* Pullin contextualizes Spark's gift for unreality: "complete frankness is not a quality that favours art." Striking a similar note in her article "The Canonization of Muriel Spark," Sharon Thompson says that she counts "Catholics, feminists, misogynists, postmodernists, Fowlerites, and those with a simple taste for a wicked tongue among Spark's supporting factions" (*Voice Literary Supplement* 9). Spark does not seem to write for the "general reader" despite her wide audience. It may be instructive to take note of how two of her characters discuss this very issue in *Loitering With Intent:*

> 'Fuck the general reader,' Solly said, 'because in fact the general reader doesn't read.' 'That's what I say,' Edwina yelled. 'Just fuck the general reader. No such person.' (56)

Pullin makes an important point linking Spark's refusal to create so-called realist fictions for the "general reader" and her position as a woman writer. In "Autonomy and Fabulation in the Fiction of Muriel Spark," Pullin argues that the subtlety of Spark's work:

> is nowhere more evident than in the treatment of her women characters.... Her women are initiators, actors, magicians whose 'real' nature, like that of life itself, can never be known. (91)

Judy Little provides what is the best feminist criticism of Spark in her book juxtaposing the works of Spark with those of Virginia Woolf. Little examines their use of comedy in terms very similar to those which we have established:

> When Spark and Woolf evaluate relationships between the sexes, and use such an ascetic norm to do so, their laughter is not content to tease follies and flail vices, or to urge a little common sense. Their laughter instead demands a radically 'new plot.' Woolf and Spark, from different directions, approach the four-thousand-year-old secular scripture and rip the temple curtain from top to bottom. (178)

Little's recognition of the ways in which Spark seeks to destroy the "secular script" of patriarchal authority through comedy implies the use of aggression and anger as weapons of comedy. Peter Kemp has noted the way "multiple instances of malice and aggression crowd the narratives" of Spark (7), but even his use of the verb "crowd" indicates his inability to see the malice and aggression as the encoded forces that will "rip" through boundaries to allow for the limitlessness, the non-closure of Spark's comedy.

Kemp is not the only one to see Spark's anger. Sharon Thompson provides a provocative discussion of the effectiveness of Spark's undercurrent of rage as women's subversive discourse in her comments on *The Driver's Seat,* pointing out those very elements that seem to make Updike too nervous to laugh:

> It takes an iron stomach to write a plot like that. I've read angrier rhetoric in fiction by women, but...no angrier plot. It's stunning—actually scandalizing. In comparison, Rhys's novels, which I love, snivel and Lessing's slop. (*Voice Literary Supplement* 9)

Indeed, Spark's portrayal of anger and refusal characterizes both her short stories and novels. In *The Girls of Slender Means,* Spark explores the imposed disingenuousness of women who are dangerously ruthless—while never forfeiting their role as ingenue. Spark explains at the beginning of the novel that, as the girls realize themselves to "varying degrees":

> Few people alive at the time were more delightful, more ingenious, more movingly lovely, and, as it might happen, more savage, than the girls of slender means. (6)

Spark herself has defended literature of aggressive intent claiming that: "the only effective art of our particular time is the satirical, the harsh and witty, the ironic and derisive. Because we have come to a moment in history when we are surrounded on all sides and oppressed by the absurd" (Kemp 14). In keeping with our argument of women's comedy as redoubling anger rather than expelling it, Kemp argues, "glycerine soothes, but acid galvanizes" (114).

Even the most "innocent" figure in a Spark novel is capable of savagery: in *The Comforters,* one character notes that "everyone can do harm, whether they [sic] mean it or not" (128). Often the most innocent figure in a Spark fiction is also the most savage, having been denied access to more acceptable forms of refusal or even participation within the dominant society. Spark's characters, in particular her women characters, are marginal, peripheral, exiled from all acceptable systems of power. These marginal figures attempt to hide their anger under conventional behavior. They try to "say anything beside the point rather than what [one] might say, at such moments, pointedly" when they "have a sharp tongue" (*Robinson* 73). But often their anger emerges, like the clear message through the scrambler, for those willing to hear.

On the one hand, a number of Spark's heroines are believed by the members of their immediate community to be suicidal, depressed, mad, engaged in espionage, possessed or even, in one extreme instance, already dead. On the other hand, a number of characters who in fact are murderous, insane, or even dead are not recognized as such. Spark does not shy away from extremes; she can be compared to the sensationalist novelists discussed by Showalter who inverted the stereotypes of traditional novels and parodied the conventions of their male contemporaries. Spark follows the same route, it can be argued, and her novels express:

> female anger, frustration, and sexual energy more directly than had been done previously...women escape from their families through illness, madness, divorce, flight, and ultimately murder. (Showalter 160)

As Kermode argues in "Sheerer Spark," the very plot of *The Driver's Seat* is an inversion of a conventional comedy. The narrative can be reduced to its essentials: girl meets boy, girl loses boy, girl finds boy. Happy ending? When that plot is carried out to its typical (what Frye would call its "normal") conclusion, perhaps. However, Spark's results are rape, murder and deviance. What is normal becomes corrupt in Spark's fiction. Lise, the main character, "is looking for her type," Kermode summarizes, "seeking on her vacation a murderer as other girls might seek a lover. She finds him on the plane, loses him, and recovers him," but the confusion dislocates comedy, dislodges it from any possibilities of stasis, comfort, reconciliation or social acceptability. Spark reshapes expectations in order to introduce the forces of chaos and non-closure, as well as her particular perfection: surprise.

Spark writes from what she calls the "nevertheless" principle, a principle which is based on the overturning of expectations. Spark writes:

> In fact I approve of the ceremonious accumulation of weather forecasts and barometer-readings that pronounce for a fine day, before letting rip on the statement: 'Nevertheless, it's raining'. I find that much of my literary composition is based on the nevertheless idea. (Kemp 7)

"There is more to be had from the world than a balancing of accounts," Spark writes in *The Only Problem* (44), underscoring her refusal to supply conventionally happy, tidy endings. Ruth Whittaker writes that Spark "has an impatience with mimesis since her real concern is with the inimitable" (168). Kemp argues that Spark keeps to "her own axiom that if fiction is not stranger than truth, it ought to be" (8). These comments point to the fact that Spark systematically refuses to accept the "absolutes" encoded within man-made cultural systems. It is significant that in *Robinson*, the only female character keeps a journal even though she remarks that "through my journal I nearly came to my death" (7). January Marlow goes on to suggest why her writings are important even though she does not consider herself an objective recorder of "reality":

> ...though I know it to be distorted, never quite untrue, never entirely true, [my journal] interests me. I am as near the mark as myth is to history, the apocrypha to the canon. (137)

January argues that writing "fetches before me the play of thought and action hidden amongst the recorded facts" (7), and it is what is hidden among recorded fact that Spark considers necessary to explore. The secret "play of thought and action" is for Spark the most important aspect of comedy.

Spark draws heavily on the multiplicitous structures of mythology. Fleur Talbot of *Loitering With Intent* comments on the necessity of the mythological in literature and argues persuasively against the systematic application of convention and closure:

> Without a mythology, a novel is nothing. The true novelist, one who understands the work as a continuous poem, is a mythmaker, and then wonder of the art resides in the endless different ways of telling a story, and the methods are mythological by nature. (Pullin 83)

The heroine of *The Abbess of Crewe* explains that as far as she is concerned "history doesn't work.... We have entered the sphere, dear Sisters, of Mythology" (16). Perhaps this is because Spark links women with mythology and in doing so reaffirms the value of the illogical, irrational and disruptive. "And it is said the pagan mind runs strong in women at any time," writes January Marlow, the only woman to survive the plane crash in *Robinson*, "let alone on an island" (9). *Robinson* is Spark's most explicit exploration of women's link with mythology and sorcery. Hoyt writes in "The Surrealist Jane Austen" that Spark "understands that the artist traces his (sic) descent from the sorcerer" (Hoyt 130), and as we see from January's own perceptions, her writing is connected to the "whole period's" being "touched with a pre-ancestral quality, how there was an enchantment, a primitive blood-force which probably moved us all" (9). Particular characters, like Georgiana Hogg of *The Comforters,* can have "turbulent mythical dimensions" (154) and characters like Dougal Douglas from *The Ballad of Peckham Rye* are out-and-out inhabitants of the fabular dimension.

Spark's use of mythology embodies the insight of the Italian proverb of which Spark is fond: "if it isn't true, it's to the point" (*Public Image* 43). Spark's fictions work towards unveiling the nature of truth as itself the deliberate construction of a "supreme fiction." Her narratives operate by:

> cutting through the barriers of overused language and situation a sense of reality true to experience, an imaginative extension of the world, a lie that shows us things as they are—a supreme fiction. (Malkoff 3)

Spark concerns herself with the ways in which innocence, particularly the innocence imposed on women, is a danger to the symbolic, patriarchal order. David Lodge has written, for example, that "Miss Brodie was not a wicked woman, but a dangerously innocent one." He quotes from a scene in *The Prime of Miss Jean Brodie* where Sandy, one of Brodie's former pupils, now a nun in a convent, speaks to a former friend: "'Oh, she was quite an innocent in her way' said Sandy [to Jenny], clutching the bars of her grille." Lodge argues that innocence is "dangerous and volatile because [it is] ignorant of real good and evil" ("Uses & Abuses" 60).

One of the more dangerous ways innocence transfigures itself in Spark is through the creation of apparently material reality initiated by belief or thought; Spark's works are informed by the "transfiguration of the commonplace," a phrase taken from the title of Sandy Stranger's (or, as she becomes in the convent, Sister Helena of the Transfiguration) treatise on psychology. Spark emphasizes the ways language shapes and creates reality since there is no objective reality; she focuses on "... the ways fiction can body forth the shape of things unknown" (Kermode 397). An example of this transfiguration occurs in *The Hothouse by the East River* where Elsa and her husband Paul are dead and living in New York. Paul believes they exist because of Elsa's will:

> His heart thumps for help. "Help me! Help me!" cries his heart, battering the sides of the coffin. "The schizophrenic has imposed her will. Her delusion, her figment, her nothing-there, has come to pass." (14)

Spark's "her nothing-there," highlights the use of absence, empty space, and the "hollows" of language and reality in women's writing. In *The Driver's Seat,* for instance, Lise's room is described in terms of absence: "the lines of the room are pure; space is used as a pattern in itself" (11). The same can be said of Spark's prose: space is a pattern in itself. Art is, in fact, linked to the nothing-there element of language, as one of Spark's characters explains in her short story "The Playhouse called Remarkable":

> And if ever you produce a decent poem or a story, it won't be on account of anything you've got in this world but of something remarkable which you haven't got. (*Collected Stories* 103)

In perhaps her most elegant use of absence as pattern, Spark ends *The Public Image* with an image of space, but space which contains the infinite. The main focus of the book, Annabel, has been described by her vicious husband as all surface, an empty shell. But Spark revises the damning phrases of the husband with his limited vision to create a benediction of the limitlessness contained within Annabel and within all women:

> She was pale as a shell...[and had a] sense weightlessly and perpetually within her, as an empty shell contains, by its very structure, the echo and harking image of former and former seas. (192)

Absence, echo, space and the hollows of things supply meaning. In contrast, substance, the material manifestation of apparent reality, can be misleading and should not be trusted. In a brief essay on a fresco by Piero della Francesca, Spark comments that "today we know more about substance than ever before, but the more we know the more it is recognized that we know nothing."[3] Spark claims, in the third act of her play *The Doctors of Philosophy,* that "realism is very flimsy." The only difficulty for the characters, usually women, who realize the flimsy nature of reality, is convincing others, usually men, of what they have discovered. Elsa of *Hothouse by the East River* argues to her husband Paul that while he might seem to accept what she says, he will refuse to accept her truth. It becomes useless, according to Elsa, to attempt explanation: "[y]ou'll believe me, yes, but you won't believe that it really happened. What's the use of telling you?" (4). However, women who recognise the flimsy nature of reality learn, like Elsa, to use the power of their own beliefs to revise the pliable substance of reality.

Everything created by language "involves a tangled mixture of damaging lies, flattering and plausible truths" (54). Kemp notes that in her study of John Masefield, Spark exclaims: "how sharp and lucid fantasy can be when it is deliberately intagliated on the surface of realism" (40). According to Kemp, Spark is writing not primarily as social chronicler but as "an artist, a changer of actuality into something else" (85). Things can be transfigured, as we have noted, through language.

Through a sort of language-transubstantiation, the "real" can be created. In *Robinson* we learn that "the awful thing about... insinuations" is that "you never know, they might be true" (123) or that they might become true through sheer belief. For example, we learn in *Hothouse* that if "Paul could be induced to believe this man's somebody else, then he will become somebody else. It's a matter of persevering in a pretense" (38). *The Comforters* contains the most consistent playing out of the idea of the transubstantiation of the apparent absolutes of reality, such as material existence. In a telling remark, Carolyn, the novel's protagonist, explains to her fiancé, who believes in "objective existence," that things "might have another sort of existence and still be real" (70).

Spark's female characters initially spend a great deal of energy attempting, like Elsa, to convince those around them that what we perceive as real is no more substantial than the imaginary. These characters abandon the attempt after realizing that they are in fact in control of situations that they had originally perceived as outside of their sphere of influence. This is the pattern of comedy in Spark's novels: the gradual knowing of the absurdity of the absolute by male as well as female characters. Spark's central characters come to understand that so-called reality can be revised, reshaped and undermined by the power of the peripheral, powers more accessible to women than to men. Men and women, explains January of *Robinson,* can be "on the same island but in different worlds" (144). Women characters, like Carolyn of *The Comforters,* have a unique understanding of the multiple layers forming apparent reality. Like Carolyn, they understand that "the voices are voices. Of course they are symbols. But they are also voices. There's the typewriter too—that's a symbol, but it is a real typewriter. I hear it" (75).

It is not surprising that Carolyn, who is writing a book on twentieth-century fiction entitled "Form in The Modern Novel" is "having difficulty with the chapter on realism" (62). Kermode comments that "[t]he relation of fiction and reality is uniquely reimagined" in Spark's novels, claiming that Spark requires the reader to undergo "a radical re-appraisal of this relation." Kermode argues that Spark accommodates "different versions of reality, including what some call mythical and some call absolute" (131). Spark rarely deals in absolutes. Like other women writers, especially writers of comedy, she refers to the subjective nature of even the most superficially objective "givens." Very little indeed is universally perceived:

> There were other people's Edinburghs quite different from hers, and with which she held only the names of districts and streets and monuments in common. Similarly, there were other people's nineteen-thirties. (*Jean Brodie* 50)

Spark's fictions depend on our perception and understanding of what she calls the "shifting ground" (*Comforters* 107) of reality. The "picture" or subjective reality replaces the "truth" or objective reality. For example, in *Hothouse by the East River,* someone wants "the picture, the whole picture and nothing but the picture" (17). Spark articulates through her novels the concept that the conventional pattern has no authority and must be understood to be the dominant fiction rather than the "truth." This leads, as we should expect, to the refusal to portray, even in the comedic context, a secure world. "Nowhere's safe," says a character in *The Girls of Slender Means* (155). The implications of non-closure, subversion and revision for comedic narrative are clear.

One critic, for example, castigates Spark for "her refusal to be committed, to solve her fictional situations, for her readiness to abandon all for a jest, for her random satire" (Stubbs 33), for precisely those elements which we now see are functional determinants of women's comedy. Spark explores the peripheral boundaries of fiction and is unapologetic about refusing to supply conventional comedic closure. Spark links the forces of creation and chaos with her usual (and much discussed) economy of method in a number of novels. In *Robinson,* for example, a character explains that "if you choose the sort of life which has no conventional pattern you have to try to make an art of it, or it is a mess" (84). The ability to overcome conventional patterns is of enormous importance in Spark's fictions. She actually views the writer-as-anarchist as a subversive figure, armed with humor against the dominant ideology:

> There is a kind of truth in the popular idea of an anarchist as a wild man with a home-made bomb in his pocket. In modern times this bomb, fabricated in the back workshops of the imagination, can only take one effective form: Ridicule. (*Girls of Slender Means* 69)

Kemp quotes Spark on the subject of writing-as-subversion: "I would like to see," she writes, "a more deliberate cunning, a more derisive undermining of what is wrong, I would like to see less emotion and more intelligence in these efforts to impress our minds and hearts" (114). He also presents her views on fiction as undermining or at least forcing us to recognise the "ridiculous nature" of what is passed off as reality:

> 'We have come to a moment in history,' Mrs. Spark claims, 'when we are surrounded on all sides and oppressed by the absurd': and what this means for literature, she argues, is that 'the rhetoric of our times should persuade us to contemplate the ridiculous nature of the reality before us, and teach us to mock it. (146)

It is worth considering in brief the manner in which Spark's subversion of realism has been dealt with critically. Spark often displays the destruction of boundaries between the "real" and the imaginary through events of great emotional violence by which she shifts our perspective and reveals what Malkoff has categorized as the "bizarre underpinnings of the superficially conventional" (3). Kemp argues, noting the dialectical interplay between the apparently acceptable/conventional and the subversive/chaotic in Spark:

> Many of [Spark's] fiction's features are immediately recognizable: what makes its effect disorienting and, indeed, almost hallucinatory is that the pattern into which they would normally fall has been violently deranged. (141)

Faith Pullin characterizes Spark's fiction in the very terms we have established for women's comedy when Pullin argues that "the nature of Muriel Spark's fiction is its duplicity; she specializes in the subverting of expectations. As she herself claims, in the well-known 'House of Fiction' interview, 'what I write is not true—it is a pack of lies'" (Pullin 71). Valerie Shaw agrees in her article on Spark entitled "Fun and Games with Life-stories." She proposes that there is "clearly a strong case to be made for [Spark's] work as being actually subversive of realism" (46). Vera Richmond calls Spark's central characters "shape shifters" (74). Caroline of *The Comforters* asks at one point "Is the world a lunatic asylum then? Are we all courteous maniacs discreetly making allowances for everyone else's derangement?" (196) and the answer, with a smile from Spark, is "yes."

Spark's comedy in fact rests on its being able to undermine the valid currency of the dominant ideology by "shifting the ground" of her narrative discourse. "Once you admit you can change the object" of a belief, she writes in *The Girls of Slender Means,* "you undermine the whole structure..." (23). Spark depends on the traditional systematic acceptance of convention, it is true, because otherwise she would be unable to subvert expectations as regularly as she does. This point has been noted by a number of critics, although few of them link the undermining of convention directly with comedy. Miles, for example, writes that "convention...has to be understood as the basis for nearly all of Muriel Spark's fiction; she assumes our familiarity with its precepts in order to be able to undercut and diminish them" (58), while Hoyt sees in Spark "an almost irresponsible impertinence towards everyday reality" (128). Alan Bold believes that Spark:

> confronts realistic detail with surrealistic tension, invests natural incidents with supernatural overtones. Her fiction is not contained by a rigid narrative frame-work; it unfolds in a visionary dimension. (9)

Spark's uncanny ability to make the ordinary conversation take on a surrealistic quality has received much attention. The "visionary dimension" in her work can quickly accommodate the commonplace by illustrating the ways simple misreadings take place, the ways in which those uninitiated in language systems and thereby uninitiated in the language of authority attempt to find meaning. Lise of *The Driver's Seat* is probably Spark's most marginal figure in that she is on the very periphery of social acceptance. She has no friends, no family, no socially prescribed role except the one supplied through employment. She cannot recognize deviance when she meets it since she has little sense of the norm. In the following exchange, for example, Lise attempts to hide her marginality, not even aware of the marginal nature of the man's own discourse. She thinks he must be making sense because he is a man. Lise thinks she should understand him, and so, illustrating the most damaging sort of duplicity, she pretends that she does:

> "You know what Yin is?" he says.
> She says, "Well, sort of" ... "but it's only a snack, isn't it?"
> "You understand what Yin is?"
> "Well, it's a kind of slang, isn't it. You say a thing's a bit too yin ... ";
> plainly she is groping.
> "Yin," says Bill, "is the opposite of Yang." (33)

Even the health-food addict appears more in control than Lise because he perceives himself as an authority; Lise, however ultimately controls the actions of the novel despite her inability to grasp yin and yang.

Judy Little provides one of the few arguments defining the comedy in Spark's narratives as gender-based.[4] "In Spark's fiction possibility is assured," Little argues, "in effect, guaranteed—by an absolute, eternal openness that judges and shocks any human effort at easy closure" (187). This, of course, supports the theory that women's comedy is itself characterized by the limitlessness of its endings, by the refusal to construct a conventional sense of finality at the end of the narrative. "Knots were not necessarily created to be untied," writes Spark, and continues: "[q]uestions were things that sufficed in their still beauty answering themselves" (Kemp 156).

But Spark does not only provide passive resistance to the narrative conventions which she refuses to employ; she sees in non-closure possibilities beyond those usually identified with the twentieth-century British novel. Returning to the figure of the writer as bomb-throwing anarchist, she writes that:

Any system...which doesn't allow for the unexpected and the unwelcome is a rotten one....Things mount up inside one, and then one has to perpetrate an outrage. (*Robinson* 162)

We must remind ourselves often that, as Spark writes at the end of *Robinson*, "all things are possible" (174). We must *retain*, she insists in *The Prime of Miss Jean Brodie*, "a sense of the hidden possibilities in all things" (119) and be even "unnaturally exhilarated" like Caroline in *The Comforters*, "by a sense of adventure" (64).

Spark informs her readers about "a lot of subjects irrelevant to the authorised curriculum," as one character calls alternatives to the prevailing authority-system in *The Prime of Miss Jean Brodie*. Spark herself teaches the literary equivalent of the "rudiments of astrology but not the date of the Battle of Flodden" (10) by providing narratives that undercut the system while remaining within it, much as Brodie teaches astrology while the girls in her class hold up their history textbooks in case the headmistress should walk by the class. In a fashion similar to the one Brodie uses when she keeps a multiplication question on the board during math hour while she speaks to her girls about art, sex and how witch-hazel is better for skin than soap and water, Spark provides a narrative "cover" for her subversive text. Sandy, Brodie's star pupil and ultimately her betrayer, learns to uncover the subtext of the most apparently innocent utterance under Miss Brodie's influence:

Sandy, who had turned eleven, perceived that the tone of "morning" in good
morning made the word seem purposely to rhyme with "scorning," so that these
colleagues of Miss Brodie's might just as well have said, "I scorn you," instead
of good morning. (79)

And even as Miss Brodie encouraged her girls to recite, with feeling,
"The Lady of Shalott," she also assured them that "the people perish" and
bids Eunice to "come and do a somersault in order that we may have a
comic relief" (13). Comedy is the mainstay of Spark's fiction. In fact,
Spark has described her reactions to the writing of full-length fiction after
the poetry and criticism she had earlier attempted by saying "that the novel
enabled me to express the comic side of my mind and at the same time
work out some serious theme" (Kemp 11).

In "Muriel Spark's Fingernails," Malcolm Bradbury discusses Spark
primarily as a writer of comedy. He sees the precision and economy of
Spark's comedy as shaped by a "tactic of indifference" which provides
"poise" for her aesthetic manner. He writes of Spark's "splendid impu-
dence" in creating a "decidedly strange view of the world and of human
potential and the human condition" (138) but, like Hoyt, who see Spark's
"uncomfortable and distinctive humor" as departure from the "humane
world of the traditional, realist novel" (169), Bradbury perceives Spark as
providing clever but not particularly revolutionary texts.

Kemp's framing of Spark's comedy provides, in addition to Little, the
only viable way to accommodate the non-closure and consistent use of
subversive humor throughout Spark's texts. Kemp quotes the response of
one critic to *The Girls of Slender Means:* "I enjoyed it as a joke until it
stopped being a joke." Kemp argues that:

[t]o read Muriel Spark in this way is to mistake the varnish for the picture. Her
books are never simply jokes, though they invariably contain them; they are not
eccentric jeux d'esprit, ephemeral and whimsical. Comic, it has to be stressed in
any approach to these novels, does not equate with trivial, any more than solemn
does with valuable. It is a commonplace to describe certain works as deeply serious: the books of Mrs. Spark are deeply funny....(8)

The "deeply funny" nature of Spark's work draws on the power of the
marginal and the magical. In obvious parallel to Updike's reference to
Spark's "ominous...witchcraft" which, as we noticed, prevented him from
laughing, stand the figures of the hysteric and the sorceress urging laughter
and abandon. Spark's comedy is tied in some way to the primitive ritual
of exorcising evil, a number of critics have claimed, but what might appear

"evil" to Spark and other women writers might be the very thing which to others appears as the embodiment of "good." Spark does not accept convention; she mocks the most strongly accepted norms. Like one of her own favorite writers, John Henry Newman, Spark could reply to critics who criticize her for being overly satirical that "what they think is exaggeration, I think truth."[5] In response to the inevitable refrain of a man telling a woman "that's not funny," Spark offers the following exchange:

> "I don't see what there is to laugh at," Paul tells her....
> "...it has its funny side," she says. (*Hothouse* 133)

Lodge writes that "it is perfectly true that her imagination is fascinated by revenge, humiliation and ironic reversals, and that she looks upon pain and death with a dry, glittering eye" (169); nevertheless, he also sees Spark as primarily a writer of comedy. Her comedy is undeniably informed by her anger. She presents us with "something between a wedding and a funeral on a world scale" (*Girls of Slender Means* 16). Instead of leading us to reconciliation and regeneration, Spark's comedy, like that of other women writers, is directed towards recognition and realization, even if this process marginalizes the characters even further from the dominant ideology. Richmond calls it "hilarity and rueful recognition" (79). Perhaps the process of moving further from the vortex of power, the pull of false "reality" as the most desirable choice, should be couched not in "even" but in "especially."

"If it were only true that all's well that ends well," writes Spark at the beginning of one novel, "if only it were true" (*Hothouse* 3). Spark dislocates our expectations continually, rebelling against the cyclical nature of traditional comedy which reaffirms the standing order. "Spark uses laughter as a dynamic... weapon," asserts Hoyt.

Spark addresses the issues of language and creation throughout the reworking of "givens" or cliches such as the "all's well" and "I wish I were dead" syndrome. For example, in her story "The Go-Away Bird," a young woman who is unhappy in both her African and her English existences cries "God help me, life is unbearable" and is promptly shot dead. Words have enormous power, as we have seen, especially for someone like the inescapably self-reflective figure Spark creates during a brief aside in *Robinson*, "MURIEL THE MARVEL with her X-ray eyes" who can "read your very soul" (61). Like MURIEL who has "dozens of satisfied clients," Spark is concerned with her audience's reactions and has said she likes to "make them laugh and to keep it short" (Lodge 60).

Comedy is, of course, a defense as well as a weapon. Often intelligent women like Caroline Rose or Sandy Stranger resort to humor as the only way to make sense of an obviously ridiculous reality. For Sandy, "fear returned as soon as she had stopped laughing" (*Jean Brodie* 60).

There is another form of comedy for women, usually exhibited by minor characters in Spark's novels but nevertheless acting in significant counterpoint to the more subtlely dangerous mocking of the protagonists. This form of comedy is the laugh of the hysteric, the "cackle" of Wilt's matriarchs. The non-participatory women in Spark provide the broadest broom to sweep away convention. They can barely contain their laughter at the absurdity of the universe before them; one such figure from *The Driver's Seat* "gives out the high, hacking cough-like ancestral laughter of the streets, holding her breasts in her hands to spare them the shake-up" (14).

Spark's comedy forces the very issue of the "happy ending" that has so unnerved critics of her work and the works of so many women writers of comedy. In *The Only Problem* she considers the question outright, wondering if:

> ...Job would be satisfied with this plump reward, and doubted it. His tragedy was that of the happy ending. (176)

"Make it a straight old-fashioned story, no modern mystifications," is the advice given to Caroline at the end of *The Comforters* as she sets out to begin her novel. "End with the death of the villain and the marriage of the heroine." Caroline laughs and replies, "Yes, it would end that way" (222). *The Comforters* itself ends with the marriage of an elderly couple, not the marriage of Caroline herself. A religious woman is drowned and Caroline can only manage to save herself by allowing the woman to go under. Hardly the "normal" happy ending. Yet the book finally ends with a framed "look of one who faces an altogether and irrational new experience; a look partly fearful, partly indignant, partly curious, but predominantly joyful" (74) and this emphasis on the play of emotions, rather than the unity of emotion, is characteristic of Spark and of women's comedy in general. Spark's comedy presents "a series of pictures, distinct, primitive, undisdainful, without hope, without pain, without any comment but the grin and laugh of a constitutional survivor" (*Hothouse* 58).

NOTES

1. Frank Kermode, "The Prime of Miss Muriel Spark." *New Statesman* 27 September, 1963: 397.
2. John Updike, "Between a Wedding and a Funeral." *New Yorker* Sept 14, 1961: 192.
3. Muriel Spark, "Spirit and Substance." *Vanity Fair,* December 1984; 103.
4. Newman, *Apologia pro vita sua,* ed. Martin J. Svagli, 296, quoted in *Muriel Spark: An Odd Capacity for Vision.* Ed. Alan Bold, (New York: Vision and Barnes and Noble, 1984) 61.
5. For an excellent discussion of Spark's humor, see John Glavin's "Muriel Spark's Unknowing Fiction" in *Last Laughs: New Perspectives on Women and Comedy* ed. Regina Barreca (New York: Gordon and Breach, 1988) 221-241.

WORKS CITED

Bold, Alan, ed. *Muriel Spark: An Odd Capacity for Vision.* New York: Vision and Barnes and Noble, 1984.

Bradbury, Malcolm. "Muriel Spark's Fingernails." *Contemporary Women Novelists.* Patricia Meyers Spacks, Ed. Englewood, New Jersey: Prentice-Hall Inc., 1977: 137-149.

Hoyt, Charles Alva. "Muriel Spark: The Surrealist Jane Austen," *Contemporary British Novelists.* Ed. Charles Shapiro. Carbondale and Edwardsville: Southern Illinois University Press, 1965: 125-143.

Karl, Frederick R. *The Contemporary English Novel.* New York: Farrar, Strauss and Cudahy, 1962.

Kemp, Peter. *Muriel Spark.* New York: Barnes and Noble, 1975.

Kermode, Frank. *The Sense of an Ending.* New York: Oxford University Press, 1967.

___. "The Prime of Miss Muriel Spark." *New Statesman* 27 September, 1963: 397-398.

Little, Judith. *Comedy and the Woman Writer.* Lincoln: University of Nebraska Press, 1983.

Lodge, David. "Marvels and Nasty Surprises." *The New York Times Book Review.* 20 Oct. 1985: 1-4.

___. "The Uses and Abuses of Omniscience: Method and Meaning in Muriel Spark's 'The Prime of Miss Jean Brodie.'" *Novelist at the Crossroads.* Ithaca: Cornell University Press, 1971.

Malkoff, Karl. *Muriel Spark.* Columbia Essays on Modern Writers, 36. New York: Columbia University Press, 1968.

Miles, Rosalind. *The Fiction of Sex.* London: Vision Press, 1974.

Pullin, Faith. "Autonomy and Fabulation in the Fiction of Muriel Spark." *Muriel Spark: An Odd Capacity for Vision.* Ed. Alan Bold: 71-93.

Richmond, Velma Bourgeois. *Muriel Spark.* New York: Frederick Ungar Publishing Co., 1984.

Shaw, Valerie. "Fun and Games with Life-stories." *Muriel Spark: An Odd Capacity for Vision*. Ed. Alan Bold: 44-70.

Showalter, Elaine. *A Literature of Their Own*. Princeton, New Jersey: Princeton University Press, 1977.

Spark, Muriel. *Collected Poems 1*. London: Macmillan, 1970.

___. "How I Became a Novelist". *John O'London's Weekly 3*. (December 1960): 683.

___. "Keeping it short." Interview. *The Listener* 24 Sept, 1970.

___. *Loitering with Intent*. New York: Coward, McCann and Geoghegan, 1981.

___. "My Conversion". *20th Century* 170. (1961): 58-63.

___. *Robinson*. London: Penguin, 1964.

___. "Spirit and Substance" *Vanity Fair* 12/84.

___. *Territorial Rights*. New York: Coward, McCann and Geoghegan, 1979.

___. *The Bachelors*. London: Macmillan, 1960.

___. *The Ballad of Peckham Rye*. New York: Putnam, 1960.

___. *The Comforters*. New York: Putnam, 1957.

___. *The Doctors of Philosophy*. New York: Alfred Knopf, 1966.

___. *The Driver's Seat*. New York: Putnam, 1970.

___. *The Girls of Slender Means*. New York: Alfred Knopf, 1963.

___. *The Hothouse by the East River*. New York: Viking Press, 1973.

___. *The Mandlebaum Gate*. New York: Alfred Knopf, 1965.

___. *The Only Problem*. New York: Putnam, 1984.

___. *The Public Image*. London: Macmillan, 1968.

___. *The Stories of Muriel Spark*. New York: E.P. Dutton, 1985.

___. *The Takeover*. London: Macmillan, 1976.

___. *Voices at Play*. New York: J.B. Lippincott Company, 1962.

Stubbs, Patricia. *Muriel Spark*. London: British Council, Longman Group Inc. 1973.

Thompson, Sharon. "The Canonization of Muriel Spark." Review. *Village Voice Literary Supplement*. (October 1985.)

Waugh, Evelyn. "Threatened Genius." *The Spectator*. (July 7, 1961): 28.

Waugh, Evelyn. Review of *The Comforters*. *The Spectator* (Feb 22, 1957): 256.

Whittaker, Ruth. "'Angels Dining at the Ritz': The Faith and Fiction of Muriel Spark." *The Contemporary English Novel*. Stratford upon Avon Studies 18 New York: Holmes and Meier, 1980: 157-179.

Witt, Judith. "The Laughter of Maidens, the Cackle of Matriarchs." *Gender and the Literary Voice*. Ed. Janet Todd. New York: Holmes and Meier, 1980.

AUTHOR INDEX

Adams, Joey 67, 68
Aiken, Joan 125
Aldrich, Sarah 124
Amis, Kingsley 112, 113
Aristotle 202
Atwood, Margaret 125
Auerback, Nina 43
Austen, Jane 5, 9, 10, 102, 106, 108, 127, 223
Ayres, Pam 119

Bacon, Josephine Dodge Daskim 159
Bakhtin, Mikhail 17, 209, 196
Barcus, Francis E. 70
Barr, Roseanne 39-45
Barreca, Regina 41, 59
Beatts, Anne 41
Behn, Aphra 7-8, 9
Benchley, Robert 157
Benedict, Paul 94
Bem, Sandra 8
Berenstain, Janice 66
Berger, Arthur Asa 70
Bernhard, Sandra 94, 96
Betjeman, John 119
Bier, Jesse 70
Blanchard, Martha 66, 74
Bloom, Harold 116
Bold, Alan 235
Bond, Dorothy 69
Bombeck, Erma 67
Boosler Elayne 97-98
Bork, Ruth 31
Bourne, Randolph 159
Bowen, Elizabeth 224, 225
Bradbury, Malcolm 237

Bronte, Charlotte 4, 201, 203
Burnett, Carol 67, 91
Bush, George 40, 98
Bush, Robert 169, 170, 178

Cable, George W. 170, 172
Calcagnino, Alfonso 219, 220
Carson, Johnny 86
Carver, Catherine 186
Chan, Jeffrey Paul 146-147
Chin, Frank 146-147
Chodorow, Nancy 19
Chopin, Kate 169, 170
Cixous, Helene 43-44, 194
Clay, Andrew Dice 33, 97
Clement, Catherine 43-44
Conquest, Robert 113
Cope, Wendy 111-122
Croly, Herbert 161

Daly, Mary 7, 69
Darrow, Whitney, Jr. 73
de Bourdeille, Pierre; see *Duke of Brantome*
della Franchesco, Piero 231
de Mille, Agnes 160
d'Este, Cardinal 214, 215
d'Etampes, Madame 214, 215, 216, 218
Diller, Phyllis 93
Dimier, Louis 215-217, 220
Drabble, Margaret 4, 101-109
Dreisner, Theodore 105
Duke of Brantome 217-218, 219, 220-222
Duke of Ferrara 214, 215, 216, 219

Eakin, Paul John 148
Eastman, Crystal 160
Eastman, Max 70, 78
Elfenbein, Anna Shannon 169, 176,
  177, 181
Eliot, George 106
Eliot, T.S. 107, 111, 112, 114,
  117-118
Empson, William 172
Erdrich, Louise 135, 141
Erikson, Eric 72

Farb, Peter 3
Fields, Todie 93
Finley, Karen 47-56
Fishman, Pamela 29
Flieger, Jerry Aline 58
Foulcault, Michel 14-15
Francis, Dick 119
Freeman, Mary E. Wilkins 170
Freud, Sigmund 48, 50, 56, 58, 62,
  202
Fry, William F., Jr. 78

Gaffney, Maureen 89-99
Gagnier, Regenia 43
Gale, Zona 160
Gallagher, Catherine 7
Gallop, Jane 58
Gibson, Mary 73
Gilbert, Sandra 158
Gilder, Richard 172
Gilligan, Carol 19
Gilman, Charlotte Perkins 160
Ginsberg, Allen 114
Glaspell, Susan 160
Goldberg, Whoopi 90, 92, 96
Goldwaithe, Bobcat 97
Goodman, Ellen 166
Gorris, Marleen 196, 197, 198
Griffin, Christine 34

Griffin, Gail 206
Gubar, Susan M. 158
Guracar, Genny Pilgrim 77

Habegger, Alfred 186
Harding, D.W. 5
Harris, Sidney 29
Heaney, Seamus 111
Heilbrun, Carolyn 196
Henderson, Marjorie 73
Heyer, Georgette 124-125, 127, 129
Hokinson, Helen 74-75
Hollander, Nicole 30, 57-63, 77
Howard, Greg 77
Howe, Marie Jennie 160
Hoyt, Charles Alva 229, 235, 237,
  238
Hughes, Ted 111, 118
Hulme, T.E. 116
Hurley, Bob 79
Hurley, Peggy 79
Hurst, Fannie 160

Irigaray, Luce 144, 194

James, Henry 108
Jennings, Elizabeth 112-113
Jewett, Sarah Orne 170
Jones, Anne Goodwyn 169, 174-
  175, 179, 182
Jung, Carl 161, 163

Karl, Frederick R. 224
Katz, Claire 190
Kaufman, Gloria 79, 80
Keller, Helen 13-22
Kemp, Peter 224, 226, 227, 228,
  231, 233, 234, 237
Kermode, Frank 224, 225, 227,
  228, 232
Kerr, Jean 66, 67

King, Allen 68
King Francis I 214, 215, 216
King, Grace 169-182
Kingston, Maxine Hong 143-145, 147-149, 151-152, 153
Kinison, Sam 97
Kirby, David 169
Kristeva, Julia 58

Lacan, Jacques 15, 52, 55, 61
Larkin, Philip 111-112, 113, 114, 118-120, 121
Leacock, Stephen 65
Legman, Gershon 70, 78
LeMieux, Kathryn 77
Lennox, Charlotte 4, 6
Leno, Jay 97
Letterman, David 86
Links, Marty 73, 76
Little, Judith 7, 196, 225-226, 236, 237
Lodge, David 224, 230, 238
Loos, Anita 158
Lorde, Audre 194
Luhan, Mabel Dodge 159
Lurie, Alison 106

Malkoff, Karl 234
Maltz, Daniel 31
Mandell, Howie 85
Mann, Brenda 34
Markow, Jack 66
Marshall, Robert 79
Martin, Michelle 125, 131
McAllister, Richard 75
McCarthy, Mary 106
McGhee, Paul 43
Mencken, H.L. 166
Mercilee, Jenkins 31, 32
Miles, Rosalind 235
Miller, Alice Duer 159

Miller, Margaret 150
Mindess, Harvey 78, 79
Mitchell, Carol 7
Moers, Ellen 190
Morrison, Blake 113
Mulkay, Michael 25, 26, 27, 33, 34, 35

Najimy, Kathy 89-99
Newman, John Henry 238
Newton, Judith 203
Nichols, Loxley, F. 187, 188, 191
Nye, Robert 121

O'Connor, Flannery 185-191
O'Connor, Regina 187, 188
O'Donoghue, Bernard 112
Orben, Bob 68
Ostriker, Alicia 117, 121

Parker, Charlie 114
Parker, Dorothy 158, 166
Parsons, Elsie Clewe 160
Petty, Mary 73
Pole, Anthony 108
Potter, Jonathan 25
Pound, Ezra 107
Press, John 113
Proust, Marcel 114
Pullin, Faith 225, 234

Quayle, Dan 36

Richmond, Vera Bourgeois 225, 234, 238
Rivers, Joan 67, 93
Rowland, Helen 159
Rosenthal, Rachel 52
Ross, Harold 157, 158
Russ, Joanna 7
Russo, Mary 62

Schechner, Richard 48, 52, 54, 55
Schroeder, Pat 79
Seabury, David 163
Seabury, Florence Guy Woolston
  159-161, 163-166
Sexton, David 112, 121
Shange, Ntozake 9
Shaw, Valerie 234
Shermund, Barbara 66, 74
Showalter, Elaine 227
Smart, Christopher 114
Sontag, Susan 56
Spankie, Sarah 122
Spark, Muriel 223-240
Spivak, Gayatri Chakravorty 144-
  146, 151, 153
Spradley, James 34
Strong, Patience 119
Swords, Betty 66, 80-84

Tannen, Deborah 26, 31
Taylor, Helen 169, 172, 174, 175,
  179, 182
Thomas, Dylan 112
Thompson, Sharon 225, 226
Thurber, James 157-158, 161, 166
Thurley, Geoffrey 101
Thurston, Carol 123-124
Tomlin, Lily 90, 92, 96
Toth, Emily 7
Trollope, Anthony 108

Updike, John 224, 226, 237-238
Utley, Kristine 35

Walker, Alice 196
Walker, Mort 66-67
Walker, Nancy 6, 7, 43, 101-102
Warner, Charles Dudley 173
Waugh, Evelyn 102, 106-107, 223
Weimer, Joan Meyers 170, 171
Weisstein, Naomi 41, 43
Weldon, Fay 5, 8, 9, 102, 104,
  105, 106
West, Donald 29
Westling, Louise 187, 191
Wetherell, Margaret 25
Whittaker, Ruth 228
Williams, Gurney 66, 74
Wilt, Judith 5, 7, 209-210, 239
Woolf, Virginia 8, 225
Woolson, Constance Fenimore 170

Yeats, William Butler 112

Zimmerman, Bonnie 124
Zimmerman, Candace 29

For Product Safety Concerns and Information please contact our EU
representative GPSR@taylorandfrancis.com
Taylor & Francis Verlag GmbH, Kaufingerstraße 24, 80331 München, Germany

www.ingramcontent.com/pod-product-compliance
Lightning Source LLC
Chambersburg PA
CBHW071416290326
41932CB00046B/1897

* 9 7 8 1 0 3 2 2 2 6 8 0 4 *